Two Candles for Maureen

Two Candles for Maureen

A DIARY OF AN INCREDIBLE FRIENDSHIP
AND A TRIBUTE TO A SOUL MATE

Margaret Darling

authorHOUSE®

AuthorHouse™
1663 Liberty Drive
Bloomington, IN 47403
www.authorhouse.com
Phone: 1-800-839-8640

Published by AuthorHouse   08/22/2012

ISBN: 978-1-4772-2301-7 (sc)
ISBN: 978-1-4772-2302-4 (e)

Acknowledgments

With Grateful Thanks to Lillian King who gave me the courage to proceed with this book and kindly edited it for me. To Maureen's Family for being such wonderful hosts for my visit to West Sussex. Also to my daughter, Judith, without whose computer skills, this book would have never been finished, and to the Macmillan Cancer Support charity whose forum enabled me to meet Maureen

PART ONE

In July 2008, I was diagnosed with Inflammatory Breast Cancer, a rare, aggressive form of the disease.

Life was good. For fifteen years I had worked as a Medical Secretary, with the local GP Practice, a very rewarding but busy job but my husband, David and I were now both retired. I was sixty three and David a year older. We originated from Kent and moved to Scotland in 1983 when Chatham Dockyard closed and were lucky to get a transfer to Rosyth. We never looked back. Since David was paid-off from Rosyth Dockyard in 1997, he had a part-time job at the local Police Station, driving police cars, delivering DNA samples to laboratories, evidence to Court proceedings and doing general handyman duties.

We had two lovely grown-up children. Our daughter Judith had just landed herself a good job and would at last have money in her pocket. Chris, our son, had his own joinery and building business that was doing very well. He and his wife Lorna, a midwife, had a beautiful ten month old son, Lucas, our first grandson, the apple of our eyes.

In June, we spent a lovely holiday in Kos with good friends. Aaah . . . sunshine, good food, wine and relaxation. One night, in bed, I noticed a tenderness in my left breast. I sleep on my tummy so put the soreness down to no more than the notoriously uncomfortable Greek beds. We have encountered equally uncomfortable beds in Corfu and Zakynthos so felt it must be a cultural thing. I therefore disregarded the tenderness until I got home, lifted my grandson on to my left hip and felt the same tenderness. I did take notice of it this time and examined myself. I thought I could feel a lump, but then imagination sometimes springs into action on these occasions and I wasn't sure. My experience as a medical secretary, however, told me to get myself to my GP. I arranged an appointment for 7 July and to my dismay, she confirmed the presence of a lump which indicated it was not just a simple cyst. I remember pulling a face at my GP. I had felt the lump was tethered which even I knew meant was not a mobile cyst. Maybe a little knowledge is a dangerous thing.

I was given a leaflet with information about urgent referrals and was told to telephone the hospital the following morning when I would be given an appointment within two weeks. This was arranged instantly for 29th July. Prior to this date, however, I was to have a mammogram so that the results would be available for my appointment at the Breast Clinic.

The mammogram duly took place on 17th July after a nail-biting few days when a phone call came from X-ray saying the machine had broken down and the mammogram would have to be delayed.

Arrival at the Breast Clinic was an uncomfortable experience, purely because once you are directed to Waiting Room No. 4 and travel past three quite ordinary waiting rooms, with plastic chairs and lino-covered floors, the fourth is full of deep armchairs and sofas, soft carpet, dim lighting and flowers. Bells start ringing immediately as you get the feeling you are being treated very gently and sympathetically. Also, there were other patients waiting to be seen, some wearing headscarves as obviously their hair had been lost to chemotherapy. My thoughts were "What am I doing here? What am **I** doing here?"

The way Breast Clinic works is that you have your ultrasound scan, biopsies and consultation with the Breast Surgeon for your results all at the same appointment. However, although I went *through all the procedures, it was too late in the day to get my results and I was asked to go back for these two days later.*

I duly presented again on 31ˢᵗ July. This time, my Breast Nurse was also in the room. This was so good because I had already met Marlene as we both sat on the Fife & Forth Valley NHS Research Ethics Committee. A small comfort at least.

One lymph node under the arm had been biopsied and I can remember every word the surgeon said to me.

"The good news is that the lymph node is clear. Unfortunately, the rest is cancer."

It must be dreadful to have to give someone this news.

"How did I know you were going to tell me that?" I said, more of an exclamation than a question.

"Now we have to decide how to treat it," he replied.

I said straightaway that I wanted a mastectomy as psychologically I would feel that the cancer had gone. Then came the most damning comment.

"Well, I would like to do drug therapy first as we feel that the cancer has spread into your skin. If I operated now, there would be every chance of spreading the cells into the scar and the cancer would just come back very quickly."

I realised now that this would be chemotherapy treatment and mumbled something about "Well, I won't be feeling very well then, will I?"

"Not necessarily," he said kindly, "Chemotherapy will take place every three weeks and for at least the last week you should feel back to normal."

I was to go straight round to Radiology for a chest X-ray. An appointment with the Oncologist was arranged for 5ᵗʰ August and one for a bone scan the day after. The Surgeon also mentioned that he would like to do a different type of biopsy, a core biopsy, on the enlarged lymph node as he wasn't convinced it was clear. This did make me feel as though I was in really good hands because he could have just accepted the first result without question. I could tell by now that my feet were not going to touch the ground.

The Oncologist told me the type of chemotherapy I would receive and that my first cycle would be administered on 13th August. The speed at which I was being ushered towards treatment was really impressive. Hey, we were only 13 days from diagnosis! A prescription for a wig was given with the fantastic news that I would lose my hair after the first chemo and before the second, that was within three weeks. I was also told to expect six cycles of chemotherapy, followed by surgery, followed by more chemotherapy and then radiotherapy. I was obviously going to get the works. The merry-go-round had started and it was at this point I realised life would never be the same again.

I was very nervous at having my first chemotherapy cycle and the evening before, we visited my son and his wife. On leaving, Chris handed me a small velvet pouch containing something. He told me to open it when I got home. Inside was a beautiful fob watch complete with inscription:

"If You're Feeling Sad and Low, Have a Look And You Will Know. Thinking About You Everyday And With You Every Step Of The Way. All Our Love Chris Lorna & Lucas."

I am not sure who shed the most tears that evening.

One of the hardest things was telling the family, although I had warned them before the results that I had a bad feeling about what was happening. When I told my sister, she had already been researching the internet and mentioned to me that my symptoms sounded like Inflammatory Breast Cancer. This name had not been mentioned by any of the professionals I had seen up to now and with all my fifteen years at the surgery, I had never come into contact with a breast cancer of that name. I then did the very thing someone in my situation should never do. I looked it up on the internet. True enough, I did have identical symptoms and certainly the route taken for my treatment plan also indicated *that this was the case. However, the really frightening part was an explanation that quite often this type of breast cancer was so aggressive, and sometimes mistaken by GPs for a breast abscess or infection and treated with antibiotics that by the time it is properly diagnosed, it has already spread to other parts of the body. Also, the survival rate for this type of cancer appeared to be two per cent of cases. I certainly didn't like what I read and I felt the need to find someone else who might be coping with the same type of breast cancer or who, indeed, had survived it as the prognosis did not look good.*

I visited the Macmillan Cancer website where you can register yourself as a patient, carer, or family member of anyone undergoing treatment for cancer. I trawled through those women who were undergoing treatment.

I found Maureen. And so started a beautiful friendship.

It was the end of September when I first emailed Maureen. Her profile stated that she had just been newly diagnosed with Inflammatory Breast Cancer. Not knowing what to expect, she was also feeling a bit scared, as indeed I was. I don't, unfortunately, have the email I first sent to Maureen as that was via the Macmillan website, but I remember saying "At last—someone with the same breast cancer as me! Please let me know what your symptoms are, what your treatment plan is."

I know I got a reply straightaway but again, unfortunately do not have the actual email. I found out, however, that Maureen was fifty eight, so there wasn't a great difference in our ages. She had four daughters and four grandchildren and lived in Arundel, West Sussex. As I live in Dunfermline, we were miles apart and it became very interesting later on to compare our treatments for the same disease.

I had been diagnosed at the end of July, so was a couple of months ahead with my treatment and was a mine of information already.

The story of how our friendship evolved into an extraordinary journey through difficult times, dealing with our problems with humour as well as sadness is told in our diary of emails from the earliest I still possess. I have left the text and punctuation exactly as was written in the hope that our personalities emerge.

17th October 2008

Subject: Re: (What Now?—a Cancer Community) Inflammatory Breast Cancer

Dear Margaret,

Thanks for your latest update and for giving me loads of info on what is likely to happen after my first chemo. I have an appt on 29th in the Macmillan centre, where I will be getting my chemo, for a wig fitting, also turban and scarves. If I don't like, my daughter is going to take me elsewhere she has heard of, so that's all positive. Just to let you know I have only had my laptop since my birthday at the end of May and am a real novice. Guess what. On reading your last e-mail and seeing your fantastic photo which I was going to save and file, my laptop started to upgrade and get cookies which I know nothing about and when I eventually got access, your e-mail and photo had disappeared. My daughter is coming over to see if she can find you so fingers crossed. I'll keep you informed. I was interested to read your daughter has moved to South Shields as my sister lives in Jarrow. Has been up there for about 17 years now. I hope my wig looks as fantastic as yours. You are certainly a young 63. Will send a picky in due course when I am rigged out. I am originally from this part of the country (West Sussex) but met an Irishman who I married in 72 and we went to live in Ireland. We came back in 2000 as kids were all back here also my Mum who is now 83. I settled back well but Liam still yearns for the green country. He has no choice now has to look after me!! Hope you have a good night out in Edinburgh and that your chemo went well and everyone is still pleased with your progress. Talk soon. Luv Maureen xxx

When Maureen refers to "talk" she means by e-mail. It is not until much later that we actually speak to each other by telephone. The trip to Edinburgh was a meal out for me with a group of friends. However, I was still only two days after a chemotherapy cycle and was anxious I might not be able to enjoy it.

I would also like to mention here that our treatment plans differed slightly from the beginning. I was on three drugs (FEC) in my chemotherapy, Fluorourocil, Epirubicin and Cyclophoshpamide. Maureen was to receive two of these same drugs—Epirubicin and Cyclosphosphamide. We race ahead to November now when, after four cycles of chemotherapy treatment, everyone concerned was delighted to find that my tumour had shrunk enough for surgery. This was earlier than expected. The surgeon went for his diary, said he had a meeting cancelled on 12th November.

"How would that do?" he asked.

We were cooking with gas. My surgery was uneventful. There was no choice other than a full mastectomy but I was absolutely over the moon at my next appointment with the surgeon after surgery when they go through the histology of the tissue removed etc.

The surgeon said "Well, we found it very difficult to find any cancer at all. We could see where it had been but there was no trace."

At the end of November, I had been for a lovely walk in The Hermitage, near Dunkeld with my husband, a friend and our dog, a miniature schnauzer called Barney. I had longed for an autumn walk to see all the beautiful colours of the leaves (who knew whether I would be around to see them this time next year?)

It was glorious. The walk was beside a rushing river, complete with picturesque waterfall and we took a few photographs, one of which I sent to Maureen. This happened to be one of me, my friend Pat, and Barney, the dog, amongst all the fabulous scenery and as you will see, this photograph revealed the first of many coincidences we came to share.

My Breast Nurse phoned me to say I could have my permanent prosthesis fitted before Christmas. I was looking forward to this as the "softee" given to you when discharged from hospital after surgery left rather much to be desired.

20 December 2008
Subject: Re: Update and piccies

Dear Margaret,

Have had a busy week at work and am feeling really tired so am having a chilled weekend. So glad you will have your permanent prosthesis for xmas. As you say, a very good service. I bet you cannot wait.

My blood count was 14.9 last time lowest so far was 13.9 so not too bad, like you say don't understand all the other numbers.

Hope you enjoy doing your mini xmas meal tomorrow and don't go overdoing things! It all sounds lovely and so nice to have your family around you. We went for our xmas lunch at work on Thursday with our 3 residents. I ate everything I was given and so enjoyed it all. The residents cleaned their plates too. I never ate another thing when I got home I was so full.

I will be glad to see the shortest day come and go. I am so looking forward to spring whatever it may hold. Has to be better than the last few months for us both. I was diagnosed on the 24th September.

Have sent photo of my daughter's dog Fern who is a mini schnauzer. She said Barney looks similar breed. We just have a pussy called Boomerang who was a stray. Hence the name as she would not go anywhere else kept coming back so we decided to keep her.

Hope you are still feeling fairly good as I am. Always get a little apprehensive before next treatment but feeling good.

Love to you especially and remember me to your family.

Luv Maureen xxx

This e-mail reminded me that Maureen was still working in a residential care home for the elderly and the reference to her blood count is because your count has to be above 10 to enable chemotherapy to be administered . . . The patient has to have a blood test the day before the chemo appointment to check that the level is normal which, at 14.9 is easily normal. I was lucky too, that my blood count didn't drop considerably throughout treatment. There were levels of other things to be taken into consideration—neutrophils, etc but this is unknown territory to the layperson . . .

I had to have two more chemotherapy sessions after my surgery just to mop up that one cell that might have escaped during surgery, according to the surgeon. My last chemotherapy was 29th December and in February, when I had started my radiotherapy, which continued almost directly after the chemotherapy, Maureen was about to have her last chemo before her mastectomy. I must mention here that I had also found a friend, Jeni, who lived near me who was a radiotherapist undergoing treatment for breast cancer herself. She was such a help to me in advising me to wear silk next to my skin during radiotherapy and giving me names of websites for lovely hats and scarves. It was strange going to the Western General Hospital in Edinburgh for the radiotherapy where everyone knew Jeni because that was where she worked. I was actually on the machine she normally would be operating.

11

2 February 2009
Subject: No more chemo!!

Dear Maureen

Good luck for tomorrow. It will be the best feeling in the world to know you have no more chemotherapy. I am, I think, only now beginning to feel the real benefits of not having had any more since 29th December. I fancied there was a smell about me all the while I was having it. This appears to have gone now. No-one else noticed it but me. I mentioned it once to the Oncologist and he said he had had 3 patients remark on that but it was rare. The radiotherapy, at the moment, is not making me feel any more tired than usual but I do go to bed at 10 p.m. and sit down all evening. My skin is a bit pink but not sore or peeling as could be expected half way through so perhaps my silk vests are working!! I shall be thinking of you tomorrow. When will you be seeing someone for the next step? I am as excited as you as things progress for you.

It's snowing here at the moment but we haven't had anywhere near what has fallen in Kent and S E England. Have you got much? I hope it doesn't get too bad for getting over to Edinburgh every day for my radiotherapy. The main roads will be OK but it's the side roads.

Had a very lazy weekend. Did our Tesco shopping on Saturday morning (yawn yawn). Have started counting points for my WeightWatchers again. I am so stupid though. I weighed myself on Saturday and got the shock of my life 10st 13lb. I weighed 9st 2lb before the big C. Anyway, decided to count points again and stop having sandwiches for lunch and go back to making a nice salad. Thought I would weigh myself again this morning and I weighed 10 stone 1.3 lb. I must have misread the scales on Saturday and thought it was 10st 13lb!

Thank goodness! Only 1 stone to lose instead of 2. Dozy wotsit, that's me. I hope I will lose that stone by the summer otherwise none of my summer clothes will fit me.

I still can't pick up my books. The last one I could not put down was The Island by Victoria Hyslop. It was about Crete and as we are complete Greekophiles, I could relate to a lot of what was going on. I, too, like Maeve Binchy and I used to read all Catherine Cookson and Victoria Holt. I usually read 2 books on holiday. I still feel a bit guilty if I sit and read when things need doing. I think that's my mum's fault. We were never allowed to sit down.

My brother is out of hospital (did I tell you he had a heart attack last Sunday). I told him he was only trying to go one better than me! What a fright. He lives on his own so things are not going to be easy for him. Spoke to him yesterday but he sounded very vague about everything. Luckily his son is helping him, plus my sister and niece. He usually comes up to visit us at Christmas but I called it off this year being in the middle of chemo and everything. Hopefully he will be able to come up in the summer for a break.

Keep in touch and hope the chemo doesn't make you feel too bad this time. Go with the flow!

Speak soon. Lots of love.

Margaret xx

It was almost another eighteen months before Maureen and I realised we both had brothers named Peter, who were the same age and who both lived alone.

I did not enjoy putting weight on through cancer treatment. I have struggled with my weight for years and had managed to stay at my goal weight of 9st 2lb since 2005. The prospect of having to lose a stone again was not made any easier by the Oncologist telling me that steroids (part of chemo treatment) change your metabolism and make it even harder to lose weight.

Throughout my treatment, I continued with pastimes I enjoyed, singing with Dunfermline Choral Union, which was like therapy; and with my work as a member of the Fife & Forth Valley NHS Research Ethics Committee. Neither chemotherapy nor radiotherapy interrupted either of these. My next e-mail talks of my "Russian chest." That was because I had a big Red Square through radiotherapy treatment.

22 February 2009

Subject: Hi again

Hello Maureen

Nice to hear from you and that you had a really nice break. I think we appreciate these things more now—at least rejoicing in feeling OK after another chemo cycle.

The Choral Union are having a band call this afternoon so I have to meet my friend who drives us at 1 p.m. Our concert is on 7th March so we haven't got long to knock things into shape. We had a rehearsal on Monday evening with the children's choir but it didn't go very well. Hopefully, today will be better.

We have booked our holiday. We are going to Corfu which is our comfort zone. We have been going there on and off since 1991 and have made a lot of Greek friends there. They welcome us to their homes like family (we have had to get to like olives!!). We haven't been for 3 years so felt drawn back now. I know I will have to be careful where I had the radiotherapy. Apparently you are very sensitive to the sun for the first year or so. I have been advised to use high factor (do anyway) and cover up.

I have to say my chest is a bit sore and has blistered (like sunburn) under my arm. I am a bit concerned about some bony pain I have in that arm. Only when I lift the kettle or the big milk carton—anything a bit on the heavy side. I suppose I will have to mention it if it doesn't go. Red Square is getting even more red. Isn't it strange how radiotherapy carries on working after the treatment has finished. I will be seeing my Breast Nurse on Thursday. She runs a support group at the hospital and has asked me if I will go. I think they do a lot of fundraising (Relay for Life, Debenhams fashion shows etc) I'll see if it's my cup of tea but I'm not sure yet. Well, I sure can talk! I had better get myself organised to go out. We have a lovely sunny day here today—cold. The bulbs are making more progress now and Chris (son) actually has daffodils out in his garden which is particularly sheltered. Spring is on the way . . . hooray.

Take care then. Hope all goes well on Tuesday. Let me know if you have any news.

Bye for now—Margaret xxx

I don't appear to have kept Maureen's e-mail to me telling me the good news that she was finally ready for surgery but I do have my reply.

26ᵗʰ February 2009
Subject: Yahoo!

What fantastic news Maureen! I know how I felt when I was told I was going for surgery. Psychologically it was such a big leap. I felt that once the breast was gone, the cancer had gone with it. I told you your feet wouldn't touch the ground after Tuesday. Another coincidence—your surgery on 12th March, mine was 12th November. 12 must be our lucky number. Only two weeks to get prepared. I said to you at the time (I believe) that the surgery was a doddle compared to what had gone before. You will be out by the following Tuesday (I wonder if you will be let out for the weekend like me, drains and all!) I am so delighted for you as you are like me and probably can't wait to get things moving on. You will be seeing light at the end of the tunnel once you have had your op. Ooooh I could hug you.

Just think, no more chemotherapy at least until after the op + 23 days (I was told I couldn't have my extra 2 until 23 days after surgery) but you may not need it of course. That is such a good feeling as well as you can imagine. The radiotherapy is fine too. My chest is still very "Red Square" but not sore and I haven't had any of the fatigue that some people get. You will be like me, I know, and sail through it all. With our positive outlook and determination not to let anything get us down, we fare better than some I think.

I am off to the support group at the hospital tonight. It's called Bosom Buddies. I am not sure I need an actual support group—not when I've got you!! However, I would like to put something back so if I can help with fundraising I will. My daughter has decided to do the Race for Life with me this year on 21st June.

Well, Maureen, I expect your last chemo is kicking in again but hang in there, it won't be for long.

Allelulia to your news.

Lots of love—Margaret xxx

With reference to being "let out" of hospital for the weekend (for good behaviour?) complete with drains, mine even went to Tescos with me.

I have obviously deleted a few of Maureen's e-mails about this time but fortunately my replies do reflect what has been said and I hope this takes care of the missing ones. I am certainly envious of the English weather as Maureen had been sitting in her garden and our weather in Scotland had been nowhere near warm enough for that.

2 March 2009

Subject: Full steam ahead

Dear Maureen

Lovely to hear from you again. Glad you are coming out the other side. It is fabulous not having to have any more of the old chemo, although I have to say it felt strange to me and, at the time, it was like losing my security blanket. That was only until I had my surgery though. Your appointment on 10th March. Is this your anaesthetic check (fitness for surgery)? I was told to be prepared to be at the hospital for at least 2 hours but in fact I was out in about 40 minutes, blood test and all. Masses of questions. The Anaesthetist even checked my teeth. I don't think he believed me when I said they were all my own and no crowns! That reminds me; I had a sore throat when I came round from the op so they must put tubes here, there and everywhere.

Sitting in the garden would have made you feel really good. Just to feel the sun on your face. We haven't been able to do that yet but the daffodils are coming out and the birds are very busy. We have had some beautiful bullfinches in the garden (hope the cats don't fancy a bullfinch dinner!) They are eating the seeds from the sycamore wings and we have hundreds of them on our grass because there are massive sycamore trees surrounding our garden (not our trees but we get all the leaves and wings!)

The support group was good on Thursday. We had people from Debenhams there doing skin care. We got some free samples. The lingerie dept were there too with bras to look at. Also some swimwear which I would have been interested in had they been suitable but my radiotherapy goes quite high up so I don't was anything too low as you need more protection from the sun for a while. There were a few new members there, all at different stages. Some hadn't finished their treatment. Still nobody with Inflammatory though! We must be really special (ha ha. Lucky us, said she ironically).

Well, keep me informed Maureen and I look forward to hearing from you soon. Hope you've got the wash bag filled up with nice little goodies for the hospital. Love from Margaret xx

I was suddenly on a downer. I sent Maureen an e-mail. I was looking forward to a telling off in reply!

6th March 2009
Subject: Counting down!

Hiya Maureen

You have coped so well with your chemotherapy. Glad to hear you are feeling better. I'm sure your energy will pick up more each day. It is good to hear you have been shopping and got a nice shirt and blouse. I found I was very short of button through things which became an absolute essential after surgery with all the check ups etc. I had to struggle to get things over my head (with the wig).

Isn't it funny how things can suddenly come over you? I hope you don't mind me saying when you are going through such a positive time but I need a kick up the backside and I know you can do it! There was not much on TV last night and we looked round the channels and saw a title that said something about Britain. We tuned in thinking it was travel but it was just about different people round Britain and what they were doing. The last person was a young man who had had breast cancer. No mention of this is the title. It was really interesting and he showed his chest and mastectomy scar etc. He still had a red square from his radiotherapy (like me). Anyway he was full of beans and determined to make the breast cancer work for him. He set up a website with his story and got to see Max Clifford who got him into some modelling for a Breast Cancer Care fashion show—my how he got cheered. He had photos taken with famous people as well. It really lifted me up and then at the very end they announced that they had some sad news. It was that after 2 years the cancer had come back. It just seemed so sad when he had been so positive the first time. They said he was as determined as ever to beat it but it just hit me. Is this going to happen to me? I have been so positive and so lucky but everyone I have been in contact with lately has got it back. Even at the support group there were several who had got it back. I suppose you just have to think it won't happen and if it does you just have to get on with it the same as the first time. I am feeling a bit tired. Maybe that's why it has affected me. I think my body is really using all its energy now to repair the radiotherapy. See—I'm telling myself all the time to shut up and give myself a slap. I suppose it's inevitable we have these moments. I am sure it won't last long but look forward to you telling me off! I am sorry to burden you with these feelings at this time. Dave cannot talk about serious stuff—what a shame. He is all right if I'm all right but I don't think he knows how to cope when I get the jitters.

I wait to hear more about your hospital whereabouts—will it be Chichester General Hospital or Infirmary and your ward no. or name etc.

Lots of love and thanks for your support.

Margaret xxx

7th March 2009
Subject: smiley face and a slap

Dear Margaret

First of all I've sent 2 slaps, the second in case the first one wasn't hard enough! Ha! Ha! No seriously please don't worry as those thoughts are always in the back of our minds and there is so much going on especially in the media at the moment—I just have to switch off. All my bad thoughts have been firmly pushed away, even buried, and won't get an airing as I cannot even think that our cancers are going to rear their ugly heads again—no way will we allow it!! That is what I am here for so that you can air your concerns, a shoulder to cry on god knows you have been there for me over the past 4 months I cannot think how things might have been without you—my rock thank you so much. How are you feeling today, has the mood passed for you? I do hope so think positive remember!!

Met my cancer doctor who is also doing my operation on Thursday, a lovely lady whom I have every confidence in. I have to be in Chichester for 7.30 am as I am to be first on the list. I have to have a right mastectomy and lymph nodes from under the arm—same as you. She has said that I can come home on Saturday as I long as I do nothing whoopee!! I am so pleased. On Tuesday I now have a mammogram at 9 am, breast nurse at 9.30 then a blood test. Will then come home and go back for my pre op assessment at 3 pm the only time they had left on Tuesday. I still cannot believe everything is moving so well. Fancy actually looking forward to going into hospital and having surgery—must be mad.

Hope I've managed to cheer you up sorry you have had to wait till today, don't forget to keep that chin up!

Luv you loads Maureen xxx

What a woman! I told Maureen how much she had made me laugh and my bad mood faded away.

7 March 2009

Dear, dear Maureen

Thank you so much for the 2 slaps—legs still stinging (ha ha). You just made me laugh so much. You are such a good friend to have. Yes, the mood has passed and I have been at Choral Union rehearsal this afternoon for tonight's concert. Getting nervous now but looking forward to a good sing. I am right in the front for this one so had better wear a bra! We are all in black so not too bad but would feel more comfortable facing my public (ooooooh!) and keeping decent.

Not long now. Again, we are so alike. I was looking forward to my surgery like it was Christmas and birthdays all in one. You really won't feel bad afterwards. No stitches or staples to have out. I had a continuous suture beneath the scar which just stays there. They put plastic all over the operation site and nobody touched it until I saw the surgeon the following Tuesday (from the previous Wednesday) and he removed it. I was told this was to prevent infection as the less it was touched the better. I expect you will find someone nice to chum up with in your ward. I did. I was also comforting all the old ladies in for various things, putting their socks on for them etc. Can't help it!

We all had a laugh, especially when me and another mastectomy lady performed the exercises we were given by the Physio after breast surgery as if we were the cabaret! I did these exercises religiously when I got home for ages as I did not want any complications.

So Tuesday it all starts, leading up to Thursday. I shall be looking at my clock at 7.30 a m on Thursday and thinking of you getting your pre-med. My op took about 2 ½ hours. Take a note of the time when you go down and when you are back in the ward just for curiosity.

Thanks again for cheering me up—I knew you would. By the way, lost a pound at Weightwatchers this morning to pleased about that as well.

Take care, I will be in touch before Tuesday and you can let me have any news you have got when you've had your mammogram etc.

With lots and lots of love from (what would I do without you)

Margaret xxx

I made sure I had the address of the hospital and the ward Maureen would be in as I wanted to send her a card and also telephone the hospital to see how she was. I wished her good luck and hoped she would make the most of all the TLC.

11 March 2009
Subject: Chichester address

Dear Margaret

The address is St. Richard's Hospital, Spitalfield Lane, Chichester, West Sussex. They haven't given me a ward as yet just have to report to reception. Had a good day there yesterday felt I know everything that is going to happen and feel confident. The chemo has virtually left no trace of any mass or tumours, nothing showed up on the ultrasound or mammogram at all, so was very pleased as you can imagine.

Apparently I'm superfit for surgery so that's nice to know. I can come home Saturday even with my 2 drains as a District Nurse will visit every day to check them and remove when ready. I cannot see me going anywhere till they are, very cumbersome looking. Thanks for all your good wishes and cannot wait to feel like a new woman! Will e-mail you when I get home at the weekend all being well.

Hope you are feeling good and take care.

Luv Maureen

The 12th March dawned and Maureen was very much on my mind. I kept looking at the clock and wondering how things were going. The next day, I decided to telephone the hospital just to make a general enquiry about her. The very helpful young lady I spoke to on the phone calmly said to me "Oh, I'll just put you through to the phone beside her bed".

"Woah!" I was taken aback. I had never spoken to Maureen before. Supposing she wasn't ready for such intimate contact—suppose I wasn't . . . What was I to say? I didn't have very long to ponder on such questions.

I just heard the "Hello?"

"Hello" I replied.

"Who's that?" asked the voice.

"It's Margaret" I said weakly "from Scotland"

"Oh, what a lovely surprise. How did you get this number?"

Well, we had our first conversation.

15ᵗʰ **March 2009**
Subject: Well done you!

Dear Maureen

Fancy getting an e-mail from you so soon. It was, indeed, lovely to talk to you—you sounded just as I expected you to sound (don't laugh). I had been thinking about you so much, and also reliving my op with you. I was phoning the hospital to find out how you were, not knowing you had a phone beside you! That was a bonus. Isn't it great, as you say, no needles, no chemo etc. I found my op so uplifting (if you'll pardon the pun). It made me feel I could see light at the end of the tunnel. I feel it is the same for you. You will be getting a "5 o'clock shadow" where your hair starts to grow very soon. I found my hospital experience wonderful (apart from not sleeping too well). Some people complained about the food—not me!! It was lovely having it brought to you.

Make sure you get plenty of rest—sitting in the garden sounds good—weather not quite good enough here for that but it is bright and airy and had a good walk with Barney this morning.

I am feeling on top of the world again—that day was just a minor blip. There again, I think we are alike inasmuch as if we do feel a bit down, it doesn't last long. I have started wearing a bra and my "softee" again as my skin looks very nearly back to normal after the radiotherapy. My check up for that is 31ˢᵗ March but I'm sure the oncologist will tell me it's fine. I still have a bit of fluid towards under my arm but this should go by itself but might take a while. Again, it doesn't bother me at all so nothing to worry about.

I am still excited for your progress (our progress actually) and take care. I've got the family all coming for dinner today. Good old roast lamb!

Lots of love—Margaret xxx

At this point, I gave Maureen my phone number and suggested she phone me if she felt like a chat. I stressed that if she preferred to stick to e-mails that was fine. I was ever conscious of being too pushy in this relatively new friendship, although it was obvious to me it was growing stronger day by day. I was e-mailing Maureen daily at this point and was pleased to receive the first of many phone calls from her. This pleased me greatly as I felt we were on the same wavelength and conversation came easily.

18th March 2009
Subject: Chat

Dear Maureen

Went for a long walk (seemed long to me anyway!) up to see a friend who is not well. This friend has also been a great support to me over the last months, calling with flowers and lavender bags and the like, so I took her some daffodils to cheer her up. She lives up a hill though and I had to stop and have a drink of water (seem to have a dry mouth since radiotherapy and carry a small bottle of water in my bag—hope her neighbours didn't think I was swigging vodka!) Anyway she was pleased to see me and it is an absolutely gorgeous day so I'm sure the walk will do me good. Still trying to build up my fitness after so much sitting around. Like you, got fed up with the four walls. It will be nice to go shopping—once upon a time the shopping was a bit of a chore but now it can be the highlight of my day!

It was great to talk to you. I am so glad you phoned. Likewise, I feel I have known you for ages and have always enjoyed our "chats" by e-mail. Now we can chat properly as well and I will phone you next time.

Well, Maureen, hope your chest won't be too sore. I remember having difficulty at night as could only lie on one side and I was sore doing the exercises until things got moving a bit. I did mine twice a day—first thing in the morning and before I went to bed. Had to lay on the floor for two of them. Bit of a job to get up these days! It was under my arm that was uncomfortable. I wonder how many lymph nodes you had removed—I believe I had 5. I expect they will tell you on 27th.

Thanks again for phoning. Take care and I look forward to another chat soon.

Love from Margaret xxx

Maureen and I still e-mailed each other but there were unrecorded phone calls as well. I feel my e-mails, however, will reflect what was going on. One phone call I particularly remember was when Maureen was feeling anxious before her return visit to the hospital to be told of the histology and the way forward. I was relieved to have had the two extra chemotherapy cycles and the radiotherapy and told her to go onward and upward and look forward to having kicked that big C right out! Maureen mentioned it was soon to be her mum's birthday. We found yet another astonishing coincidence here as we realised that our mothers shared the same birthday—3rd April. This revelation brought to light that her grandson's birthday was 9th April. Mine is 8th, and my sister's 7th April. April is obviously a good month.

21st March 2009
Subject: Zzzzzzz

Hello Maureen

I had a lovely day in Perth yesterday and a nice lunch with friends. One friend wanted to "do" Marks & Spencers,

Debenhams, Matalan, an art shop and various other shops in between. We didn't get home until 5.15 p.m. I had a good sit down when I got home and slept well but this morning I did not know what to do with myself. I felt I couldn't walk straight, I was lightheaded and felt really awful. I could only put it down to the fact that I am really not ready yet to go traipsing all over the place.

It's only natural you will be anxious before your hospital appointment. From what you said about the ultrasound, it should all be good news as mine was the same. I was told before surgery though that I would have 2 more chemotherapy cycles after surgery and then the radiotherapy as a 'top up' after chemo and surgery. So, I feel confident now that everything has been zapped. It may be that you won't even need any more chemo but I think you said in the beginning you were told you would be having some radiotherapy. Still, that is a doddle compared to the chemo so nothing to fear there. We are still to go onward and upward Maureen. Hope you have a lovely relaxing day tomorrow. Lots of love and take care (will phone Monday)

Margaret xxx

On 24th March 2009, The One Show on BBC TV did an item on breast screening. The TV doctor was there. There was no mention of the fact that Inflammatory Breast Cancer does not show up on screening mammograms. I had a clear screening mammogram in January 2008 before being diagnosed in July 2008. My surgeon suggested the cancer could have been there since then and even thought it might be an exercise for staff training to pull out my mammogram films to see, in retrospect, whether anything was visible. The TV doctor also suggested that if there was pain in the breast, it was unlikely to be cancer. This is another misconception as regards Inflammatory Breast Cancer as it was the tenderness in the breast that sent me to my GP. I went to the One Show website and left a comment: "Women should be aware that this type of breast cancer does not show up on screening and that if you have any pain in the breast—get it checked anyway because I had tenderness." I called myself brave Nutmeg (Meg being short for Margaret and because I am a bit of a nut!) Maureen had now let me have her home address and via telephone let me know she had been told her treatment had been successful and she was now to go for radiotherapy.

28th March 2009
Subject: Quick reply

Dear, dear Maureen

I am delighted with your news as you must be. Again, we have had similar results and must praise our treatment for the fact that it worked so well for us. As I said to you before, the radiotherapy is a doddle compared to the chemotherapy. The only drawback is the travelling (as we know ourselves). However, you soon get into a routine. In fact, I still look at the clock at about ten to two and think "Oh, better get going"! All my appointments were at the same time, 2.50 p.m. but if I got there early, they always took me early and we were out in 10 minutes.

That's brilliant that you have no fluid build-up. I still have a little but it is definitely going gradually. Exercises loosened the arm so keep up the good work. Your family must be over the moon for you—and no more chemo! I had to have two more sessions after surgery and before radiotherapy. Brilliant to think you will have no more jelly legs! Enjoy your weekend and revel in your good news (that's when I went to the Abbey to give thanks). I couldn't believe I had been so lucky.

Lots of love Margaret xxx

Later, I was to question the reasoning behind Maureen not having the extra chemotherapy but not that much later. My appointment with the Oncologist on 31ˢᵗ March 2009 was as anticipated and everything was fine. I was given permission to use perfumed soap, creams and deodorants again.

31ˢᵗ March 2009
Subject: Update

Dear Maureen

Lovely to talk to you this morning

I asked the Oncologist this afternoon if I could regard myself as having no cancer now and she said that as far as they were concerned that was the case. So, that's me finished now until I get called back to see the Surgeon in a year which will be November time. It feels really good. When I sat in the waiting room at Outpatients, I felt completely different. Then I realised that I was sitting there actually feeling well whereas before, sitting there I must have been feeling unwell, without realising how unwell I was feeling! I don't suppose that makes much sense but all I know is I sat there feeling really well and it was a different feeling from all my previous visits!

Anyway, Maureen, let me know when you get your appointments through for your radiotherapy and don't forget to ask your radiotherapist about getting tattooed. Also, I was told that wearing silk next to your skin when you are having your radiotherapy helps any soreness. I loved the silk things!

Look forward to hearing from you again and have a lovely lunch with your Mum on Friday.

Lots of love

Margaret xx

Once again Nurse Margaret put her hat on to advise Maureen about her radiotherapy. Regarding tattooing, I should explain that a patient has to have the area to be treated with radiotherapy very carefully marked. This may be carried out by marker pen or by "tattooing" which becomes permanent. The marker pen option means the patient cannot shower during treatment, but the tattoos do not wash off. These tattoos are the size of pin pricks and do not really show once treatment is finished. Facetiously, I asked my radiotherapist if she would "do me a butterfly somewhere at the same time!" She replied "You really wouldn't want me to do that". Obviously her artwork did not extend beyond pinpricks.

21ˢᵗ April 2009

Subject: Hospital tomorrow!

Dear Maureen

Thinking about you and hoping you get on fine tomorrow. I wonder if you will be having 4 weeks radiotherapy same as me—we shall see.

Went swimming with Judith today—first time since BC (before cancer). We had been doing 36 lengths of the pool but I only managed 14 which I though was brilliant because it was a while ago when we last went and I have obviously lost fitness.

Well, good luck again for tomorrow—I'm still right behind you. Take care. Lots of luv from Margaret xxx

22nd April 2009

Subject: Re: good news

Dear Margaret

Thanks for your last e-mail which I have just read. Just back from Chichester. Will have to have only 3 weeks radiotherapy so am very pleased as St Mary's isn't exactly on my doorstep. Will be just having the radiotherapy to the breast area and not to the underarm area so it is all good news as well. Signed the consent form and am now waiting for my next apptment to get started on the last bit of this journey.

So glad to hear you have been swimming well done with your 14 lengths which most definitely was brilliant—no better exercise for us. I presume your swim boob is made of a foam?

Went for a quick visit this morning to one of the girls I used to work with and then carried on to Arundel Cathedral as wanted to visit their gift shop. It was quite a steep walk and my legs certainly knew about it but at least it was downhill home . . . Sat in the garden reading until time to go to the hospital.

Thanks for thinking of me so much won't be too long now before everything will be finished.

Take care. Lots of luv as always. Maureen xxx

I had a niggling feeling regarding the fact that Maureen would be having just three weeks of radiotherapy when I had four, also, the fact that she was not offered two extra sessions of chemotherapy after surgery. However, I thought this must be because she maybe had had better reactions to everything.

22nd April 2009

Dear Maureen

Thanks for letting me know your news so soon. Kept looking at the clock and wondering how you were getting on. That is good news indeed . . . 3 weeks. You will be done and dusted in no time. It all gets very exciting when you know you are getting near the end of all your treatment. I still wake up and have a job to believe that this time last year I had no idea what was in front of me but now it's all over. It's a lovely feeling.

Yes, the swim prosthesis is made of foam but doesn't dry out very easily. I have made a net bag (out of 2 Persil tablet bags!) with a drawstring at the top. I thought I could hang it somewhere sunny to dry on holiday.

I expect you will hear very soon when you will be starting your radiotherapy. It is almost a pleasure after all the chemotherapy. I had a good clean through the house today—kitchen tiles as well as they had not been done for a while so it looks quite nice—well I can see the difference myself anyway.

Look forward to hearing from you again—and we will definitely keep in touch even when all our treatment is over. I don't feel we can just be ships that pass in the night, do you?

Take care and let me know when you get your appointments through.

Lots of love from Margaret (and well done again!!) xxx

24th April 2009

Subject: Re: update

Dear Margaret

Lovely to hear from you as always. We have just returned from my mum's where Liam has just cut her grass in the garden. Only a small piece so didn't take too long.

I didn't get to meet any radiotherapists on Wednesday only the clinical oncologist. Hopefully at my next apptment.

Ruby has just taken her first steps on her own, about time as she is well over 15 months now. No rush of course but I think her mum and dad are pleased she has started. Mind you once she starts getting everywhere they might change their minds.

Will ring you on Monday morning. Take care. Luv Maureen xxx

I realised from this e-mail that I also had a grandson the same age as Ruby. I sent Ruby a big X for being a clever girl. I have also by now found out that Maureen's birthday is the same day as my closest friend's in Scotland.

28th April 2009

Subject: Today

Hello Maureen

Lovely to talk to you yesterday. Today I have been swimming. Jude and I set off about 8.45 and were in the water by 9 a m. We did 22 lengths of the pool today (14 last week) so well pleased. I know I hold Judith back. I keep telling her she should not wait for me. She is a brilliant swimmer. The pool was quite crowded though. We were home by 10 a m and it made us feel really good. I'm still keeping half an eye open for things for the holiday. Also I want to get a nice bag for the present I got for my friend's daughter's new twins. (I'm glad I didn't have twins).

Dave is still working hard on THE DOOR. I expect I shall be more interested when we get on to decorating the utility room itself.

I am joining in with this year's Relay for Life which is held in Dalgety Bay. I went in last year as a survivor but I had only just been diagnosed so felt a bit of a fraud. This year I am also going in as a survivor (we just do a lap of honour—the rest do 24 hours relay walking). I have been sent a posh T-shirt to wear and a badge. With it came a leaflet about "sharing your story". It is inviting people to "share your story and help raise awareness". Well, I couldn't resist than could I? I have just filled a form in online. It's probably because Inflammatory Breast Cancer is rare that I want to tell everyone about it. I wonder if they will contact me? This is all done by Cancer Research UK. It will be interesting to see if they pick it up.

My friend Pat (birthday same day as yours 29th May) is off to the USA on Thursday. She is worried about swine flu and trying to get a mask to wear. They have 2 days in New York where I think 20 people have been diagnosed. I think she is worried about flying home with the air conditioning on the plane spreading germs. There is always something to worry about. I think it will be like bird flu and will just go out of the news very quickly. You don't hear anything about bird flu now do you.

Well, I must get myself organised to go up the town.

Hope you hear about your appointments soon.

It's a very cold day here today! (Bet you are sitting in the garden—I'm only jealous)

Lots of love—Take care Margaret xxx

The reference to THE DOOR should be explained. My husband has always wanted a door into the garage from the house. He had always had to go outside to gain entry. Fitting a door and subsequent decoration took almost a year to complete. However, it probably helped take his mind of other things.

28th April 2009
Subject: Re: Today

Dear Margaret

Lovely to hear from you as usual and so nice to have a chat on the phone. What did you buy for the twins? Clothes or toys. There are some lovely things out there. Glad to hear Dave is still working on the door. Do hope Cancer Research UK pick up on your story.

Yes, bird flu disappeared very quickly and if people are sensible this swine flu should be contained and go the same way. It has been lovely again this morning but we have heavy showers now and much colder. It won't be long till your holiday where you will have some lovely sunshine to enjoy.

Met up with Elaine my breast nurse this afternoon and at long last have my silicone prosthesis. It is lovely and so comfortable and looks so natural in my bra under my t.shirt. Another thing to do crossed off the list. No word from Portsmouth yet!

Hope you had a nice afternoon in town with Jude. Did you spot anything for the holiday? Taking Mum out tomorrow. Won't know where till I arrive on her doorstep. Have a lamb stew for dinner tonight.

Talk soon. Take care. Luv Maureen xxx

Amongst all Maureen's lovely chat, she mentions cheerfully that she has had no word from Portsmouth yet. This is for her radiotherapy appointments. Bearing in mind Maureen had her surgery in March, I was beginning to feel it was rather a long time to be waiting, considering I went straight from chemotherapy to radiotherapy just as a top up. Belt and braces, if you like.

29th April 2009
Subject: Re: Today

Dear Maureen

Here we are again. I am just back from a walk right round what we call the Dalgety Bay loop. Our town is shaped like a figure eight and I walked both halves. It took me exactly one hour and it worked out (on my pedometer) to 2.57 . . . miles. I feel really good that I have done that and am only realising now how much stronger I feel. Now I think I'll be able to do the Race for Life (about 3 miles) so that's good. Your email encouraged me to try my silicone prosthesis again and I am amazed at how it feels now. I was obviously the wrong shape for it before with the fluid hanging around and now it fits beautifully and feels so comfortable. I can't believe it. You are still helping me you see! Judith said it looks much better than my softee with the T-shirt I have on today so I feel really chuffed.

I got the twins each a little romper suit from Next (I don't know how they make them for the cost—£4.50 each). One has "I love Mummy" on the front and the other one has "I love Daddy". They are obviously not identical although the twins are, but I thought they are little individuals anyway. (James and Alexander). I hope we get some nice warm weather so that they can wear them, little short sleeves and short legs. I shall see some photographs tomorrow when I meet up with the Thursday girls. I expect proud granny will have plenty to show us.

Well, lunch time almost so had better get my skates on. Pat is off to the States tomorrow. We are taking her to the station. We are treating her to a birthday meal on 29th May. She will only have been back two days so hope she is not too jet lagged. Pity we couldn't all celebrate yours and hers birthdays together!

Bye bye for now. Lovely to hear from you as ever.

Margaret xxx

The Thursday girls are a group of friends I have known since moving to Scotland. I was lucky to land beside one girl who met with six others once a fortnight. This started when as neighbours with small children, they would go to each other's houses for a drink and a blether as they couldn't get out easily any other way, and has continued for at least thirty years. It wasn't long before I was invited to join the group and this gave me an instant circle of friends for which I am ever grateful

*A telephone conversation brought to light another coincidence. Maureen's daughter Mandy worked for the Norwich Union. I had worked for the Norwich Union, years ago, admittedly, but previous to that post, Mandy had worked for the RSPCA at their Head Office. My daughter had worked for the Scottish SPCA, first at Head Office and then as Assistant Manager at the Stirling Animal Welfare Centre. Also, as we chatted about our daughters, and their love of animals, I mentioned that Judith had three rescue cats, Josh, Billy and Jaffa because he was orange (groan). Maureen amazed me by telling me that one of **her** daughters also had a cat called Jaffa because of something to do with Jaffa cakes.*

1ˢᵗ May 2000
Subject: Weekend again!

Hiya Maureen

It's a lovely sunny evening here after a day of showers. We looked after Lucas today for Chris & Lorna. One of their friends tragically took his own life last week and it was his funeral today. We are all devastated for the family. He has a three year old daughter Amy too. We took Lucas for another walk in the woods—he seems to love that and then we thought we could manage our Tesco shopping (ha ha) We ended up with two trolleys, Lucas in one with the fruit and veg and all the other shopping in another one. He didn't want to sit in the proper trolley seat for some reason but agreed to sit in the trolley itself. He had a shot on Thomas the Tank Engine (in store) and we then brought him to our house as apart from unpacking the shopping, Lucas wanted to see Barney and the cats. We gave him lunch and Judith had a play with him. We then took him back to his own house for a sleep although he had different ideas. I knew he was tired but he cried so hard when I put him in the cot. He was calling "Gran, Gran". It was heartbreaking! Still, I just left him and he was asleep in five minutes. It was lovely having him but hard work, of course.

I used to work for the Norwich Union Life Insurance Society back in my early twenties. I was secretary to the Life Inspector at Chatham Branch and had to deal with public plus work out all the insurance quotations and process all the new business. Doubt if I could do it now. It's the Research Ethics Committee meeting on Tuesday afternoon but not too much reading this time so the meeting shouldn't be too long.

Well, hope you have a lovely weekend and the weather is kind to you. Just heard the first case of swine flu passing to someone in this country who hasn't been near Mexico lives in Falkirk! Won't be going there then (wasn't going anyway).

Take care, write soon. Lots of love from Margaret xxx

As my treatment had finished and Maureen was still waiting for her radiotherapy appointments, our exchange of emails is about everything and nothing, which all added to finding out about each other and our families. We chat about various tournaments, snooker, horseracing and tennis as they take place on TV.

5th May 2009
Subject: Brrrr

Hello Maureen

You sound as if you have had a lovely weekend—lucky you with your weather! We are freezing here and we are getting the rain also. Not good. However, Chris & Lorna came for dinner on Sunday and enjoyed themselves. Lucas eats well.

Well, John Higgins won the snooker. We follow it too, especially Dave. Stephen Hendry comes from Dalgety Bay. His aunty lived in our street when we first moved to Scotland and Stephen went to Inverkeithing High School, same as our children. His aunty always used to cut his hair and the children would hang around the house for a glimpse of him. When we moved here I remember phoning Dave's mum telling her to watch Junior Pot Black as he was on that. I think he was 14 then.

Tried to phone you this morning. I wondered how the Nicola Jane lingerie shop measured you for your mastectomy bra. I received their brochure and decided to measure myself the way they tell you to do it but my bra size came out at 40D. I was so shocked I phoned them. All they said was that I could try a 38 if I thought the 40 would be too big. I have always been a 36. Couldn't imagine wearing a 40.

Had my cholesterol test OK having fasted since tea time last night. I enjoyed my breakfast when I got home. I have to go back next Tuesday afternoon to see the nurse about the results and to get my blood pressure checked. This is because I take medication for hypertension and the surgery keep tabs on me once a year.

It was also my NHS Research Ethics Committee meeting this afternoon. We were out by 4 p.m. for a change. It's usually 6 or 7 p m but am still tired tonight. I'm going to the hairdressers tomorrow morning for advice. I am not sure whether I should be having what little I have trimmed into a shape and also whether I could have a colour put through it to make it look a bit decent on holiday if I want to go without my wig during the day at least. I have a feeling she will say it is still too short to do anything with but at least she will tell me what's best. I went to Tesco's yesterday without the wig (I know all the girls there). They all had a good laugh. They are putting on a "Stars in your Eyes" on Saturday for Breast Cancer (Cancer Research UK) and they are also all doing the Race for Life. We are going to see what they get up to on Saturday. It will make a change for us. When is your Race for Life (you have probably told me)? Ours is on 21ˢᵗ June, just after we get back from Corfu.

My goodness, it's blowing a gale outside! Glad I haven't got to go out anymore tonight.

Speak soon and let me know if you got in touch with the hospital about your radiotherapy.

Best love, as usual, Margaret xxx

I think our holiday neighbours thought my husband had two women with him, one with lovely blonde bobbed hair, and one with hardly any. My last sentence of the above email speaks volumes about what I was thinking to myself. Time was marching on.

*On 7ᵗʰ May, Cancer Research UK contacted me about "Share your Story." I had a long, interesting conversation about my cancer journey with a very attentive young man who introduced himself as Tom. I also told him about Maureen and how we had met, and he thought that really **was** a story. Later the same day I had an email from Tom.*

7ᵗʰ May 2009
Subject: Cancer Research UK—Share your Story

Dear Margaret

Thank you again for your time speaking to me earlier and for contacting us with the Share Your Story form. If you were able to email over some pictures that would be really useful for our database. It would be wonderful to hear if your friend in West Sussex was also happy with the idea of speaking to us—there's no pressure at all and no worries if she is not keen. As I said on the phone, it is difficult to know exactly what or when opportunities that might arise, but I hope it is ok to be in touch when something suitable comes up. Please don't hesitate to get in touch with me if you have any queries at all. I look forward to hearing from you.

All the best,
Tom

I phoned Maureen straightaway, but knew in advance that she would be up for it. Bring it on, she would say. I emailed Tom again:

7th **May 2009**

Subject: Cancer Research UK—Share your Story

Dear Tom

Thank you for speaking to me this morning.

I have contacted Maureen, my friend in West Sussex (Arundel) and she I more than pleased to speak to you should you so wish. We are delighted to have met each other in the way I described to you. She was diagnosed after me and is just about to commence 3 weeks radiotherapy. Her treatment will then be complete. She gave me her full permission to pass you details of her email address, home address and telephone number. We have, indeed, been able to support each other over the past few months, mainly because only we know exactly what the other is going through with inflammatory breast cancer. It is so uncommon, Maureen remarked that neither of us had met anyone else, or made contact with anyone else with this type of breast cancer so to have found each other was fantastic. Thankfully, our cases have had such similarities inasmuch as all her pre-treatment scans were clear, as mine were—an indication that this cancer had not spread by the time of diagnosis. Anyway, she will tell you all about her case and her side of our friendship if you contact her.

Regards,

Margaret Darling

The rash of emails continued

7th **May 2009**
Subject: RE: Cancer Research UK—Share your Story

Dear Margaret

It was an absolute pleasure to speak to you this morning. Thank you so much for all the pictures, which are lovely and for the information about Maureen—it is such a fantastic story about the way you have been able to support each other and I will definitely be getting in touch with her very shortly. I will also be contacting my colleague who looks after the press in Scotland—I am sure he will be delighted to hear about all of the Cancer Research UK activities that you support. I look forward to speaking to you again before long.

All the best

Tom Bourton

7th **May 2009**
Subject: Cancer Research UK—Share your Story

Hi Maureen

Thought you might like to see the exchange of emails with Cancer Research UK. I sent Tom the photo of me in my wig and also one of me with my WeightWatcher group after we had done the Race for Life last year and the other one was of me doing the survivor's lap of honour at the Relay for Life in Dalgety Bay last year just after I had been diagnosed. These are obviously events all arranged by Cancer Research UK so he sounds pleased!

He was very easy to talk to and is genuinely interested in everything you say. I am sure he means what he says and will be contacting you shortly.

Thanks for agreeing to talk to him also. Lots of love as usual,

Margaret xxx

Via telephone conversations I found that Tom soon contacted Maureen. We were both excited about possibly getting a little bit of publicity. I also had word from Maureen that she now has her radiotherapy dates all set

9th May 2009

Subject: Ooooooh!

Hi Maureen,

Well, our Tom doesn't hang around does he? Still, I think ours is a good story. I don't know what I would have done without you.

I am excited for you now you have your dates all set. I am sure you will sail through radiotherapy. I expect you will get your little talk about not using any perfumed soaps, shower gels, deodorants and powders. It was suggested I should go without a bra for the duration and I just wore my silk camitops and loose clothing for comfort.

You are really nearing the end of your treatment now. Isn't is wonderful?

Do you know, it is absolutely pouring with rain here and it's freezing! We have had gales too and it's still quite windy now. I'm still in polo neck jumpers and winter coat. Even Barney's nose twitches at the back door and he takes ten steps back. I was going to have a wee look round the town when I was up for WW this morning (lost ½ lb so that makes 5 ½ lb altogether so far) but I was so cold and it was so miserable I just went to Marks and then got the bus home. By the time I got home I was ready to emigrate!

We have lovely rhododendrons in the garden, particularly a scarlet one and a bright pink. They are being spoilt by the rain and wind. Our lilac tree is extra good this year too. The wood pigeons were being such a nuisance taking the young leaves or buds off the plum tree. Don't really know what they are eating but there were four perched on top yesterday. It is just a young tree so not very big. They had great difficulty hanging on! Anyway, Dave decided to hang a CD in the tree and it is blowing and shiny. Now the pigeons are sitting on the ground wondering what to do.

Keep me posted if you hear any more from Tom as I will you, and let me know how it goes on Wednesday. I've got the dentist on Wednesday (by the way, I still had my check up when I was having my chemo—nobody told me not to). I didn't have to have any treatment though and I had to add that I was on chemotherapy on my health sheet so the dentist would know. We are also looking after Lucas on Wednesday afternoon as Lorna has her first scan. Chris is going with her. She has a little podge already.

Bye for now and lots of love to you. Margaret xxx

11ᵗʰ May 2009
Subject: Re: Hi!

Dear Margaret

Hello again, how did Saturday night go, great I'm sure. You must have sent the Scottish gales down here as it is blowing one this morning. Lovely and sunny but impossible to do anything outside in case my wig goes sailing off on the horizon! Had a fab day as Mandy & Graham along with Fern turned up and took us off to The Black Rabbit at Arundel for a roast lunch. Only about half mile from the Wetlands we were at last week.

We sat outside with the dog yes it was warm enough and then went off for a walk along the river Arun smashing.

On your advice I also bought a silk camisole ready for radiotherapy, so am looking forward to wearing it. Probably won't bother with a bra either for those 3 weeks. Congratulations on losing over 5 lbs with weight watchers—brilliant. Keep up the good work. Have read about that CD tip in a magazine so it seems to work.

I am sure you are looking forward to seeing the picture from Lorna's first scan Such an exciting time. As we are both busy on Wednesday will give you a ring early on tomorrow and then we can carry on with the writing again.

Have swept and washed kitchen and bathroom floors this morning and baked a batch of small cakes for Liam for his lunchbox. Have just had one whilst warm—lovely. Have collapsed now into the chair catching up with my e-mails.

Hope you had a lovely weekend another week dawns. Take care.

Luv as always. Maureen xxx

14th May 2009
Subject: Marking up

Dear Maureen

Glad to hear everything went well yesterday. I think I had seven tattoos (?? bigger boobs!!!) Anyway, now you have all your times you can plan your days accordingly. My appointments were all at 2.50 p.m. We always got to the Western about 2.30 p m as we thought we had to leave plenty of time for traffic. They managed to take me early so sometimes I was out even before my appointment time. It's really good to know you are definitely now on the homeward stretch (literally by the way we have to position our arm in the machine!)

My cholesterol was fine at 4.9, my blood sugar was 5 which is within normal limits (so no diabetes, thank goodness) and my blood pressure was really down (keep taking the tablets). So that's me for another six months and then it is just a blood pressure check.

We went over to Chris & Lorna's about 12.30 yesterday. Lucas was having his sleep. They went off to the hospital for Lorna's first scan and Lucas woke about 2 p m. We took him for another walk in the woods nearby. He loves it and Dave hides behind trees and we have to hunt for Granddad—you know the score. We met the local nursery children in the woods too, all having a great time climbing on tree stumps etc. It is good to see that health and safety are not interfering too much with what the children are allowed to do. They were all wearing lovely red jackets so could be easily seen. Lucas was mesmerised by them and what they were doing. We lifted Lucas up on to a tree stump and he thought he was in the tree tops. "Up tree, up tree . . . gain, gain". After that we took him to our house to play. About 4.30 p.m. Chris phoned to say Lorna wasn't too good. She had a heart rate of 220 and was being monitored. I said Lucas could have his tea with us and we would take him home and bath him etc. However, about 5.30 p. m. he phoned again to say she could go home at 6 p.m. They actually got home just before 7 p.m. Lorna had said she hadn't felt well the day before at work but she was with a woman giving birth and couldn't get away for her lunch and thought it was just that. So, I think they call it tachycardia (fast heart beat) and she has been put on a betablocker. Hope she will be OK. Saw a picture of the baby and Lorna was told she is 13 weeks. I think her due date is 17th November. Hope you have a nice lunch today and shopping. Jude and me been for another swim this morning so feel well exercised this week. Got my Thursday girls tonight. We are going to the local Bay

Inn for our meal. A couple of our crowd are on holiday and one up to her eyes helping her daughter with the twins. Lovely to hear from you Maureen. Take care and I have put 26th May in my diary. Hope they have a birthday cake for you on 29th when you go over. Lots of love Margaret xxx

I can tell from reading my own e-mails that my mood is high and I am feeling very much back to normal after enduring seven months of rigorous cancer treatment. It happens without realising. I found that going from wall-to-wall hospital appointments to nothing had felt like abandonment for some time. Maggie's Cancer Caring Centre was a great help in this respect. They were going to run a course on the Transition Back to Normal after Cancer and asked me if I would like to put my name down. I remember Maureen asking me if I felt weird once treatment had all finished and I really did. At first it was like having crutches kicked away from under me, that is losing the support of the hospital doctors and nurses. It hit me finally that I had had cancer. Cancer, me! How could I? Supposing I had not survived. All sorts of thoughts came crashing in that never entered my head whilst I was too busy concentrating on getting through chemotherapy, surgery and radiotherapy. How much exercise should I now be doing? Can I tell everyone I have HAD cancer—or have I still got it? It became a big subject. The course at Maggie's convinced me that it must be quite normal to be feeling the way I was. It seemed that the road back to normality might take longer than anticipated with highs and lows on the way.

15th May 2009

Subject: Hello

Dear Margaret,

Do hope Lorna is feeling better. Glad you saw the picture. My Dad's birthday was on 17th November—another coincidence. Babies never arrive when they are supposed to though. He died 11 years ago when we were in Ireland of a massive heart attack—was a heavy smoker.

Had the double glazing people here today to replace a misted up window. Only took 20 mins so a good job done. Haven't ventured out as didn't want to miss them. Due at noon but arrived at 11.45 a m so just as well. My runner beans have just started to peak through so will have to get some more canes for them to climb up as haven't got enough. My beetroot and carrot seeds are appearing as well, so must be ding something right.

Hope you enjoyed your meal last night with your Thursday girls. It's good to have a chinwag. Will be popping over to work tomorrow to have a cup of tea with them all and catch up with the gossip. One of my friends, we were at each other's weddings rang me up this morning. She is still working full time but has Monday off so is calling to see me before I start my radiotherapy as it will be hard to fit anyone in once that starts. I haven't seen her since she had her birthday bash when she was 60 last July so am looking forward to her visit.

Hope you all have a great weekend. We will be going to see Leisha, Matt and Ruby on Sunday and staying for lunch. Other than that a quiet weekend. Bye for now. Luv Maureen. xxx

18th May 2009
Subject: Update

Hello, my friend

What a day—rain, rain and more rain. Got soaked walking Barney round the shore and we had a lot of running about to do today so it wasn't that pleasant. We wanted to get our holiday euros through Marks & Spencer (get points to spend) and that meant going to a big shopping centre between here and Edinburgh. We left about 9.20 a m and all went well. Did some shopping at the same time—new suitcase for me as mine is a bit of a state.

We had a quiet weekend this week which gave us a chance to sort through what needed washing for going away. Oh, by the way, as we are to be away for 2 weeks, do you have a mobile phone and, if you don't mind, I can send you a few texts just to keep in touch? I would like to know how your radiotherapy goes along and it's too long to wait until I get home.

You sound as if you are a good gardener. I wish I was. To think you are growing beetroot and carrots. I eat beetroot every day as I love it so much but not the sort in vinegar—just plain, lovely, sweet beetroot. It's difficult to get it here, to cook yourself, that is. We have strawberries and raspberries coming along nicely (thanks to Dave) and a few plums on the tree. We took down an apple tree last year as it wasn't doing very much but I'll still miss the few apples we got. They stewed beautifully. Managed to get Pat (birthday 29th May, same as yours) an old boot ornament at the garden centre. We are going to plant it out for her (like yourself, she is a brilliant gardener—must be the Gemini star sign). It is a bit of joke too, as she will be 70 so we are going to say she is now officially an old boot herself so it's an old boot for an old boot. Aren't we awful! It will stand nicely on her patio though.

Hope you enjoyed your friend's visit. There were only three of us Thursday girls last week (holidays kicking in already) but it was still nice and makes a change

Perhaps I can give you a ring on Thursday unless I hear to the contrary. We are swimming tomorrow and Wednesday I hope to go to Edinburgh on the bus to get a few more bits for the holiday (sun creams etc).

Take care and start crossing off those days!

Lots of luv Margaret xxx

I gave Maureen my mobile phone number and she was happy to give me hers. It felt good that even though I would be miles away in Corfu I could still find out how Maureen's treatment was going.

19th May 2009

Subject: Re: Update

Dear Margaret

Lovely to hear from you as usual. You have had a lot of rain. We had heavy rain Sunday night but yesterday turned out sunny again with a strong wind. Cannot seem to get rid of the wind. Liam was out in the garden most of yesterday sorting out the water feature as the pump had broken. We must have had half the beach in pebbles to move out to get to the bottom. I went off to the dentist and left himself and Graham to get on with it all. The dentist went well just had to have a clean. A different dentist this time I don't know if my regular was on holiday. I had a young girl very nice and was very careful when cleaning so didn't hit the roof at anytime! Said my gums were a bit inflamed and to brush them as well and hopefully things will improve. Anyway when I got home my water feature up and working. When Liam came in for his dinner and changed his t-shirt vest his shoulders and neck were all sunburnt. He had to apply lots of aftersun. Lucky I had bought plenty ready for myself!

I like your idea an old boot for an old boot! A lovely present I'm sure she will be thrilled. Got some more canes for my runner beans. I have Fern today arrived at 8.15 a m so will be doing the river walk with her later. She has had a play with her toys and is now stretched out on the carpet having a rest while I do my e-mailing. Boomerang who doesn't like dogs is curled up fast asleep behind the sofa. She will probably head down to the bedroom when Liam gets up.

It would be lovely to text whilst you are away. I have programmed you into my mobile phone. I will ring you on Thursday morning before I go off shopping with Mum, otherwise I might miss you.

Look forward to speaking on Thursday. Take care.

Luv Maureen xxx

22 May 2009
Subject: Re: Hi

Dear Margaret

Do hope you got on alright in Edinburgh yesterday with your Debenham's purchase. It has turned so warm here really lovely. Where I was out walking with Mum on Wednesday have ended up with a red neck so am back to wearing my check shirt with a collar. It is a bit sore and itchy this morning so want to clear it up before Tuesday. Don't want to be getting told off!! Will have to sit under the parasol when I go in the garden now. Never mind it is so good to feel the warmth.

After shopping yesterday my hairdresser texted me to say she had a half an hour between clients so I popped into Arundel and we had a cup of tea together and a catchup. She liked my lilac headscarf which I had put on as my wig was just too hot. I have it on this morning. Just taking Mum out this morning as won't be able to see as much of her next week. Must catch up with some housework at the weekend as haven't done any this week. Do hope you have some sunshine too. Makes a difference to the day, doesn't it? Have a lovely Bank Holiday weekend. Take care. Luv Maureen xxx

22 May 2009
Subject: Re: Hi

Dear Maureen

Thanks for the email—I just want to move to West Sussex! Get some sunshine. Well, we do have sunshine but in between the showers. So, still not sitting in the garden weather. Never mind.

I had booked an appointment with my hairdresser to have a colour put through what little hair I have just to cheer it up for the holiday. I mentioned it to someone in Tescos where a member of staff on the deli had breast cancer. She had been told that because she had been on chemotherapy she couldn't have anything put on her hair for a year! I thought I had better find out more and phoned my Breast Nurse. She confirmed that we shouldn't put anything chemical on our heads but for six months, not a year. Still, it is not six months for me yet so have had to cancel the appointment and will just have to look like Barney—steely grey and white. Least of worries anyway. I wonder if you have been told anything like that. However, like you, I find the wig a little on the warm side so am going without it quite a bit. I look a bit masculine I'm afraid. Dave says it's fine.

Looking after Lucas on Sunday so they can get packed—off to Portugal on Monday for a week. They are then coming to me for their dinner. Have got a nice piece of leg of lamb—I think Jersey Royals will be the order of the day. I have some lovely apple mint growing in the garden. I do my lamb making slits in the skin and inserting garlic slivers and rosemary sprigs (also from the garden) . . I then cover the top with orange slices and ground black pepper, cover with cling film and leave over night . . . It does something to the flavour and I think the orange must help tenderise it. It's very good anyway. I'll make the carrot and coriander soup which is not too heavy and easy to make so will be busy from now on.

I got my top changed in Edinburgh and can't wait to wear it now (big kid). Will save it for the holiday though. I got factor 50 suncream for myself, as I am a bit nervous about really hot sun this year. I think I was told that once you have had radiotherapy, you burn easier, I suppose just in that area but am going to be extra careful.

Have a lovely weekend. The time goes so quickly. Can't believe your appointments are almost here now. Hope to speak to you on the phone next week to see how you are getting on. Lots of love to you.

Bye for now, Margaret xxx

28 May 2009
Subject: Life in the fast lane

Hello Maureen

Hope radiotherapy still going OK. Thinking about you lots.

Things a bit hectic here—I always feel you REALLY need a holiday after all the preparations. The washing machine is never off and there seem to be a million and one things to think of. No doubt we shall get to Corfu whatever.

Pat got home from the USA last night. Dave met her from the station and she came back for a cuppa. She was full of it. What an experience—Queen Mary II and all the millionaire type houses over there. Her body clock still all up the creek so hope she will manage to enjoy her birthday tomorrow. I tried to get a balloon to put on the back of her chair at the restaurant as a surprise (not one bearing her age though!) and two card shops in Dunfermline had no helium which threw me a bit. Still I have to go back up to the salon tomorrow (hope they can knock my wonky eyebrows into some kind of shape now they have grown a bit) so hopefully I'll get one tomorrow and we can take it to the restaurant in advance. We have planted her old boot with young geranium plants. I think they will look lovely when they flower.

We were shopping for a jacket for Dave to take to Corfu as it gets quite chilly sometimes in the evenings. What a trial that was. The shops must think men like going upstairs to shop. Every one we went in all had their mens' clothes up a million stairs. I was absolutely shattered by the time we got back to the car—even four flights of stairs to car park. I must just notice them more I expect. I do find many stairs a bit gruelling still though.

Well, Maureen, hope you are crossing off your appointments as you have them so it looks less and less day by day. My friend Issy—we usually go on holiday with Isabel & George—had her knee replacement op yesterday and came through OK. Honestly, we all seem to start falling apart after a certain age. She is the same age as you though, so quite young to be having a replacement but she has been struggling to walk so hopefully this will have her jumping around like a spring lamb again—well, sort of!

I will ring you early tomorrow and you can let me know if you have anything planned for your birthday other than another lazy 5 minutes on the radiotherapy machine (ha ha). And your facial, of course—heaven.

Byee xxx

Wonky eyebrows—oh dear. Whilst one expects to lose hair from one's head, it came as quite a surprise that all body hair gradually disappeared, even down to nasal hair! I had such a drippy nose and it was only then I realised why. At least I didn't have to pay for leg waxing during this time. Every negative has a positive.

28th May 2009
Subject: Re: Life in the fast lane

Dear Margaret

Gosh you will have to slow down or you will be a wreck before you get to Corfu. Glad Pat got back from her holiday ok. I am sure you will all have a lovely day together tomorrow. It looks like your weather is going to be good for you before you go on holiday. The same here for the weekend.

Treatment going well no problems so far. Just the travelling; accident going into Portsmouth this morning so ended up 20 mins late for my apptment. Ended up arriving home 45 mins later that I should have but never mind just have to go with the flow.

Look forward to your call in the morning. Your parcel has arrived so will be up early in the morning to get stuck in.

Bye for now. Luv Maureen xxx

30th May 2009
Subject: Re: Bon Voyage!

Dear Margaret

Do hope you all had a lovely day yesterday as I did. Got home from the hospital at 5 pm. Not bad for a Friday. All going well so far 4 down, 11 to go.

Going to church this evening. Tracey is down from Peterborough, staying with Mandy so will catch up with her in about an hour. Had an email from Grant in Afghanistan and seems to have settled in ok. All the family are coming here tomorrow for a barbeque at 2 pm, thought it would be nice since the weather is good and we are all together for a change. Have been to Tescos and got all the necessaries. We get all our meat from an organic butcher so much nicer.

I am so excited about your holiday you would think I was going!! It will be wonderful for you both to relax and enjoy after the past few months. I shall look forward to a text now and then to keep up with your activities. Plenty of sea and sunshine what more could a body want.

Do have a super time and don't be too stressed getting ready tomorrow. It's great you have Judith at home to look after Barney. Hope he doesn't miss you too much.

Take care. Luv Maureen xxx

P.S. Thanks again for my bracelet (haven't took it off) and my cute bear so apt. Haven't done anything with my seeds yet!

For her birthday, I sent Maureen a "Life after Cancer" bracelet I purchased from our local Maggie's Cancer Care Centre—a wonderful haven of peace and help for all sufferers of cancer. The bracelet was not pretty but very symbolic and was a mark of the success of the journey we had been through together. I wore mine with pride and I hoped she would do the same. I also sent her a "Forever Friends" small bear. It was wearing a headscarf tied at the back just as ours had been whilst having chemotherapy. The flower seeds were to plant in recognition of our growing friendship.

31 May 2009
Subject: Up, up and away

Hi Maureen

Thanks for the ever welcome e-mail—shall miss them over the next 2 weeks. Anyway, it's 3.20 and apart from getting myself nail polished and stuff, I think everything is about ready. Just put the hoover round for the last time and tidied up. What a mess you make getting ready to go away.

It's absolutely glorious here again today. Barney really feeling the heat. It would be fantastic to have a barbeque same as you. I'm sure there will be lots on the go, making the most of the weather. I hope you enjoy yours. Does Liam do the cooking on the barbeque? Usually all the men have a shot don't they. Great stuff.

Make sure you don't overdo things whilst you are having your radiotherapy. It takes a lot of energy from your body to repair what is happening (so I'm told). I made sure I was in bed earlier than normal and had a good 8 hours. I then felt I could carry on as normal during the day. It seemed to work anyway.

I shall be thinking of you whilst I am away and sending you a few texts. I am also going to be wearing my bracelet. I do feel a certain comfort coming off it somehow and I hope you will too.

I will definitely think of you having your radiotherapy at 7 p.m. tomorrow. It will be 9 p.m. in Corfu and no doubt we will be having our first evening meal (probably in the open air). We will raise a toast to you and me and ours for our future good health, so think of me as you climb on that machine and what we are doing all those miles away in Corfu at the same time.

Well, Maureen, it won't be long before your sessions are over and you can look forward to *your* holiday (well earned, I feel). Still find it incredulous that this time last year we were still unaware that anything was untoward and here we are all done—hooray.

Best love. Take care and love to all the family.

Margaret xxx

Off we sailed, into the sunset . . . well, no, Glasgow airport actually. We were so looking forward to getting to Corfu. We would be staying in apartments owned by Effie and Takis in Sidari, a very popular resort these days. We first went in 1991 and fell in love with the place and the people. We have got to know Effie and Takis particularly well. On arrival, Effie came out to greet us, arms outstretched.

"Oh Effie," I said "Karkinos, karkinos," which is Greek for cancer. She looked shocked, stood back and said "Oh! Me too."

We hugged understandingly. This was Effie's second time having breast cancer and she was having chemotherapy as before. This was in addition to running her apartment complex, cooking in their taverna and serving drinks until the last person left the bar in the evening; no small feat considering Effie was in her sixties. We had such a laugh one evening, sitting with Effie and Takis enjoying a glass of red wine. We looked knowingly at each other as we surveyed our glasses. My Greek may not be very good, nor Effie's English but we laughed, eyebrows raised, as we both knew we were comparing the red wine to our pee! Epirubicin—one of our chemo drugs—turns your urine red. Both of us had the same thought and the communication was unbelievable. I now also realised how much we take our situation in this country for granted. I had to travel just two or three miles to Dunfermline for my chemotherapy. Effie had to go to Athens which meant a two hour bus ride to the ferry terminal, six hours on a ferry and an overnight stay in the hospital and, of course, a return journey. She had to do that every three weeks.

16th June 2009

Subject: Re: welcome home

Dear Margaret

Welcome home. Do hope you had a reasonable journey home and everything wasn't too tiring. Hopefully you have brought the good weather to Scotland with you. It is lovely and sunny here and quite warm.

Yes, my last radiotherapy, yesterday, we got back home at about 1 p m so had a nice lazy afternoon in the garden. I cannot believe that all the treatment is over and everything is behind me. Did you feel kind of weird? My skin has turned pink like a red square as you said. I have an itchy bit mid chest which I keep putting my cream on so I don't scratch anything. I handed my blue form in on leaving, so will get a six week apptment sent to me.

My next apptment is 22nd July with my Oncologist which will be at Chichester. I promised myself on leaving St. Mary's that I would not be back.

I am sure Barney was glad to see you lots of licks. It will take a few days for you to settle back into a routine again. Will be going to take Mum out this morning as haven't seen her since last Wednesday. Boomerang has sat on my lap since I started this e-mail after walking all over my laptop first and she is no lightweight. Obviously not getting enough attention!!

Anyway Margaret do hope I shall hear from you soon and know everything is OK.

Take care as always both of you.

Luv Maureen xxx

20th June 2009
Subject: Chat

Dear Maureen

Glad to hear your cold on the way out. Summer colds can be a nuisance.

It's our Race for Life tomorrow. I went back to WW this morning (have put 3 ½ lb on—must be the wine!) They have been running a raffle to help sponsor all of us that are doing the race. Over £200 collected. This will be shared out between all the members who are taking part so I thought that was brilliant. Trust me, though, I slipped on the stairs leading down to the room where the meeting is held and twisted my foot. It's not too bad but hope it doesn't get too stiff overnight. I'll have to take a couple of paracetamol perhaps. Of all the times to do that!

Yes, the washing eventually got sorted. I spent all Thursday morning ironing, 3 hours in the morning. We then took Barney for a walk further up the coast to a little fishing village called Dysart—very pretty walk—and then I did more ironing when we got back. I always manage to leave something in the basket though.

I am fed up with my hair. Everyone tells me it's fine without my wig. It feels more comfortable without it now but I still find my own hair very, very short. I have tried spiking it up a bit (very trendy, ha ha) but I think I look a fright, or look as if I have HAD a fright. We have to get new passports soon and I don't know whether to have the photo done with, or without the wig. They already stipulate no glasses so I will look more like a convict than ever maybe. Oh well, all in good time, eh? How's yours coming along?

Thought I would attach a couple of photos. The one of Dave was when he got to drive our boat on the East Coast Cruise. He loved it! Don't laugh—the one of me in the pool with my arm across my front is because I didn't have my swim boob in the swimming costume. I thought I could get away without it but then thought I looked a bit flat. No-one else around anyway.

Well, have a nice Father's Day. I am cooking Dave his favourite roast. We shouldn't be away too long for the Race for Life. Have to meet everyone else at 10 a m.

Glad you liked your tea towel. It was a lovely shop full of nice kitcheny things. Couldn't resist.

Bye for now—speak soon

Lots of love from Margaret xxx

This also reminded me that whilst on the East Coast Cruise, when we passed the nearest point to Albania, approximately one mile off their shores, I received a message on my mobile phone that said "Welcome to Albania. Enjoy your stay." That, I thought, might be awkward if I had for any reason to prove my whereabouts on that day!

21st June 2009

Subject: Re: race for life

Dear Margaret

Thank you for the lovely piccies you sent of your holiday. The sky is so blue and the two of you look as though you are having a ball. Your hair looks really good. Mine is similar but still quite short. I haven't been brave enough to go without a headcover so wear my scarves. I bought 3 in different colours and designs. It was pink today as I wore a fuchsia t-shirt and white crop.

Congratulations on your race for life walk this morning. I was thinking of you at 11 a.m. Do hope I get as good weather as today it was perfect here, hopefully the same for you. How is your ankle, wasn't too painful for you I hope. Sometimes it can get worse before it gets better. Plenty of ice.

We went to The Coach and Horses for a roast lunch today. First time we have been there and was really impressed. Very children and dog friendly which means a lot with our family. All the Dads got a miniature cognac and a bowl of fudge to take home! My mum has picked up my cold which has gone on her chest so she's not too happy at the moment. Will pop and see her tomorrow.

Well another week approaching how time is flying by. Liam has the dentist on Tuesday but apart from that nothing much going on.

Enjoy your week. Take care. Luv Maureen xxx

22nd June 2009
Subject: Race for Life

Hi Maureen!

What a great day we had. The sun shone, the atmosphere was fantastic and Jude and I completed the course in 53 mins—that's 6 minutes slower than I did it last year so didn't think that was too bad. However, I was absolutely bushed by 9.30 p m and had to go to bed. You must be careful not to overdo it when you have so recently finished your radiotherapy. I was honoured by one of our group, Yvonne our WW leader, the one in the hat, ran the race for me. She had put "For her brave friend Margaret who fought and won". Wasn't that great. You will see one of our members had the race number 666, poor thing, but another member gave us pink fluffy devil horns to wear, in the circumstances.

Anyway, I've attached a few photos of our group etc and hope you can make out what I put on my back. You will see Jude No. 898. I raised £77 and Jude got over £100 so I think we have done very well.

Hope to hear from you soon. Best love, Margaret xxx

When Maureen and her daughters complete their Race for Life a few weeks after mine, I noted they too did the course in 53 minutes, the same time as me. The message I carried on my back read as follows:

"I race for myself and my dear friend Maureen. We fought and survived inflammatory breast cancer together. We were diagnosed 2008. Now both completed our journey". Little did we know then what was to come.

I had noticed a red patch across my mastectomy scar. As it didn't seem to be going away after a few days, I decided to have a word with my Breast Nurse. I telephoned her at 9.30 a m. She phoned me back after ten minutes and asked me to be at the hospital for 11 am the same morning. By 11.30 am I had seen the Breast Consultant, had a biopsy and was on my way home—whew. One of the symptoms of Inflammatory Breast Cancer is redness and heat so one can't take any chances. I was anxiously waiting for results of the biopsy and very relieved to hear I was clear. The opinion was that the redness was nothing more sinister than as a result of my radiotherapy, incredible after all this time.

25th June 2009
Subject: Hi

Hello Maureen

Thanks for your ever-welcome email. What a lovely day we had yesterday. Lorna had to go for her 20 week scan, everything OK, so we looked after Lucas whilst they were at the hospital. We are enjoying some really hot days so I managed to get a small paddling pool from our post office. Well, it kept Lucas busy for about 1 ½ hours. Jude had her feet in it too! It was great. We then got him dressed and walked him down round the shore and up our woodland trail and got home just as Lorna & Chris arrived.

We all had our meal in the garden. I had some lovely melon. I made Greek salads (still in holiday mode!) with spaghetti bolognese and garlic bread and then just some Scottish strawberries and cream—would have cost you £20 at Wimbledon I expect!). We sat in the garden until it was time for them to go home . . . If only we had more sunny days like that. You feel so relaxed.

No results yet. Was a bit anxious yesterday as can't help hoping I haven't got to start all over again. Still, trying not to think that way. Just going to get stuck into some ironing. I am out with the Thursday girls tonight so looking forward to that.

I expect your square is looking quite prominent by now—I wondered when mine was ever going to stop getting brighter. I did blister too—not sore though. I still have a square, albeit just a bit darker than my other skin now. Will keep you up to date as soon as I hear anything. It comforts me to know you are thinking about me.

Bye for now. Lots of love Margaret xxx

We both enjoyed the tennis and we were both hoping Andy Murray would do well.

27th June 2009
Subject: Re: good news

Dear Margaret

So pleased to hear your good news on Thursday another crisis over thank goodness. It is so good we can share our ups and downs together it helps so much.

Have had to come indoors as it is just too hot in the garden and am getting a headache—not good. Will be watching Andy later today. Kieran is 3 today so having his family party tomorrow so should be lovely for a barbque. I might have my first Pimms or a weak white wine spritzer tomorrow. Haven't felt like a drink so far but I do now!! Am I moving on at last.

Glad everything is going well with Lorna's pregnancy so far. Is your weather still good in Scotland? What are you up to for the weekend.

My red square is still itchy and bumpy but hopefully settling down. Of course this hot weather doesn't help.

Lots of love to you from us here in Sussex. A big hug as always.

Luv Maureen xxx

27th June 2009
Subject: Re: good news

Hi Maureen

Lovely to hear from you. We have lost our good weather I'm afraid. Quite cool today and a bit damp. The garden could do with the rain. We have strawberries coming along nicely in the garden. Dave got some straw and netting to keep the birds off.

Funny you should say about not fancying a drink. I was exactly the same but I did enjoy a glass of wine on holiday. I thought I was never going to enjoy any alcohol again! Not that I have ever taken very much.

Andy's match just finished. I felt sorry for his opponent, can't spell his name ?Trioscki? Anyway I enjoyed it. Thought with the Roddick match running on it might not have finished this evening. Did you see that flash of lightning? We seldom get storms here. We used to get loads in Kent—the children loved them then.

I hope Kieran has a lovely party and you can have it outside. I must get my thinking cap on for Lucas' birthday present. He will be two in August and I have no idea what to get him yet. Any ideas?

Hope your red square is behaving itself. Thank you for being at the other end of the phone when I had my biopsies on Tuesday and for the results on Thursday. Only you would really know how that all felt.

Anyway, enjoy Sunday and we can 'speak' again soon.

Lots of love from not so bonny Scotland—at the moment.

Margaret xxx

1st July 2009
Subject: Hello

Hiya Maureen

Hope your mum is making good progress now. She must have been pretty miserable.

This week is turning into a very busy one. Today I have been invited to lunch at a former colleague's new house. Kymm is a lovely young girl who came to work with me at the medical practice when she left school—she is now 28. We got on very well considering the age difference and I am like an aunty I think. She had her first baby (Lewis) in last June and this is the family moving from a little old bungalow to a brand new 4 bedroom det res. Kymm works at the Queen Margaret Hospital now. I am looking forward to seeing the wee one. I love to see the young ones getting on in life and Kymm and Stuart are a lovely couple. They started going out together at the age of 13 and neither had any other romances.

Friday morning we are having Lucas as Lorna on nights Thursday and needs some sleep. Her mum and dad are going to Paris with their neighbours to celebrate a 50th birthday. They would normally be having Lucas.

Dave also going to doctors tomorrow. On holiday I noticed a flat mole on his back which I had not noticed before. When you look closely it is a different colour round the edge so I thought he better get it checked out.

My papers have arrived for the NHS Ethics Committee meeting next Tuesday and there are seven projects to read this time! Bad timing with Wimbledon on the go. Andy plays today—can't miss it. Just about had a heart attack during the last match. Great game though.

So, feels like the fast lane for me this week Maureen. Oh, yes, I am doing a Survivor's lap of honour in the Relay for Life (Cancer Research UK) on Saturday as well. It's a good day out and I shall definitely feel differently doing it this year as I had only just been diagnosed when I did it last year and didn't feel like a survivor as I do now. Keep forgetting to tell you I am so upset because I lost my bracelet on holiday. I never took it off but we went swimming one day in fairly rough seas and can only think it came off then. I didn't miss it immediately. I am going to try to get another one although psychologically it is not the one I had at the end of treatment. Daft, I know.

Well, hope you are having a good week and managing to watch as much tennis as possible. Hope you are now getting more used to not having to get to a hospital so frequently.

Look forward to hearing from you.

Take care now—not long to your hols. Lots of love from Margaret xxx

4th July 2009
Subject: Hello again

Dear Maureen

Here we are again . . . happy as can be, as the song goes. It's another glorious sunny day here today—just right for the Relay for Life. All us survivors have to meet at the Registration Tent at 11.30 a m. 12 noon we have the opening speeches by local celebrities (Chairman of Dunfermline football team). We are told the Relay opens with a BANG this year so don't know what to expect. Probably frighten all the children present if too loud! 12.15 it is the Survivors' lap on honour and 12.45 is our lunch. I've got my T shirt at the ready and will be marvelling at what efforts everyone makes to raise money for cancer research. Our Tesco girls have a team again. The teams will be walking from noon today until noon tomorrow. My Breast Nurse and Surgeon are involved in their teams and there will be many stalls there hoping to raise plenty of money—wonderful.

I forgot to ask you how your red square is coming along? Is it settling down yet?

The steristrips from my biopsies haven't dropped off yet but are beginning to peel at the edges! Not sore. Still very relieved.

Have a lovely weekend Maureen and I'll speak to you some time during the week. I'll let you know if I get another bracelet. I have decided I do want one.

Lucas is a bit off colour and he's got conjunctivitis—probably because he has started nursery. He wasn't his usual boisterous self yesterday but a cuddly boy instead.

Hope your mum is back to normal.

Love to everyone. Bye. Margaret xxx

July brings more news of babies. My son and his wife are expecting a November baby and now Maureen's daughter Tracey and her husband, Grant expect a baby at the beginning of December. We are both to become grannies again round about the same time. Everything seems very peaceful and normal again, although Maureen still has to be given the complete all clear. She is off on holiday to the Isle of Wight, a well-deserved break with family and dogs. Our friends, Lin and Colin who live in Kent were also holidaying in the Isle of Wight at the same time as Maureen. I jokingly asked Lin to approach any woman wearing a headscarf and ask if she was Maureen. I have replaced my bracelet and will make sure I don't lose this one.

5th July 2009
Subject: Re: Hello

Dear Margaret

Lovely to hear from you and do hope you had a good day yesterday with your survivors lap. It all sounds wonderful so hope lots of money was raised and the weather held. Still lovely here but not so humid so that's a blessing.

Yes, my red square isn't so red and itchy now just settling down at the right time although it has spread to under my arm now but that's ok. Mum is much better thank goodness but still has a sore chest. Finds it takes her longer to recover from anything nowadays.

Have been looking out knitting patterns for babies and needles ready to have a go after the holiday as this will be a winter baby. Haven't done any knitting since November so am quite keen. Hope the result of your weekend is good and peaceful. Talk soon.

Lots of luv as always. Maureen xxx

19th July 2009
Subject: Hi, again

Hello Maureen

I am glad you enjoyed your holiday. Our friends had a lovely time too, with lovely weather—always a bonus. Now it's back to all the washing.

I am probably a bit late wishing you luck for the Race for Life as you will have done it by the time you read this. I look forward to hearing all about it later.

I have got my new bracelet and am pleased to say it feels just the same as the other one. I'll make sure I don't lose this one. It was lovely at the Maggie's centre where we went to pay for the bracelet. There was a large group of ladies all on a "Feel Good, Look Good" workshop with makeup demonstration etc. I have enrolled for a Nutrition workshop on 3rd August and have put my name down for a new six week course starting in August on the transition back to normal after cancer. I think it should be good. You know yourself it feels strange to have suddenly finished all your treatment etc. This is obviously quite normal otherwise they wouldn't be running such a course. Anyway, I might not fit in all the talks as we go away in September for ten days so I'll see how it goes.

Looking forward to hearing all your news.

Lots of Love (and a hug) Margaret xxx

19th July 2009

Subject: Re: Home sweet home

Dear Margaret

Hello. Boy am I tired!! We all had a lovely week I had forgotten how hilly the Isle of Wight is. Went swimming everyday so that was a bonus. Have caught up with the washing and have just done the ironing that's why I'm knackered. The children had a ball and were very good as were the dogs.

We all met up again for the race for life today. Have sent some piccies for you to see. Well Margaret we completed the course in 53 minutes, I was determined to get under an hour. As it is my first I shall treasure my medal. It was bright and breezy here perfect walking weather. We raised £500 between us to very pleased. Glad your new bracelet feels good. I was petrified of losing mine on holiday but thankfully came home with it. The courses you have enrolled on sound perfect. I'm sure you will enjoy them.

Tracey goes home tomorrow but will be going up to her for the weekend around the 7th August. We all went back to Leisha's today for jacket potatoes, sausages and beans. Yummy. Thanks for the Vita magazine I loved it. Haven't seen it before so sent the coupon away today to get the next issue.

Talk soon.

Lots of love Maureen xxx

Maureen's Race for Life message she carried on her back was "I race for life for 2 survivors of breast cancer myself and my bosom buddy Margaret. Friends for life." I was really proud of us both.

22nd July 2009
Subject: Re: Good News

Dear Margaret

Just to let you know that I got the all clear from the Oncologist and I am now cancer free!! Just have to have 4 monthly checkups for 2 years and a yearly mammogram as a precaution, probably the same as you. Feeling so good today we all had a little cry. Relief I think. Taking Mum shopping tomorrow. Weather looks good here for the weekend so will enjoy that.

Hope you are well and glad you liked your IOW bits. A bit blustery here today are you the same? Off to e-mail my other friends the good news. Talk soon. Take care. A very big hug from Maureen xxx

We rejoiced together in Maureen's good news. My follow-up treatment was a little different. Annual check-up and mammograms for me for the next ten years, not two as in her case. Maureen had showered me with gifts from the Isle of Wight, all lovely, useful things.

22nd July 2009
Subject: Re: Good News

Dear Maureen

Good news indeed! Isn't it great to hear the oncologist say we are cancer free. Yippee. I am sure we will be well looked after in future. I had a little cry too! You can't measure relief can you.

Have just taken Barney round the block. Best part of the day. We are getting very heavy showers and had a lot of thunder and lightning last evening. Chris was afraid it was going to waken Lucas but it didn't. He is waking up very early at 5 a m every morning at the moment.

I am using the bookmark you sent me. I am reading Colleen Nolan's Autobiography. Jude read it and thought I would like it. She was right. I really love the shopping lists and magnets you also sent (too nice to use) and I just can't resist a new tea towel! Truly, a lovely surprise.

I'm off to Glasgow on the bus tomorrow to meet my friend Agnes so looking forward to that. I also had my hair shaped today and a bit of silver put through it. I am really pleased with it. The hairdresser even managed to get a hot brush through the top. I might keep it short now.

Well, Maureen, I know how you must be feeling and the word is F A N T A S T I C. I'm sure our positive attitudes have had a lot to do with our recovery. YIPEE again!!

Best love, bye for now

Lots of love (and thanks for the big hug) Margaret xxx

Margaret, very pleased with her wig!

Margaret, Pat and Barney (Miniature Schnauzer)

Fern, Maureen's daughter's Miniature
Schnauzer

Maureen's granddaughter Ruby
(Same age as Margaret's grandson Lucas)

Margaret's grandson Lucas

Margaret in Corfu on first holiday after
completion of treatment

Margaret's Race for Life message

Group picture at Race for Life 2009.
Note number 666 plus devil horns!

Treatment finished!
Maureen and her husband Liam enjoying a
holiday on the Isle of Wight

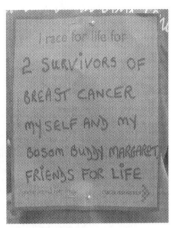

Maureen's Race for Life July 2009 Message

'Thumbs Up'
Maureen with daughters Sheena and Leisha
Race for Life July 2009

I said a prayer and lit this candle in Zakynthos
when I heard from Maureen that her cancer had
returned

Lucas with baby Zak

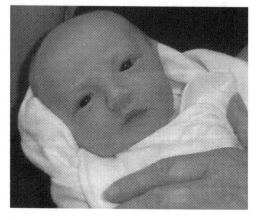

Sophie, Maureen's new granddaughter born 16th December 2009

Maureen's Family including her beloved mum

Margaret on Holiday
"The blonde bombshell"!

Maureen and Liam on her 60th birthday -
29th May 2010

Maureen and Granddaughter Ruby at
Family Wedding - July 2010

First photo in hospital

Waiting to be admitted
10 September 2010

Maureen, Liam and Margaret saying final goodbyes
at the hospital - 12 September 2010

PART TWO

25th July 2009
Subject: Lovely Day

Hi Maureen (smiley face)

We have a lovely day dawning here, hopefully replacing the torrential—and I mean torrential—showers we have been having for a few days.

I hope you are still feeling on top of the world and looking forward to a nice weekend.

I was at a lovely "do" last night. One of the GPs I used to work for is retiring and all us "oldies", meaning former members of staff were invited along. We had a lovely meal and a wonderful time reminiscing. What a laugh when we spoke of all the fashions we used to wear. Shoulder pads, big glasses, afro hairstyles, perms etc. I worked at the surgery for 15 years and loved it.

Chris, Lorna and Lucas are coming for dinner tomorrow so think I'll make some red pepper soup. It's one of their favourites. I have a nice piece of lamb too and the new potatoes roast up so well.

There's me talking about food again and I am literally just off to WeightWatchers! I have been asked to sit at the welcome desk this morning and give out the cards. Better get my skates on.

Love to all in West Sussex

Speak soon

Margaret xxx

25ᵗʰ July 2009
Subject: Re: Lovely Day

Dear Margaret

Yes we have a lovely day here as well thank goodness and hopefully a good weekend. Have had showers like yourselves but didn't last too long. Gosh you were up early this morning. I have to confess I didn't get out of bed till 9 a m this morning and it was the same yesterday. Am I becoming lazy?

Went to Pulborough yesterday to see past friends I used to work with to share my good news. Some I haven't seen for a couple of years so it was lovely. Other than that I haven't done a lot. Changed the bed this morning, have a wash on now, at least will get it dry today and am going to bake some cakes after a cup of tea of course. Once I get going I'm fine it is just getting going!! Still get tired how about you?

How are you getting on with your Colleen Nolan book? Haven't done any reading at all this past week. Bought some lemon wool and have just finished a first size cardigan for the new baby. Was thrilled but so small it didn't take long. Am going to start on a flecked white matinee coat later on today, probably this evening as I want to sit in the garden whilst we have the sun. My runner beans are doing well picked some for dinner yesterday with my steamed cod—lovely and tender. The strawberries have finished now but were lovely and sweet.

Your hair sounds lovely well done. I think I'll keep mine short as well. At the moment when I get up every morning I have a piece of hair which just sticks out over my ear at all angles. Have to get the water on it to smooth it down. Hope weight watchers went well and to enjoy tomorrow with your family I do love a bit of lamb myself. Am going out for the day on Monday with my sister who is down from Newcastle. She has been catching up with her 3 children who all live Worthing so haven't seen her yet. Hope the weather holds so we can have a nice day out somewhere.

Anyway Margaret this won't get my washing pegged out. Have a lovely weekend and talk soon.

Lots of luv and a big hug Maureen xxx

I was feeling very, very tired—over tired in fact and thought I ought to see the doctor in case there was something not quite right. My GP was quick to remind me that I couldn't expect to get back to normal so soon.

"Your body has been battered by strong chemicals" she lectured, "you must keep life simple." That, for me is something much easier said than done. I would try—maybe.

28th July 2009
Subject: Holiday Photos

Dear Margaret

Thought I'd send some more holiday photo with the pets. Hope you like them.

Had a lovely day out with my sister Marilyn yesterday. We went to Hotham Park near Bognor Regis. We had the grandchildren with us so they had a great time running around exploring whilst we caught up. We all then went for a pub lunch which was good, before returning back home.

We hope to have a barbeque on Sunday for her before she goes back to Newcastle on Monday, weather permitting.

How have you all been? Give Barney a hug from Fern.

Lots of luv for now—Maureen xxx

31ˢᵗ July 2009
Subject: Weekend already!

Hi Maureen

Can't believe it's Friday again. I think I will be having a quiet weekend this week. Dave is off fishing with Chris on Sunday 5.45 a m start !!! I think Judith and I will be going over to Edinburgh to Toys R Us to see what we can get Lucas for his birthday. Still haven't got a clue. He is having new bedroom furniture from his mum and dad and will be going into a big bed rather than his cot so I don't know if we can get anything for his room.

It is exactly a year today I got my diagnosis. It was on the Thursday though so yesterday by day, but today by date. I guess I shall be going over things step by step again. I can't help it. I think I have caught your achy arm—quite sore today—upper arm though. I cleaned the cooker and hob yesterday and it's probably all the scouring I had to do (remind me to do it sooner next time). Most hated job but when it's all done it looks lovely.

My sister phoned yesterday to say she had been to see my brother who is convalescing at his son's house. He seems to be very well and in good spirits. I think he is enjoying the company and getting looked after as he lives alone normally. Heart operations seem to be very much routine these days and he doesn't even have a big scar where they took a vein from his leg for the bypass.

Well, I had better get myself dressed and get Barney out. Have a lovely weekend. Speak soon, take care, lots of hugs, and anything else nice I can send you! Margaret xxxx

Before her cancer was diagnosed, Maureen had been receiving treatment for gallstones, but this was put on hold until she

finished cancer treatment. The reference to gallstones becomes quite significant later.

Maureen is well into racing at Goodwood at this time. Her husband was a professional jockey and show jumper before he retired as was his father before him. Liam never missed the racing either watching it on TV or making it a day out. I watched this day and we both enjoyed seeing Rip Van Winkle. I think he was the Queen's horse.

31st July 2009

Subject: Re: Weekend already!

Good morning Margaret.

I see you are up nice and early today and on your computer at 9 a m. Managed to get up at 8.30 a m today. Slept much better last night as most nights I wake up constantly throughout the night as I get so uncomfortable. Glad to hear that your brother is still progressing well.

After I spoke to you on Wednesday an appointment came for me to attend the Upper G I clinic for my gallstones. It is on Wednesday so should be interesting. Haven't had any symptoms for a couple of months now but I do watch what I eat. Will have to have a blood test done and an ultrasound scan so there I was thinking I had finished with hospitals. Sorry to hear your arm has been playing up but as you say probably due to your excess use of it whilst scrubbing the cooker!! A job well done.

How exciting another holiday in September. Where are you off to this time? Hope you manage to get Lucas something for his birthday. I know how difficult it can be. Anyway it will be nice to go and look.

My sister is returning on Monday so are meeting up on Sunday as I said, the weather is looking promising to far. We have a lovely morning here the sun is shining. Am picking Mum up and taking her to a garden centre this morning. Liam will be tuning into Goodwood when he gets up. Got your text glad you enjoyed watching Rip Van Winkle run. They had dreadful downpours there yesterday.

Anyway Margaret do have a lovely weekend up North and we will be in touch next week. Take care with lots of hugs and kisses as always.

Luv Maureen xxx

I had started the course on the Transition Back to Normal after Cancer at Maggie's Centre with other cancer sufferers. It was enlightening to me to know how different we all are in our approach to this most fearful illness. One lady I recall who had suffered leukaemia had decided she would take the homeopathic route to recovery that meant no chemotherapy. She consulted a homeopathic specialist who advised her on diet—she was to eat nothing from the pig—and exercise. Amazingly, to me, she said her blood count recovered and she was in remission. Another told us that she, too, had decided to let her body heal itself, refusing a mastectomy, but using prayer and meditation. She had a young daughter and again, I didn't realise some people would make these decisions. Personally I felt both these ladies to be incredibly brave.

5th August 2009
Subject: Re: Maggie's

Dear Margaret,

Lovely to hear from you again. My didn't you do well in Toys R Us. Everything sounds just perfect for Lucas. Ruby is going through a similar stage loves computer buttons and phones as well. She goes to Merry Melody's every Monday for an hour which she just loves. They do songs and singing and nursery rhymes of course with all the actions, has been going since six months old. Started nursery this week on Tuesday afternoon and seems to be doing fine. Brought home what she made and a written report of what she had done during the afternoon.

Gosh those girls from your workshop are so brave. Like you I never questioned any treatment as it was all tailored to my needs for getting better. I hate to think where we would be now if we had refused chemo and the mastectomy. Got on well at the hospital had my blood took and the ultrasound done. Checked my liver which was fine and then the gall bladder. Yes I am full of little small stones all the way through so looks like the gall bladder will be removed. Have a follow up appointment on 30th September to see the way forward, so at least nothing till then. As you say not long till you will be off on your travels again. I'm so glad we don't have to wear our wigs this warm weather, they were great in the winter. It is so humid here today real headachy weather with no sun. It was nice to walk round the chiller area in the supermarket—so cool.

Myself and Liam are off on the train to East Croydon tomorrow to sort his railway pension out ready for October. Haven't been there before but we have a map of where we have to go. Better go and make a cup of tea, cannot do without that!

Take care, lots of luv Maureen xxx

I really enjoyed Maureen's chatty e-mails and hearing all about her family, grandchildren and their respective cats and dogs. The happiness she is experiencing is obvious. I think as cancer patients, we appreciate everything in life much more and rejoice in just being alive. We are now coming up to my grandson's second birthday. Last birthday, I had just had my first chemo. Will these memories ever fade?

10th August 2009

Subject: Weekend in Peterborough

Dear Margaret

Had a lovely weekend in Peterborough. Took us four hours to get there on Friday as traffic around the M25 Heathrow was very bad. Lovely and sunny when we got to Tracey's so unpacked and sat in the garden. Liam took the dog out for a walk so I got dinner ready for Tracey who got home at 7.10 p.m. We all sat down and ate together. Saturday we went shopping in Peterborough and had lunch out. Came home had a rest and then went to Stamford about 4 miles away where we fed the ducks and swans and Boris had a lovely long walk along the river. Had chicken for dinner when we got back. Watched Neil Diamond Saturday evening—had seen it before but still enjoyed the music. On Sunday another lovely day so sat in the garden whilst Liam tidied the weeds. Went back to Stamford at noon for a roast and left Tracey at 1.50 pm. Got home at 5.40 pm. Bad traffic at Heathrow again and much hotter coming home than going. Had to have a shower once in to cool down. I have done 2 lots of washing today, got it all dry, ironed it and put it all away. I am now knackered!!

Will be popping along to my homeopath lady Sally after that. Still see her every couple of months. What are you up to this week? Another busy schedule knowing you. I don't expect Barney likes this hot weather either.

Anyway, take care must get back to the knitting had a break over the weekend. Bye for now, Luv as always, Maureen xxx

10th August 2009
Subject: Weekend in Peterborough

Dear Maureen

Great to hear from you after your lovely weekend. We must have all been doing the same things! We had Lucas on Sunday as Lorna was at work and Chris wanted to get on with some decorating. We decided to take him to Beveridge Park, Kirkcaldy to feed the ducks. When we got there, as we made our way to the pond, there was a flock of geese on the grass. They started walking towards us so I got the bread out and we fed them too. Lucas was very brave and let one take the bread from his hand when he saw me doing it. We saved some for the ducks too. There were some wonderful climbing things for Lucas' age as well but unfortunately the heavens opened and we couldn't stay as long as we would have wished. However, he enjoyed it and was trying to tell everyone how the geese had taken bread from his hand. We had chicken for dinner AND watched Neil Diamond on Saturday. We have it recorded from when we watched it before but still enjoyed it. He is one of our particular favourites. I like September Morn. We also have the film The Jazz Singer on DVD. Good stuff. I have to say I am very tired today after being so energised last week. It must be something to do with having Lucas all day. Next weekend will be the same as we are having him on Friday afternoon and Saturday is his birthday. I have been seconded to sandwich making etc. They have about 18 coming to the house for his party so will be quite hectic. Last birthday I had just had my first chemo!

You have worked so hard with all the washing and ironing. It's good to get it al sorted in one day though. We are just back from a Barney haircut. He has been feeling the heat although his coat was no longer than usual. He actually bit the groomer! I felt terrible. She said she was doing his back legs and he doesn't usually mind but he just went for her. Dave said it's all part of her job. I know that but I wish it had been someone else's dog. He is becoming a grumpy old man—Barney that is, not Dave.

Tomorrow we are going to Glasgow. I went a couple of weeks ago to meet up with my friend Agnes. Well, her father passed away last Wednesday and the funeral is tomorrow. We never met her father but will go to support Agnes, James and the family.

Pat has friends arriving from Australia on Wednesday. We are all going together to the Edinburgh Tattoo next Monday. Really looking forward to that. Watch it on TV if you get a chance. It is usually televised at some point over the Festival. It takes place in the Castle, every night during the Festival and the fireworks at the end are quite spectacular.

I can't get over us both being shorthand typists! I wonder what else will come to light?

Well, Maureen, take it easy now. I think I'm up for an early night tonight. Hope you like the photo. The geese were almost as tall as Lucas. I didn't realise I had such a scraggy neck—oh well, c'est la vie.

Bye for now—will be in touch later in the week. Take care.

Lots of love from Margaret and the gang xxx

13th August 2009

Subject: Re: Busy, busy

Dear Margaret

Thanks for e-mailing me twice. I am getting so lazy! I don't know how I ever fitted work in 4 days a week and do everything else. I certainly don't have time for it at present. Hope you managed to get some waterproof ponchos ready for Edinburgh next week. I should be about tomorrow morning so look forward to speaking to you.

Loved the photo of Lucas. The geese were the exact same all over the park in Stamford. Small world. Unfortunately I didn't take the camera at the weekend.

Glad the funeral went ok and you got some good ideas for your sandwiches! Don't blame you as it is always hard to decide what to do. Had the grandchildren out today so feeling quite shattered now. They all seem to want my attention at the same time. That's what I get for having 4! Anyway hope to catch up with you tomorrow, if not have a great weekend and we will speak next week.

Lots of luv. Maureen xxx

17th August 2009

Subject: Re: Busy, busy

Dear Margaret

Hope you are all well and enjoy your event at the Tattoo tonight. Looks like the weather will be ok for you. We have had a lovely weekend here very warm and sunny. Looks like it will last till Thursday. Popped round to work yesterday afternoon for a cup of tea and a catchup with everyone. Did you get all your sandwiches made on Saturday?

Had a quiet weekend just enjoyed the good weather in the garden. Liam had to work last night. Am going to Sheena's tomorrow so am looking forward to that. Will probably go to the beach or Brooklands boating park with the children. Weather permitting the residents of The Willows are having a barbeque on Saturday so looking forward to meeting up with everyone. Just have to bring a bottle. Also have a facial on Friday morning so all in all have a busy week ahead. Hope everyone well in Scotland. Look forward to hearing all about your weekend. Talk soon.

Lots of love Maureen xxx

Our lovely, chatty, newsy e-mails reflected summery occupations. I fear we both still thought we could carry on completely as we had BC (before cancer) but repeatedly mention how exhausted we are. Neither of us seemed prepared to keep life simple as had been advised.

18th August 2009
Subject: Happy but frazzled

Dear Maureen

Yawn, yawn. Didn't get to bed until midnight last night but it was worth it. The Tattoo was absolutely brilliant. The weather was fine and we had good seats. We were doubtful that we would get the last train home, but we did so everything was perfect. We had a lovely meal in an Italian restaurant—one we usually go to if we are going to the theatre in Edinburgh and the walk up the Royal Mile to the Castle was magic. Crowds of people and street entertainers. Everyone had smiley faces. Lots of lovely interesting little shops and cobblestones all the way. The buildings in Edinburgh are beautiful.

Lucas' party went very well and he had a lovely, lovely time, soon getting the hang of opening his presents! There weren't many sandwiches left by the end. Jude helped me make them in the morning. There was a great spread. Lorna's mum had made a couple of pasta dishes and provided some roast beef and ham. I had also made a big salad. Lucas' birthday cake was Fireman Sam. He is Fireman Sam mad just now.

On Sunday we took the family to our local pub/restaurant for a meal. There is a playroom upstairs so Lucas was well away. He made a little friend and although we had to keep an eye on him he was quite busy whilst we enjoyed our meal. He put his own order in for sausage and chips (he just about manages to say "sausage".) He made us laugh because the waitress came and just said to us all "what would you like" and he pipes up "sausage and chips". So, anyway, we had a lovely weekend but I now feel totally done in.

I am starting to get my stuff ready for Saturday when George & Issy come for an evening meal. I am doing a Greek meal and will try to do as much in advance as I can. I am at Maggie's Cancer Care Centre tomorrow afternoon for the start on the Transition from Cancer course and Lorna has asked me to have Lucas on Friday. Never mind it will all work out I know.

Your weather sounds great—we are very cloudy here today. Hope you have a lovely day with the family. I expect your work colleagues are all pleased to see you looking so well. It's nice to catch up with everyone.

Well, I must go and make a cup of coffee now as it is 11 a m and Dave is busy in the garage (what's new?)

Lovely to hear from you

Lots of love from Margaret xx

P.S. Think I might learn to play the bagpipes after last night!!! The Chinese entertainers were amazing. So colourful. Just like the opening ceremony at the Beijing Olympics.

19th August 2009
Subject: Re: Update

Dear Margaret,

Like you I'm worn out too!! Glad everything went well for Lucas' birthday at the weekend and he was a good little boy. I took Kieran to nursery at 11.15 a m yesterday then myself and Shaun went to Brooklands. We went out in a boat which Shaun had to steer as he said the last time he was in a boat with his other Nanny she crashed it so he had to do the steering this time. Made me laugh—so much for my driving skills. He never stops talking all the time so there's never a dull moment. He then went on a pony ride which he loved and we sat down and had an ice cream. We walked all round the park so I was well worn out when I got home. It was a hot day also which gave me a headache even with my sunhat on. We have another scorcher today so have been chilling out in the garden this morning. Off to Sainsbury's with Mum about 1.30 p m to do our shopping and that will be it for today.

It was lovely to catch up with everyone from work—yes they all told me how well I was looking and loved my hair. Told them I wasn't sure if I was coming back—I know myself no way could I work 4 days now where would I get the energy—they said no rush to take my time deciding what I wanted to do, my job would be there whenever so that has stopped me worrying about letting them down. I know I have to put myself first now.

Hope you enjoy your cancer course today. I'm sure you will let me know all about it. Seems you have another busy week ahead of you—but better than being bored. Won't be long till your holiday either. Anyway must get a drink before I head off. Won't be long till Liam is up and about. Finds it hard trying to sleep these hot mornings.

Lots of luv as always from us all down south. Maureen xxx

It has to be a first for Maureen that she is realising she now has to think of herself before others. I also find this difficult and we will have to learn to be more assertive somehow.

21st August 2009
Subject: Hi

Dear Maureen

Just waiting for Lucas to arrive (9.15 a m). At least the weather is fine and we can maybe get him out somewhere.

I still feel a bit overwhelmed with all that is going on. Went to bed at 9.30 p m last night. Should have been out with the girls but after a day cleaning the house and shopping I couldn't make it. I have made an appointment to see the doctor because I am not sure I should be feeling quite as tired as I am. I certainly didn't expect to feel this tired after finishing radiotherapy in February but I don't know. Maybe my iron is low or something. Anyway I thought I would go and see her. Got to go next Wednesday morning.

Went to the course on Wednesday. It was very good and gave us all a chance to speak. There was a physio there dealing with exercise and the course itself is run by a clinical psychologist. There were four breast ladies (one only 30 years old) and 2 bowel cancer ladies. We all came away with questionnaires to complete and a big course book. I haven't had time to study it yet. I do think the course may be aimed at those less able than myself but I'll keep going and see what comes out in future.

Hope you are OK and looking forward to a nice weekend.

I am making a pavlova tonight for tomorrow. I am pretty organised but tomorrow will be a bit of a trial. I think I always try to do too much. Still, Sunday not far away for a good, good rest (hopefully).

Sorry if I don't get to speak to you on the phone this week—it's not for not wanting to.

Will speak soon. Lots of love to you all from me. Xxx

21ˢᵗ August 2009
Subject: Re: Update

Dear Margaret

Lovely to hear from you as always. Yes, you do sound really tired and think you are wise to have the doctor's appointment just to check things out—could be an iron deficiency but best to know. I do get tired but bounce back the next day nothing quite as bad as what you are describing. Glad the course went well this week will be interesting to see how it develops. Hope you have had a good day with Lucas and that it stayed dry for you to get out. The little ones have so much energy at that age especially boys I find so outside is just perfect for them to run off their energy.

Had my facial at 9 a.m. and an eyelash tint so my reasonable length lashes you now can see! Mum's second cousin Pam is coming down from Essex tomorrow for a visit so will be going out with them tomorrow morning and then coming back to base for The Willows barbeque at 4 p m. Going up to Mandy's for dinner on Sunday so have a weekend of no cooking—hurrah. Will ring you to see how you are and have a little chat on Monday morning if that's ok but don't change your plans if not.

Hope you enjoy your meal on Saturday and put those feet up on Sunday. Have sent a photo of when my sister was down on holiday with Mandy, Leisha with Ruby (of course) and my mum. Talk soon.

Lots of hugs Maureen xxx

26th August 2009
Subject: Re: Update

Dear Margaret, Just to let you know they think I have some sort of node in the underarm. I have to go for an ultrasound and a mammogram on Tuesday and then go back for the results 2 weeks after that. The doctor said he didn't think there was any cause for concern so I think I'm ok with that. Feel much happier thank goodness.

Have attached Mandy's horse Holly for you to see.

Take care. Luv Maureen xxx

I smiled as I thought of Mandy's horse galloping over cyberspace as an attachment to my email. More seriously though, I was very concerned at the appearance of a node as mentioned by Maureen. I did not voice this to her. As a medical secretary I had limited knowledge about medical matters, of course, but maybe more than someone who does not have any dealings with health at all. I understood any enlarged node to be worrying. However, she was to get an ultrasound and mammogram. I remember wishing she didn't have to wait two weeks for her results

27ᵗʰ **August 2009**

Subject: Hello again

Hi Maureen

Thanks for phoning yesterday with your news. I would be reassured that there is nothing to worry about. I suppose it is inevitable, at least for a while, that we are going to worry if we get anything different going on. I know exactly how you must have been feeling though because of the wee scare I also had. I kept looking at the patch hoping it had gone away (it has now). I just thought it would have been truly unfair if the cancer had come back again so soon. I expect we have to trust our "all clear" a bit more. Still, neither can we take any chances.

I feel set for a lovely QUIET weekend??? Dave and Chris are going fishing on Sunday we will be away all day and I won't be cooking large meals for anyone. I'll get to Weight Watchers on Saturday and have a look round town.

What a lovely horse Holly is. My WW leader has 2 (one is her husband's) His is Molly and hers is Alfie and likewise they are beautiful creatures.

Went to Maggie's yesterday. It was all about exercise and taking things gradually. We did half hour stretching, bending etc whilst we were there and have been given sheets to follow to do at home. I do such a lot of walking I think I probably get enough exercise that way but I'll try to do a bit more.

Well, Maureen, hope you have a nice weekend. Even though we don't go to work now, I still look forward to the weekends.

Let me know how you get on Tuesday, although I know your results won't be in just yet.

Love to you all (and hugs for the wee fright) Margaret xxx

28th August 2009
Re: Hello again

Dear Margaret.

Thanks for your call on Tuesday and being at the end of the phone for support. What are we like? Have put all my negative thoughts away so hope they don't re-surface on Tuesday at the hospital. The photos you sent of Lucas' birthday are lovely. He looks so happy with his pirate ship. Glad everything went well. Lorna has a lovely bump. Tracey's is smaller now that I have seen a picture of Lorna I can compare.

We have just come back from Bognor Regis where we have just ordered a new bed. Have gone for one where we can hoover under as our divan is floor level and so heavy to move. Ended up in McDonalds with the grandchildren yesterday after a visit to the park. Not a place I frequent very often but enjoyed my chickenburger. Finished with a cup of hot water which I added my own green teabag to, I always carry a supply in my handbag. Have to take Mum to the cemetery tomorrow with flowers as it would have been my grandmother's birthday. She likes to get there at least once a year. Lived to be 91 so didn't do too bad.

Like you should have a quiet weekend so hope to catch up on jobs and just maybe do some baking. Like you say still look forward to the weekend even though not working—just habit I suppose. Well Margaret do enjoy your weekend and make sure you get those feet up!

Thanks once again for all your support and for the hugs.

Lots of luv Maureen xxx

I feel the need to reassure Maureen that as she has to wait two weeks for her results, there cannot be anything to worry about. I couldn't help remembering my experience in Scotland of same day biopsy, consultant seen and results. However, perhaps we are luckier in Scotland not to have so many people in the "frozen north," Oh, Maureen . . .

1st September 2009
Subject: Hospital and stuff

Dear Maureen

Hope you get on OK today and are not too anxious. I do feel there should be nothing to worry about, especially as you are not to expect the results for 2 weeks. Thinking about you anyway and let me know how you get on, soon as!

Did you manage to catch the Edinburgh Tattoo on TV last night (I take it was on down your end). We recorded it as I was at choir last night but watched it when I got home. It was still very colourful and stirring. Hope you saw it.

I went to Dunfermline Abbey on Sunday morning for the service which was really uplifting. The organ is magnificent and sends shivers down my spine!

Dave & Chris went fishing on Sunday in a boat off Dunbar. Chris caught 56—yes 56 mackerel and 1 cod. Dave caught 4 cod but won the prize for the biggest fish on the boat (3 lb). Chris threw most of the mackerel back. I love fish but not particularly keen on fresh mackerel. The cod will do nicely though. I am just glad I don't see them caught—what a hypocrite.

I hope you had a good Bank Holiday. Here, we must have had the wettest day of the year! Just as well it wasn't a Bank Holiday here. I went up town but it was awful walking around as it was literally bucketing with rain. It did dry up for the afternoon but came on again in the evening. At least our plums are really swelling out now. They are absolutely delicious (Victorias) and coming off the tree eight or so a day so we (meaning me) are being really greedy for them.

Better go and get dressed. Feel quite lazy these days but it's quite nice!

Speak soon, Lots of love and happy thoughts to you.

Margaret xxx

1 September 2009
Subject: Re: update on hospital

Dear Margaret

All done and dusted had a thorough ultrasound and mammogram this morning and also a needle biopsy from the lump. Have been assured it is a lymph node and nothing to worry about so do feel back to my old self today. Results in 2 weeks so glad to have all that behind me again. Yes, we watched the Edinburgh Tattoo. Had been looking out for it in the TV Times since you mentioned it. We thoroughly enjoyed all of it and as you say very uplifting. We had a lovely Bank Holiday yesterday really warm and sunny. Much fresher today with a cool breeze so looks like Autumn on the way. Sorry about your weather you will just have to come back down south you know!

Gosh didn't Chris and Dave do well in the fishing department. Yes, we love cod so don't blame you for keeping them. Glad your plums are fattening up. Mum loves Victoria ones and is always looking for them in the Greengrocers. They are so nice this time of year for jam or pies. Yummy. We just went to Mandy's yesterday and had a nice walk and picnic in the woods near her at Fittleworth. Shaun went to Fisher's Farm which is animals and rides so he had a nice time. Back to school for him on Friday.

I have shopping tomorrow lunchtime. Sheena and children on Thursday and Mum has dentist on Friday morning—another week gone.

Hope you have a good week and glad to hear you are trying to slow down a little. Off on holiday next week? Take care.

Lots of luv from Maureen xxx

Preparations are in hand for our September break with friends to Zakynthos, Greece. I have arranged for Maureen to text me whilst we are away, with the results from her biopsy.

3rd September 2009
Subject: Zzzzzzz

Dear Maureen

It was lovely to talk to you yesterday. I must apologise if I sounded a bit vague to start with! I will now confess to having a wee snooze when the phone went. I try to do most of my chores in the morning and then I like to sit down about 3.30 p m with a cup of tea, do my crossword or codeword before I make the dinner. I will not tell you how many times I nod off doing my crossword! Oh well—now we are retired we can do these things I suppose.

Mind you, it could be water on the brain! Will this rain never stop? It was absolutely torrential again last night and it is still raining at 11.30 this morning. We woke up to water on the kitchen table. All my cotton napkins were soaked through and there was water dripping out of the light fitting about the table! Well, Dave was in the loft before he had taken his dressing gown off. As we are in a bungalow and with all the rain we obviously suspected something wrong with the roof. He thought it was the lead flashing but wasn't sure so phoned Chris and he came down and was outside up on the roof in pouring rain in no time. Anyway he found a crack in the lead.

Luckily Dave had some lead in the garage so without more ado Chris was dealing with it and it is all done now. That would have cost us hundreds, I'm sure, if we had to call someone in. It's probably hundreds just to go on the roof before anything else. So, we are very lucky to have a son who does these things in his line of business. Glad it didn't happen whilst we were away. You hear of ceilings coming down and all sorts—I'm sure you will never experience anything like that in West Sussex with your lovely weather. It still looks good on the weather map for you—and Kent (boo hoo).

So glad everything went well for you at the hospital. Well, Maureen, I'll phone you before we go to Zante. I hope you will text me whilst we are away if you get some results from the biopsy. I'll text you anyway.

Take care—weekend nearly here again. My, how the time flies. Hope you have a nice one. Lorna is working Sunday so the family won't be coming for dinner so maybe a quiet one on the cards. We may go out for a meal Saturday for our anniversary. See how we feel. If the weather is terrible it's better staying in and I'll cook us something nice or get a Marks & Spencer dine in for £10—never tried them yet. See, I AM getting lazy!

Bye for now. Lots of love Margaret xxx

4th September, 2009

Subject: Re: Update

Dear Margaret,

Lovely to hear all your news as always. We had the heavy rain on Wednesday night but only a few sharp showers since although it feels very autumnal with a strong wind. The weekend looks good though into next week. Never mind you will soon be in the sunshine in Zante and topping up with your vitamin D. I expect we will be in the garden cutting grass and catching up with jobs. We have quite a few bushes which need pruning back. Hope to get to church Saturday evening. I bet you were glad your leaky roof didn't happen when you were away. When we were in the Isle of Wight there was a bad thunderstorm which cut off the electricity here for a couple of hours which put all the timers haywire. We had to reset everything when we got back.

Take care. Lots of Luv Maureen xxx

We went off to Zante and whilst enjoying the lovely sunshine, good company and relaxation, on 16th September a text came from Maureen. It was only three words long but said it all:

"Lump cancerous—gutted."

Straight to the point. It could have been my own results as I felt the shock go through me like electricity. We were in a lovely apartment in the resort of Tsilivi and at the top of the road was the smallest church I had ever seen. The church, in true Greek Orthodox style was absolutely beautiful with painted icons around the walls, and a small altar complete with lighted candles. My first thought was to go there, say some prayers, and light a candle for Maureen. I literally ran up the road to the church and I hoped she might feel comforted to know there was a candle burning for her in Greece. I took a photograph and sent it to her, but did not get a reply.

In one of the local shops I came across some pretty little china bells patterned with doves of peace. I bought one for Maureen and one for myself for our Christmas trees. I had hoped that by looking forward to Christmas we would be thinking she would be well on her way to her second recovery.

My next e-mail seems full of too many meaningless things when all I wanted to ask her was how was she feeling, was she frightened, and what was going to happen next.

23rd September 2009
Subject: Scan

Hi Maureen

Glad to hear the scan was going ahead today. I expect you were pretty hungry after having to fast from last night. I hope the liquid you had to drink was not unpleasant. Anyway, as you say, only another week to get through. It will probably feel like forever—I know it would for me.

Managed to get all the holiday clothes washed and stood ironing last night for over 2 hours (silly me). Still, I wanted to get it out of the way.

I saw my GP this morning for another BP check after coming off one of my tablets and she said it was OK and to have it checked again in 3 months. We discussed my osteoporosis problem and I have decided to start taking the recommended drug. I had been delaying it as I didn't really want to take any more powerful drugs, but that's silly if this one is going to prevent anything else later on. I only have to take it once a week but on a completely empty stomach (bang goes the early morning cup of tea) and I have not to sit or lie down for ½ hour after taking it. I have decided to start on Monday. I hope I don't get any side effects—hate taking anything really.

My blood test was OK so no anaemia causing the tiredness. Funnily enough I didn't have the feeling on holiday, nor the lightheadedness. No everyday pressures I suppose. I think I must have been made to be a lady of leisure—ha ha. Still, I haven't felt that tiredness since, so GP thought coming off the BP tablet had helped.

We have got our meal at Ibrox (Rangers football stadium) on Friday with our Glasgwegian friends. James was 65 in July and a relative gave him £100 voucher to spend in the restaurant there. He and Agnes have asked us to share it with them. I wanted to mark the occasion so managed to get James a book called "Temple of Dreams" which is a history of the Ibrox Stadium. Lots of pictures from long ago. I think he will enjoy it as he is such an avid fan. I am going to town tomorrow to see if I can get a top to wear. I want to be smart but not cold!

Chris phoned from Spain today and I spoke to Lucas, bless him. They are having a great time by all accounts.

Well, Maureen, I do hope everything went OK for you at the hospital. I look forward to hearing how you got on.

Bye for now, Lots of love, Margaret xxx

24th September 2009
Subject: Re: Scan update & thank you

Dear Margaret

Thank you so much for the gorgeous little bell you sent from Zante which will really look lovely on the Christmas tree as you say. It arrived this morning. The scan went well yesterday, everything before time as had to be there an hour before 3.20 p m so actually was finished at 3.30 p m. The liquid was fine about a pint of white stuff, thickish and actually tasted of fruit so quite pleasant. The scan then took place 40 mins after taking this. Had to change into trousers and top so felt like a member of staff! Had a cannula inserted into my hand as halfway through was injected with dye. My arms were above my head the whole time so of course brought back memories of our radiotherapy. The bed I was lying on went in and out of a Polo mint like machine. Had to breathe in and hold breaths during the 25 mins whilst in there. So, all in all everything was fine. Got home about 4.15 p m.

The girls are going up to see Tracey this weekend so I'm going as well. Liam is working so won't be going this time. They are all going to see Michael McIntyre in Nottingham on Friday evening and Limahl on Saturday. Mandy has been a fan since she was at school (Kadgagoogoo) don't know if you remember them. Don't know what is in store for me so took the opportunity to get away for a couple of days.

The weather is still beautiful here and very warm. Looked after Ruby in Worthing today whilst Mum at work. We walked to the park about 20 mins away and had a swing. Then came home and have been painting, and making shapes with plasticine. I'm having my third childhood all over again.

Glad Chris, Lorna and Lucas are all having a great holiday in Spain you will have a lot of catching up to do when they get back. Enjoy your meal with your friends at the weekend. Lots of luv as always. Maureen xxx

I am so helpless at this point and my emails reflect that with so much chat. It is only at the end that my true feelings emerge a little.

27th September 2009
Subject: Chat

Dear Maureen

I'm glad you liked your little bell and that it survived the post. I was interested to hear all about your scan. It sounds as if you coped with everything extremely well (as you always do). You were saying about memories of our radiotherapy. I have still got my square. Will we always have that, I wonder.

We had a fantastic meal at the Ibrox Stadium. We were in a cubby hole just us four at our table. There was a big window to our side and it looked straight out onto the pitch which was manicured to perfection. No match on obviously but it was quite spectacular. We had the best attention and it was a lovely menu. I had got myself a new top at guess where (M & S)—don't know what I would do if that store closed. Anyway, was a bit tired next day as we didn't get home until 11.30 p m and had to be up and out for 9.30 a m for WeightWatchers. I had to do the WW shop this week so that woke me up pronto. I only put on 1 ½ lb over my holiday which I thought was really good considering I was having wine which I don't normally.

It's dull here today and windy, but dry at least. Got out for a walk with Barney (it's his birthday today—12) and I am ashamed to say I didn't get him anything! Perhaps he'll get a bit of our roast lamb tonight.

I managed to arrange for Chris & Lorna to receive a bottle of champagne for their wedding anniversary. I got the idea and am always up for a challenge (don't we know it the both of us). Anyway, I knew the name of the people the villa in Spain was booked through and contacted them to see if it was possible. There was a lot of to-ing and fro-ing and eventually it was arranged that the owner would buy it for me and the cleaner, who was going up yesterday, would take it to the villa. Well, it all worked like clockwork and Chris phoned me yesterday. His first words were: " . . . and how did you do THAT?" What a surprise they got. It was in a nice bottle bag with a note and everything. I told the agents I would write to the newspaper to give them some good publicity for their customer service. So I must. I was so pleased it got to them.

Went to Bosom Buddies (Breast Ca Support Group) at Queen Margaret Hospital Thursday. Had a head massage—lovely. Debenhams are putting on a fashion show this week. All the models are from the support group. I was asked if I wanted to take part some time ago. They all get made up and the shop provides different outfits. I didn't fancy it myself. I'd probably fall off the catwalk, knowing me!

Hope you had a good weekend at Tracey's. I do remember Kadgagoogoo the name but that's about all, I'm afraid, unless I hear something and then say "Oh yes, of course". That's me all over.

Let's hope Wednesday won't be too trying for you. Please, please let me know how things go as soon as you can. Perhaps there won't be too much involved this time. I know it could so easily be me and I certainly understand how you must be feeling. You know you can always have a good old moan to me if you want to. Anyway, speak soon.

Take care and lots of luv as usual. Margaret xxx

28th September 2009

Subject: Re: Update

Dear Margaret

Lovely to hear from you as always. Yes, had a lovely weekend, quite hectic but took my mind off my troubles which was the idea. After arriving about 1 p m us girls went off shopping of course and managed to get some presents for Christmas so was quite chuffed got into the swing of things as at the moment don't even want to think of Christmas. Had a roast lunch out on Sunday before getting back home about 6 p m as the traffic wasn't too bad thank goodness. Liam has 2 weeks off now so went over to Mum's this morning to tackle her garden as she wanted some hedges cut down and a fir tree trimmed. Managed all that so just have to dispose of it all tomorrow at the re-cycling plant. Don't know how many trips it will take to get rid of it all but we will manage bit by bit.

Glad you had a nice meal at Ibrox Stadium and well done for only adding a little weight over the holiday with all that lovely food and wine. It is very chilly here first thing in the morning but once the sun appears it is lovely again. If we get another month of this it will be super.

There's 4 of us going to the hospital for results on Wednesday so am getting lots of support just hope they don't have to carry me out! (only kidding) my sense of humour is starting to return. Just watching tele tonight and doing some knitting. Got washing sorted and the ironing so well up to date on jobs. Are you having a busy week? Anyway will be back in touch after Wednesday so fingers and toes crossed!

Lots of luv, Maureen xxx

I think it was our mutual sense of humour that kept us afloat through everything. We always talked about having to laugh. We developed quite a dark sense of humour at times. Things like bringing a whole new meaning to "keep your hair on" when ours had fallen out and as we had both had left mastectomies saying that we hadn't got a pair between us!

30th September 2009
Subject: Scan Results Day

Hi Maureen

Well, scan result day! Just to let you know I will be thinking of you and waiting to hear from you. This so easily could be me, or might be at any time. Wish I could be the 5th person with you at the hospital this afternoon. I will be there in spirit. Take care Bye for now

Luv Margaret (keeping everything crossed)

2nd October 2009

Subject: Hi there!

Dear Maureen

I am shivering up here! Have got a polo neck jumper on *and* a body warmer. The temperature has dropped somewhat and yes, it's raining again. Autumn has come with a vengeance. Yesterday was a lovely autumn day. I walked Barney down the woodland trail near us and all the leaves are changing colour. I got down to the waterfront and it was so calm, quiet and sunny, I felt quite overwhelmed with the moment . . .

(There is nothing like cancer to bring your emotions right to the fore. I did feel quite tearful with the beauty of this moment. Everything seems more meaningful than b.c. and of course it is always in the back of your mind how much longer you might be enjoying nature and all her finest attributes. I suppose Maureen's circumstances were making everything that much more poignant. Of course, in my own inimitable style, I have to counteract my remark . . .)

silly me.

Hope you have a good weekend ahead of you. I am off to Edinburgh tomorrow with the Thursday girls to have a meal and go to the theatre. We are seeing a very Scottish play called "The Steamie" which is about the old days when Scottish women had to do their washing at the steamie. There were big white sinks and old coppers. It really concentrates on how all the women learn about each other's lives—the ups and downs, happy and sad. It's funny and sad. I have seen it on TV and enjoyed it. It will mean a late night.

Chris and Lorna travel home from Spain tomorrow and have asked to come for dinner Sunday. I thought I would do prawn cocktails to start using Chris' lettuces he grew in troughs and passed over to us as he had so many. I am using about 3 lettuces every day with my salad—they are lovely little cos lettuces. The usual roast will be what they are looking for and when George & Issy came over last time, they brought a dessert Issy had made—apple sponge—made with apples from their garden. I didn't use it and put it in the freezer so that's coming out Sunday. I'm looking forward to seeing them all as it is about 4 weeks since we saw them (before we went away).

Barney has a haircut on Monday afternoon so going to be quite busy. Tuesday afternoon is my NHS Ethics Committee meeting and I have still got some reading to do for that, but will give you a phone Wednesday before you go for your ultrasound on Thursday. However, as we always say, don't stay in. We'll always catch up later.

Hope you are still feeling nice and positive. I'm sure everything will get sorted quickly for you.

Well Maureen, I bet your weather is better than ours. If so, get out and enjoy it. Speak soon, Lots of luv from a not so Bonnie Scotland (ha ha)

Margaret xxx

Maureen and I are corresponding more frequently now. It feels like a certain need in both of us I'm sure—hugs from a distance?

2nd October 2009
Subject: Re: Catch up

Dear Margaret, Poor you with the weather, it is still lovely and warm in the daytime here but chilly in the mornings. We went off to the park with Ruby this morning with no coat or jacket lovely. A bit of a blip tomorrow then fine again Sunday although the temperatures are getting lower. The trees are just starting to shed their leaves here and the colours turning red and gold. It is a lovely time of year like spring. My two favourite seasons I think.

Cannot believe its 4 weeks since you have seen the family it will be nice to catch up on Sunday. We are going to Mandy on Sunday for dinner and church Saturday evening. I have a facial Monday morning, Tuesday the car is booked in with Fiat as there has been a recall for Pandas. Something has to be fitted (don't ask me what) but it is all free. Wednesday off to Brighton and Thursday hospital so quite busy again. Still haven't heard anything about the MRI scan yet. Will definitely catch up with you at some point next week.

Our neighbour gave us some cooking apples off their tree so made an apple tart which was lovely. Must make some cakes this weekend as haven't done any for a while Do have a lovely weekend all of you and don't eat too much of all that lovely food, sounds scrumptious.

Lots of love as always from Maureen xxx

We are both good cooks, and exchanged recipes and ideas many times. It is ironic that Maureen throws in the comment about not hearing about her MRI scan, amongst the baking she proposes to do. She obviously has her priorities right.

6th October 2009
Subject: Re: Update

Dear Margaret,

Guess what it's raining! Has been for the past 2 days. Have to say the garden does need it but we don't. Thought I'd give you a quick e-mail before we go off to the garage with the car. Heard from the hospital this morning and they have managed to give me the MRI scan on Thursday morning before my ultrasound so am pleased I won't have two trips to make. Will be a long morning but at least it gets everything out of the way. Results appointment is on Friday 16th October so not too long to wait to find out further treatment.

Hope you had a lovely weekend with all the family and lots of fun with Lucas. Hope Lorna is keeping well still, I presume she is still working. Cannot get used to looking out at rain and more rain. Mum is gradually recovering and feeling a little better it is taking quite a while this time.

Otherwise everything is good. Quite nice being pinked for breast cancer. Thought you would like that one.

Lots of luv as always Maureen xxx

My reaction to Maureen's news that her results day was Friday 16th October and her comment that this would be not too long to wait was not as complacent. Not too long? Surely, that is far too long, especially when inflammatory breast cancer spreads in an inkling. However, I would not be voicing that opinion to my dear friend. It was 16th September when the lump was found to be cancerous and still nothing in place regarding treatment.

My daughter-in-law and Maureen's daughter are now in the last few weeks of pregnancy and we are both wondering what gender our new grandchildren will be. It is good that this is taking Maureen's mind off her situation.

6th October 2009
Subject: Rain at last

Hi Maureen

Had to laugh when you said it was raining! Quite a novelty and, yes, the garden will be glad of it. Well, we have had a lovely couple of days—quite cold but bright and dry.

Had a long Ethics Committee meeting today (2.30 p m till 6 p m) so didn't get our dinner until about 7 p m. Still, it was a good meeting—we had an emergency project on the safety of the swine flu vaccine. We only got the papers to read on Saturday morning by post. I was out all day Saturday and Sunday the family were round so it was a quick read yesterday before we went off for a Barney haircut—he looks lovely—and choir. Still, apart from Chris coming down tomorrow to do some estimates, things should quieten down for me at least. Things happening your end then. Good that you have only one journey to the hospital on Thursday. I might phone the Queen Margaret tomorrow as I am supposed to have my appointment with the surgeon, with mammograms in November and I haven't received an appointment yet. I may be a bit premature but I would have thought they might have arranged one by now.

I will be waiting to hear how you get on of course. I expect you will be anxious to get on with some treatment—I would be. I am always impatient and want to get ahead of myself if I can. I think that is how I never stop doing things.

This is Lorna's last week at work. I think she looks tired even after their holiday but she is quite a size now and I remember how I felt those last few weeks.

Thank you for "pinking" me. I thought that was lovely. Sent it to a few others too.

Hope the car got sorted. I know you are off to Brighton tomorrow. Hope it has stopped raining by then. I have been to Brighton in the rain. We sheltered under the arches for ages. I remember my shoes had to be thrown away when we got home as they were ruined. I was about 7 or 8 years old at the time!

Lucas was full of beans on Sunday. He doesn't want a brother, a sister, or a baby—just says "no" when you ask him.

He is really funny now. Chris and Lorna will have their hands full I'm sure when the new one arrives.

Well, I won't be late to bed tonight. Didn't sleep very well last night for some reason. Hope I will be better tonight.

Speak soon, my pink friend Lots of love Margaret xxx

The references to being pinked were as a result of a text message that was whizzing round during Breast Cancer Awareness Week. It was one of these little emotional messages full of hearts as I remember. A thoughtful message and one was asked to pink one's friends, pink being the colour representing breast cancer care.

It was almost time for my first yearly check since breast surgery. The surgeon would be examining me plus scrutinizing the results of a mammogram. My appointment was not forthcoming and as I didn't want to get lost to follow-up I felt that maybe I should phone the hospital. However, I resisted the temptation and told myself I was not really that anxious—who was I kidding! But I was more worried about Maureen and her results.

I remember we had quite a serious telephone conversation about things and it came across to me that although Maureen was able to appear cheerful, understandably, underneath there were terrible concerns. I shared these with her but at the same time mindlessly chattering on about the ordinary things happening in my life.

9th October 2009
Subject: Weekend again!

Dear Maureen

It was lovely to talk to you yesterday and to hear that things are getting sorted out. I phoned the Queen Margaret as not had an appointment through for my check in November yet. Was told to phone again if I don't hear in next couple of weeks. Postal strikes are a bit worrying.

I have just booked us to take Lucas on what is called the "Santa Special". The Bo'ness & Kinneil Light Railway have these special events throughout the year. Last year we took Lucas to a Thomas day. The trains all have the faces of Thomas the Tank Engine, Henry, Percy etc. A member of staff was dressed as the Fat Controller and we saw the Tiresome Trucks. He loved it. The drivers all waved to the children and there was a lovely shop full of Thomas things (of course). We thought Lucas was old enough now to actually enjoy a train ride on the "Santa Special". The latest we could book near Christmas was 6th December—day after my Choral Union Christmas concert. The children get a present from Santa and festive refreshments are available (mince pies, I hope!) I am quite excited already. It will give Chris and Lorna a day to have the baby to themselves and for Lucas to have a treat with us.

Have got to go to Specsavers this afternoon for another eye check. Last time, they photographed the back of my left eye as they saw a naevus there. Said it was nothing to worry about but they always check them 6 monthly just to make sure it doesn't change in shape and size. Thought that was good. Might do a bit of shopping after.

Going to the Abbey on Sunday morning

Anyway, Maureen, take care.

Lots of love as usual from Margaret xxx

13th October 2009

Subject: Re: Weekend again!

Dear Margaret

Lovely to hear from you as always. Hope you got on alright at Specsavers and your eyes are ok. So pleased you got booked up with Lucas for a Christmas treat. I just know he will enjoy it especially this year now he is 2.

Went with Liam last week to get his flu jab and they gave me one as well so I didn't say no. The last 2 days have been lovely again although chilly nights so hope you have had the same.

I have had a bad day as when I got up I felt very dizzy and nauseous. Vomited for 3 hours on and off bright yellow bile so got a doctor's appointment for 4.20 p m. Was given some tablets to pop between my gum and lip for the nausea. Have only been able to sip water all day but managed some soup this evening and will try a cup of tea in a minute. I still have a headache but am feeling much better. Related to the gallstones which is what I thought. The doctor wants me to have another scan in due course. Am feeling pretty fed up with myself at the moment as like you I hate feeling ill. Never mind, will get over it.

Lynn Daley e-mailed me yesterday from Cancer Research. She is the south co-ordinator. As it is breast cancer awareness month they will be doing some features in the local paper and wanted to know if I would give an interview. I said that would be fine. Has anyone from their Scottish office been in touch with you as our friendship was mentioned by Lynn, obviously from Tom.

Had a nice quiet weekend so hope you all did too. I think I will be going to bed early tonight. Hope you are all well. Take care. Lots of luv Maureen xx

16th October 2009
Subject: Beautiful Day

Dear Maureen

I am sitting here with sunshine streaming through the lovely trees beside our bungalow. I can see so many different coloured leaves—it is absolutely beautiful. I will be thinking about you today and hope you are not feeling too anxious about your appointment.

We are just going to Tescos (again!!) another weekend is here and I look forward to hearing from you.

I have still not heard anything from Cancer Research UK but you go for it.

Best love from your pink friend. Take care. Margaret xxx

Maureen's mother comes more into the picture at this time as her health seems to be deteriorating and this is of obvious concern to Maureen. It brought back memories of my own mother, especially as they both shared the same birthday. I looked after my mum for nine years when she developed dementia. It was a difficult time and it meant that eventually, with the best will in the world, I couldn't give her full-time care and she had to go into a residential care home. I smile as I write, as she thought the home was her own house. I remember on her 89th birthday, when the home provided all the residents with a glass of sherry and birthday cake in her honour, mum visited every person thanking them for coming. She actually argued with one who said she lived there as well, saying "Oh no, you can't. This is my house." My mother was a wonderful pianist and still entertained everyone in the care home, practically daily. She needed no memory to play all the old wartime favourites for singalongs. She had met my father who had been a professional musician in the Army and who had presented the "Calling All Forces" programmes for the BBC from the Middle East during the war. We had one of the scripts for years and the humour was so unsophisticated in those days but still makes me laugh. One of the paragraphs went like this:

No 1: "And here is your Mastoid of Ceremonies"

No 2: "I thought mastoid was a pain in the ear"

No 1: "Yes, that's right!" I would add "boom boom" to that personally.

When he was demobbed from the Army, my father went on to become a member of the Billy Cotton band and he also busked on the streets of London with Joe Loss. I hope these names still mean something to some of you. He met my mother when he moved to Kent looking for more lucrative work and for years they had a trio, The Rhythm Group and were very popular locally, playing at weddings and social clubs.

19ᵗʰ October 2009
Subject: Beautiful Day

Dear Margaret

We have had a lovely weekend weather wise lots of sun but a cold frost yesterday morning with ice on the car first thing. Today though is grey and miserable. Mum has had a stable weekend but not much done as it was a weekend. On a nebulizer for her breathing and oxygen. Will be going to see her again today so hope to know more as she should have seen a doctor this morning. Had to get up early to let the workmen into her house to finish her bathroom. Should be the last day so at least that should be all ready for her when she eventually gets home.

Have you all had a good weekend yourselves? Managed to see the grandchildren on Saturday so that was nice. My sister was 58 yesterday so had to ring to wish her happy birthday, and update her on mum. Liam is still in bed so will probably go shopping when he emerges. Hospital visiting is 3-8 p m at Worthing so will try to be there for 3 p m. Otherwise nothing much else happening today. Hope you are all well. What have you been up to?

Take care for now. Luv Maureen xxx

20th October 2009

Subject: Blustery and cold!

Hiya Maureen

Thanks for email. Do hope your mum is getting sorted out. She won't like being on the nebuliser much, I don't suppose.

Very quiet here this weekend but went to the Abbey on Sunday morning. It is Lorna's birthday tomorrow and we are popping along this evening to take her pressie. We got her some nice perfume to cheer her up. She is a bit fed up with herself at the moment (not long to go now). I also made a big pot of our favourite soup—the lentil and bacon to take along. At least she won't have to worry about what to have this evening as it is thick enough for a main meal and very tasty. We had some friends over for lunch yesterday and I made the same soup at the weekend for our lunch. Also made some sandwiches and treated everyone (except me) to a Marks & Spencer lemon meringue cupcake. They are 6 ½ points on the WeightWatchers plan and I only have 18 for a whole day so couldn't afford one! I did have some lovely plums and a pear though.

We are babysitting tomorrow so Chris can take Lorna out for her birthday. Looking forward to seeing Lucas again. I am not sure whether we will be giving him his bath yet.

Will be thinking of you getting your results tomorrow. Hope you let me know how you get on. I must phone the hospital. Still no appointment and time is getting on.

I am looking at a lawn full of fallen leaves! It is a really cold, windy autumn day today. Time to get out the winter coat. Speak soon

Lots of love Margaret xxx

21st October 2009

Subject: Re: results

Dear Margaret,

Sorry I didn't ring but didn't get back from hospital till 6 p m and we had someone in to replace 2 radiators. He didn't leave till 8 p m and such a mess—water everywhere, soggy carpets in places—say no more!! I just feel so worn out at the moment. Good news from the hospital. No cancer in the breast, just lymph nodes. Will be having an auxiliary clearance on 12th November. She doesn't want to do a mastectomy. Only if I insist so has given me the weekend to think about it and have to ring on Monday with my decision. Am 99% sure I want one so will go from there.

Hope Lorna had a lovely birthday. Give Lucas a big kiss from me. Talk soon. Luv Maureen. xxx

I know Maureen meant an axillary (armpit) clearance, rather than auxiliary, but an understandable mistake when you are not a medical person. The medical person in me came out very quickly in my reply to Maureen the next day.

22nd October 2009

Subject: Re: results

Hello Maureen

I hope you are OK and your carpets are drying out! I have to go out tomorrow morning otherwise I would have tried phoning you again but I thought I would email instead. I was so glad to hear there was no cancer in your breast. I would, however, if it was me, want to know what they meant by "just" lymph nodes, I think. If there are any enlarged lymph nodes anywhere it is usually because they are trying to fight something. I feel the same as you. I think I would still go for the mastectomy. If I remember rightly you were told at first that the lump under your arm was just a node and then the biopsy showed it was cancerous. What would they do about the nodes in the breast if you don't have a mastectomy? Would they zap it with radiotherapy just in case? If you have the mastectomy, it will all be examined and you will know for sure what's going on. However, I am not trying to influence you in any way—only say what I think I would do if it was me. The fact they are going to do an axillary clearance will tell them something I should think but it may be that you would still have to go on to have a mastectomy after that, so might just as well have it and be done with??

Poor you. You have a lot on your plate at the moment what with visiting your mum in hospital, your own hospital appointments, and getting stuff done in the house. No wonder you feel worn out. Try to take time out over the weekend to relax and have a good think about what you want to do. Phone me if I can help at all.

Had Lucas this afternoon just for an hour or so. We went out kicking through the leaves. I think it did me more good than him! They are all coming from Sunday dinner. I've got a nice piece of pork in the freezer. Not had pork for a while so must get the apple sauce going.

Thinking about you more than ever. Please let me know your thoughts. I can truly empathise with you. Hope I am not speaking out of turn.

Lots of love Margaret xx

I found it quite difficult at this point to express exactly what I was feeling. I didn't want to alarm or offend Maureen but after my own treatment and advice from my surgeon, I found it strange the way things were being put to Maureen. Her axillary clearance was

to take place on 12th November—I had my mastectomy on 12th
November the previous year. I could see so clearly what I would do
*but that was it—it was what **I** would do, not Maureen.*

27th October 2009

Subject: Atishoo!!

Hi Maureen

I expect you have made your phone call by now. Won't have too long to wait until 12 November anyway.

I am nursing a humdinger of a cold. Don't know where I got it. I thought something was going on last Thursday when I felt a tightness in my chest and had a little cough. It has now developed into an all singing, all dancing rotten cold. I always said I would rather have a baby than a cold as you got over it quicker—perhaps that was a bit rash though.

I have a hair appointment at 11 and yes, it is raining too. We have to renew our passports so the plan was to go after I had been to the hairdressers to have our photos taken (one has to look one's best for these things, yah?) ha ha. It's got to last 10 years. I have to say I look a lot different now from the last photo but I am just going to chance sending it in without getting it countersigned again. AND I am NOT taking off my glasses as recommended (what a rebel I am). I have worn glasses since I was 9 months old and I cannot *not* wear them anywhere. They are just part of me. I'll be able to tell from the photo if it is acceptable I am sure.

Let me know how you get on with your interview. Put the lippy on for a photo shoot (!) I am really excited for you.

Got the dentist tomorrow and Maggie's in the afternoon. It is a get together of all the girls that were on the transition course. Just to see how everyone is getting on.

Well, Maureen, how do you like the dark evenings? Lights on at about 3.30 p m here. We get very short days in the winter but the really, really long days in the summer. Don't like going out in the evenings much when winter sets it. I still go to choir but until I get there and thoroughly enjoy it, I wish I wasn't going! Human nature, I suppose—or an age thing.

Better get myself ready. Keep me up to date with things your end. Love to hear from you. Speak soon, Lots of love, Margaret

I am embarrassed now to recall my visit to the Post Office to renew my passport. The assistant did say I would have to remove my glasses for the photograph. I made a stooshie and was adamant that I was definitely not taking off my glasses for anyone. As it was, I had very little hair and didn't know whether or not to wear my wig. The fact that I may have to leave my glasses off was adding to my angst. What a thing to make a fuss about when Maureen was deciding whether or not to have her other breast removed. Self-centred or what? My passport photograph is abysmal, by the way, no hair and no glasses (I did remove them in the end). Now I have to look at that for ten years.

Maureen was preparing herself for her interview with the local paper for Cancer Research UK. This, of course, was pre-arranged before her cancer had recurred and put a different slant on the article. However, I duly received a copy of the Chichester Observer and was pleased to see reference to us having become firm friends, sharing our experiences in regular phone calls and emails.

"It is nice to have somebody who understands exactly what you're going through", Maureen states.

She also says that her outlook on life has changed—you just don't worry about things so much.

27th October 2009
Subject: Re: Photo

Dear Margaret, love the hair it really does suit you, colour and length and you look quite fab in the photo, blooming again and losing weight as well, well done. Forgot to mention got my passport renewed at the end of September and as you say looked so different from the one took 10 years previous. I was worried it would not be accepted so took it to the post office who checked through everything, paid them and got it back after a week. I was very pleased there was no hassle.

Poor you with the cold. I'd nearly prefer anything too as a cold makes you feel so miserable. Hope you are feeling a wee bit better by the time you read this. Yes, made the phone call at 9.30 a m yesterday and Elaine the breast nurse was to ring me back today after speaking to the surgeon but I haven't had anything but I am sure we are full steam ahead for the 12th. As you say, not long now. Mum is progressing quite well but hasn't a lot of energy sitting, sleeping in her chair on and off during the day. Went over today and washed her hair which is all she could manage. Had a chat with my homeopath this morning so feel ready for my next hurdle. Am off to see the results of gallstones scan tomorrow (hospital again) I cannot keep away and then some shopping on the way home. Will be going to Leisha's on Thursday then off to Crawley on the 9.07 train for Liam's presentation and lunch in the Aurora Hotel. Looking forward to that.

Mandy & Graham are going up to Peterborough to help Tracey & Grant move into their new house on Saturday. They get the keys on Friday. It's all happening. Oh how I hate the short evenings haven't got used to them yet but will have to muddle through now till February. Glad you enjoy your choir so much. Singing is such a good therapy. Am worrying about my xmas shopping not getting done with this surgery coming up but hopefully I'll feel like getting out and about again fairly soon. At least I have Liam at my beck and call now he is retired poor thing.

Anyhow, will let you know of any further developments and how the interview goes tomorrow. How I would love to be doing it with you by my side.

Take care, lots of luv Maureen xxx

1st November 2009

Subject: How Are You?

Hi Maureen

Just checking in. It seems ages since we spoke but I know it's not.

Hope you are OK. 1st November so won't be long before you get that wash bag out again! You will be glad when you get started I should imagine. I phoned the hospital as hadn't heard about follow up appointment. The girl said they hadn't sent out their November appointments yet (which I found a bit strange as it is now November). However, she made my appointments over the phone there and then. I have to go on 9th November for mammogram and then on 19th to see the surgeon for results etc. As you say, will all this ever end. I know I was told it would be check ups for 10 years so I had better get used to it. Won't have to worry about postal strikes now anyway.

A funny thing! My friend Joan (one of the Thursday girls—we live in the same street) told me she had seen a clip on BBC 1 for a programme to be shown Tuesday night called "Hash in the Attic". It is about how you might not know if your neighbours were growing cannabis in their lofts. Well, Joan swore she saw her house shown briefly in the clip. She did not think it was very funny because she is a nurse, working in our own community, well known and people would recognise the house. She phoned the BBC to see if she could find out how this came about and to tell them she didn't like her house being associated with drugs. We are a very quiet cul-de-sac, off main roads and it doesn't seem feasible our road would just be chosen at random. They are getting back to her. Meanwhile, we kept a lookout for the clip and saw it ourselves on Saturday night. We also realised we had recorded it by accident on Thursday night. Dave always watches the Michael Portillo weekly chat after Question Time. It was delayed on Thursday so he recorded it. Low and behold, as we could pause it, there was our road in all its glory. You can see right up the cul-de-sac and as we are at the end of the road you can see our house as well. It doesn't bother me the way it bothers Joan but I am curious as to when it was filmed and why.

I am looking forward to seeing the report on your interview. There has been loads in our local paper this week about people's cancer stories. One was of a woman who goes to the Bosom Buddies support group I sometimes go to at Queen Margaret Hospital. She took part in the fashion show recently and there was her story. All the stories were from people who had breast cancer over six years ago and longer but who also do a lot of fundraising.

Well, Maureen, it will take you all day to read my ramblings. It's bucketing rain today (after glorious day yesterday) so not going far. Barney not keen to go out either. Have to learn something for choir so think I will get stuck into that—at the risk of spoiling everyone else's day with my caterwauling!

Lots of love to you and yours. Speak soon, Margaret xxx

The fact that our street was featured in "Hash in the Attic" was probably because the programme concentrated on leafy suburbs, although not in our area, where it was most unlikely to be involved in growing weed in the loft, but who knows? It did cause phone texts to fly back and forth between our neighbours saying "Don't forget to water your plants tonight" and "Have you got a spare spliff" to which the reply came back "Well, think you must be a dealer—you know all the jargon". What a giggle!

2nd November 2009
Subject: Re: Update

Dear Margaret, I am well thanks and yes got the wash bag out, towel, pyjamas, toothbrush, paste etc, here we go again. Wasn't expecting to need these things so soon but never mind. We have had a really wet weekend with rain and winds yesterday so didn't do much. We both had a lovely time on Friday. Arrived at 10.15 a m for bucks fizz or orange juice. The speeches and presentations followed. All the wives were presented with flowers and we also had to go and get our photos taken. We then had a 4 course lunch, lovely, with red wine, white wine or any drinks from the bar paid for. We were on table 5, 17 altogether. The setting was beautiful. Followed by tea or coffee and choccie hearts. This ended at 3 p m followed by a disco. We caught the 4.45 p m train home arriving at 5.30 p m. I was quite tired, probably all the talking going on. Anyway so glad we went. Liam received a cheque for £250 from the company and his colleagues had a whip round and gave him another £250. I now know where to go for a loan!! I'd better tell you the menu—bruschetta with parma ham with a tomato and pesto sauce, lemon sorbet, chicken breast wrapped in bacon, fancy mash with asparagus and carrot sticks wrapped with a leek leaf and caramelised onions with a caramelised apple tart to finish.

How strange your street being featured on TV and photographed. Will be out buying the local rag on Thursday to see if I am one of the people featured. Fame at last but what a way to get it! Pre-op assessment tomorrow morning. Took Mum out as the sun shone today although a little colder—her first time out for a month so we took it gently but she did enjoy it and we had a cuppa before we came home. Leisha is taking us to a bigger M & S on Wednesday to do some xmas shopping before my surgery.

Well, did enjoy reading all your news as usual and hope you are both well and Barney too. Lots of luv Maureen xxx

At least Maureen could enjoy the taste of the lovely food served to them at Liam's retirement party before she started another round of chemotherapy sessions. Everything tastes like cardboard for a while and as a foodie I found this most disconcerting. However, I made extra spicy things so I could taste something. I found myself jollying Maureen along to her operation on 12th November.

6th November 2009
Subject: Weekend again

Hi Maureen

See how the time flies—your op will be over and done with in no time. Don't forget to let me have details of the hospital again—not sure I've got the address anywhere. If you know which ward you will be in that would be helpful too.

Just in case I don't get to speak to you, have a lovely weekend. Don't know what the weather forecast is for us but whatever we have the family coming for Sunday dinner. Lorna is really fed up. Massive and hoping baby will come early. We are on emergency stand-by in case Chris has to take her in during the night. I got a fright this morning when we came back from Tescos. Lorna's car was in the drive. No-one in sight! I wondered what was going on. All it was, Chris was next door speaking about an extension he starts for them next week. His colleague had his van as his was off the road. Whew, I thought things had sprung into action for a minute!

Not looking forward to my mammogram on Monday (10.40 a m). Will be a bit anxious until I get the results on 19th I suppose. My niece comes up on 20th for the weekend. Will have to be organised if I have to go to the hospital as well. I always go a bit mad before visitors, getting everything just-so. Stupid, I know.

Hope your blood test will be OK. Do you know what that is for? Just routine, I expect.

Not many fireworks heard last night. Got the cats in early just in case and Barney only barked once. I don't think so many people have them in the garden these days. Chris said two of their friends took Lucas up to the big display in the park in Dunfermline. It meant he had a late night which didn't matter but he woke every hour during the night, seemingly a bit scared. Probably a bit overwhelming for a little one. So they are all tired today!

Have a good weekend and hopefully we'll catch up next week with all our medical bits.

Lots of love (and big hug) Margaret xxx

7th **November 2009**

Subject: Re: catchup

Dear Margaret,

Sorry I missed your call yesterday only was minding Ruby for Leisha and didn't get home till 4.30 p m. It turned out wet yesterday but sun is shining today thank goodness. The girls have gone off shopping to Bluewater today at the crack of dawn to get a good start. Do hope Lorna does not have too long to go now. That last few days seem to last forever. Will be thinking of you on your visit back to hospital. I am so uncomfortable now going every time and probably will be for a while. Yes, Thursday cannot come soon enough now but am keeping busy. The blood tests are routine—have to know type of blood in case a transfusion is required at any stage.

The ward I will be in is Chilgrove, St Richards, Spitalfield Lane, Chichester PO19 6SE, West Sussex. I cannot believe I need these details again and am packing my bag! Am off now to take Mum to osteo as she has quite a stiff neck for over a week now. Probably sleeping awkwardly in the bed, but the massage does help her. Have church tonight as am having a Mass said for my intentions. Probably won't get back for a little while. Tomorrow just us will be getting things ready. Have to have a trim at hairdressers on Monday to look good! Didn't have to worry last time as had no hair only headscarf which was very handy I must say.

The article appeared in the paper this week so have a copy for you. My picture could have been a lot smaller—you will know what I mean when you see it! Anyway Margaret have a lovely weekend with the family. Take care, lots of luv as always, Maureen xxx

Why do none of us like photographs of ourselves? I thought I would email the newspaper just to add a bit to the story as I was mentioned as her friend from hundreds of miles away in Scotland.
"I would just like to say that Maureen and I have supported each other through the same type of cancer and we both have always been very positive thinking and kept a sense of humour. What is the alternative, we always asked ourselves. I was diagnosed a little before Maureen and was therefore one step ahead and was able to let her know that chemotherapy was never as bad as you think it is going to be and that losing your hair is no big deal. I sent her

a picture of me in my wig (better than my own hair I thought).
Once we started getting to know each other, purely by email at
first and then by phone when Maureen went into hospital to have
her first mastectomy (I had mine a few months previously), it was
uncanny how much we found we had in common, other than
the inflammatory breast cancer . . . Feeling positive makes the
experience you are going through much less traumatic and in fact I
do not regard my cancer experience as a negative experience. I am
fully aware that it could return at any time but, like Maureen,
if it does, I shall face the right direction and keep on walking. It
has been lovely to have someone to share all hopes and fears and
to be able to compare treatment and effects. I am sure we shall be
Bosom Buddies from now on. Thank you for featuring her in your
newspaper".

By now I was becoming so fond of Maureen, she was like a
sister.

17th November 2009

Subject: In the fast lane!

Hi Maureen

Jaffa has decided to come and sit right in front of the
computer screen. He's looking for a fuss to be made of him
He watches the cursor going round. You must be able to hear
him purring!

Things have just got so hectic since Saturday. Lorna's trip
to the hospital on Saturday afternoon was a false alarm so
she is a bit disappointed. The baby is bound to be born next
weekend when my niece is here from Kent. Still, it goaded me
into action and I wondered how I could do something to help.
My best thing is cooking so early Sunday morning I decided
to make a chicken chasseur, a Hungarian goulash and a "shep"
pie (as Lucas calls it)—shepherds pie to put in their freezer for

when Lorna has the baby. At least they will have something to eat. I did the goulash in my slow cooker as I needed the oven as well but after 2 hours when I checked it, it wasn't switched on! I use the same socket for the kettle plug and the can opener. The kettle was plugged in and I mistook it for the slow cooker plug. I am doing some silly things lately (can't blame the chemotherapy now). We took everything round about 8 p m so it still had time to cook and they were really pleased. I was whacked after cooking our own dinner as well. Never mind.

What a shame about your washing machine—I know only too well how one thing goes and then another—let's hope not. We certainly can't do without our washing machines for very long. My mum never came to terms with me having a washing machine—she never had one, and years ago when we were little, she would get up at 4 a m to light to boiler. Then there was the mangle. I can see her now, straining away to wring the clothes. Good old days?? I don't think so.

I made the lentil and bacon soup yesterday and put in the freezer for the weekend and also today I have made another goulash (Chris & Lorna's smelt so good) to put in the freezer for dinner Friday when Carol arrives. All this hard work should pay off at the weekend, I hope.

I see you are back at the hospital on 25th. Another one for my diary. I have got the hospital Thursday for my results and see the surgeon. Be glad when it's over but whatever the outcome, I will face it.

Dave is like Liam and couldn't do enough to help when needed. I am still amazed we are let out of hospital with our drain bags. Mine even went to Tescos. I saw from the news that your area was getting quite a battering. My friend Pat has friends at Worthing and they lost a chimney pot. We are quite peaceful at the moment, weather wise, apart from a bit of rain yesterday.

Just going to order another bra from Nicola Jane. We have to wear black V neck tops for the Choral Union concert. I am not very good with V necks. Thought I'd get myself a camisole bra just in case there is any gaping. They do have lovely bras. I have two of theirs now. I think I am entitled to another prosthesis soon—one a year. I got my last one just before Christmas. Might go and see if I can get a lighter one.

Well, Maureen, keep up the good work. Look after yourself. I'll let you know how I get on Thursday. My appointment is 4 p m so quite late on.

Best love and big hug. Margaret xxx

P.S. Pulled another chair beside me and Jaffa now fast asleep on that! What a life.

18th November 2009
Subject: Re: Update

Dear Margaret, lovely to hear from you as always. My new washer/dryer came yesterday at lunchtime and am very pleased with it. The nurse didn't get here till 4 p m so was thoroughly fed up by then. It had been a nice morning and wanted to get out for a little walk which didn't happen. My drain was took out thank goodness so have been getting around more comfortably today. Will be thinking of you tomorrow as I see you have quite a late appointment. Liam is taking me to Leisha's tomorrow so the change should do me some good.

My you have been busy getting ready for your niece arriving at the weekend. It will be nice having so much prepared beforehand especially if the new baby decides to make an appearance. My friend Lesley came today, she has booked us for a xmas lunch the week before xmas, there will be 8 of us so will enjoy that. My house is full of cards and flowers again, people are so kind and thoughtful.

Do hope you are coping well with everything and you manage to have a lovely weekend with all your family. Will give you a ring next week some time.

Take care, lots of luv Maureen xxx

19th November 2009
Subject: Hospital check

Dear Maureen

Just to let you know my mammogram was fine. The surgeon examined me and said that was fine too. I don't have to see him for another year. I am not under any illusions though, and know anything can crop up at any time but it feels good today. I know it's silly of me but I feel guilty for being OK when you have to go all through it again. I am obviously pleased about myself but wish you had been the same. Still, I think with it happening to you so soon is probably better than having a few years free and then it starting up again.

The weather here is terrible. It's been raining non-stop since last night and the wind is howling. I do hope it improves for the weekend if we are to go Christmas shopping in Edinburgh. Nothing worse than traipsing round in the rain with bags of shopping. I am glad you are pleased with your new washer/drier. We used to have an Ariston but I think they stopped making them. I liked having the two in one.

The hospital told Lorna to come back next week, if not before, and she will then be induced. We had Lucas all day yesterday. He was a real poppet and is doing so well with his potty training!

Well, Maureen, just a quick note to let you know how I got on. Hope you have a lovely, restful weekend and get some fresh air. There is nothing like it. Keep me informed as to how you are.

Lots of love from Margaret xxx

I didn't really think it was better the cancer recurring sooner rather than later on. I actually felt it was so unfair that she was having to go through it all again without having the benefit of a little respite.

23rd November 2009
Subject: Hello, hello

Hi Maureen

I feel quite a stranger! What a weekend it has been. Carol (my niece from Kent) arrived on Friday morning, earlier than expected as she had such a good drive up. Good job we didn't leave all the work until the Friday as we would have been caught out. Anyway, Saturday, we got the 9.30 a m bus to Edinburgh and started her Christmas shopping in John Lewis. It was lovely having her to go shopping with.

Chris & Lorna asked us to pop over Saturday evening so we had our meal and went straight over knowing that Lucas would still be up. He opened the door, saw Carol and promptly said it was someone he didn't know! He is a case. We were exhausted and only stayed about an hour.

Sunday morning we decided to pay Dobbies the garden centre in Dunfermline a visit. It was very Christmassy (? spelling) but again some beautiful things to look at. We had a coffee. Dave & Carol had something called a banoffee waffle loaded with fresh cream. I had a fruit shortcake biscuit. I can't eat those big creamy things any more even though they look tempting. They only give me indigestion as so used to a low fat diet. We were all going out for a meal Sunday tea time and it was very nice although a bit difficult to keep Lucas entertained and sat in his place. Carol went at about 10 this morning so on her way home now. The sun is out so hope it's a nice drive for her—such a long way.

I feel now, how I felt when I had really bad fatigue. I know I didn't sleep as well as I usually do and you are on the go all the time with visitors aren't you. So, choir tonight and tomorrow I'll start my reading for the Ethics Committee meeting next Tuesday. At least I can do that sitting down!

How are you feeling Maureen, old fruit (x x). I expect you are anxious to get Wednesday over to see what, if any, kind of treatment necessary. What time is your appointment? I shall be waiting the other end of the phone if you can possibly give me a ring after. I was in and out in 5 mins for my appointment. I hope the examination was comprehensive enough. The surgeon didn't seem to do very much. Felt all under my arms and examined the other breast and that was it. He didn't ask me any questions, nor did I ask him any, although I had thought of many before I got there!

Still no baby! Lorna has to go back to the hospital Wednesday, if not before, and she has been told they will take her in then and induce her so it shouldn't be long now. Poor girl looks fit to pop!

Well, better get some lunch ready. Really looking forward to hearing from you. Speak soon, Lots of luv, Margaret xxx

23rd **November 2009**
Subject: Re: Hello, hello

Dear Margaret, so pleased to hear you had a lovely weekend with your niece. It all sounds very hectic but lovely. I was hoping to see the headline "new baby", poor Lorna but hopefully there will be news later this week if she is took in on Wednesday. I think they are so nice and snug in the womb they are in no hurry to be born. I know Ruby wasn't arriving 13 days late! Good news your niece is on her way home. Such a long drive, as you say, it's the wind that is so frightening at the moment.

We went off to Crawley xmas shopping as well. Got there at 10 a m. Did very well and had a breakfast out. Got back at 1.45 p m and like you was shattered. I just couldn't walk any more and my arm was getting sore, but glad I made the effort. I'll just have to do things in small spurts, we also dodged the rain most of the time, the sun is now shining.

My appointment arrived for Friday instead of Wednesday, the girls having already booked Wednesday off. I quickly rang Leisha before I caught the train to explain. I left it with her to ring the hospital to see if we could get it changed. She rang me in Crawley to say we have an end of day appointment at 3.45 p m on Wednesday so pleased about that. I need to move on again and find out what will be happening next. Am feeling quite good just a little sore which is only to be expected. Much better being my left side this time. Some nights I sleep quite well and then I hardly sleep at all, don't know why.

Anyhow, of course I will ring you once I get in on Wednesday, it will be nice to share my news with you. It is Liam's birthday on Thursday bought him a Bosch cordless screwdriver which he wanted. There are still plenty of jobs I have lined up for him to do, but he cannot be rushed. How he fitted in work as well I'll never know.

Take care, and talk soon luv Maureen. Xxx

Very conscious that the days were passing and Maureen had still not heard about her next visit to the Oncologist, I was anxious to hear of her way forward. Our new grandson arrived on 25th November, and was named Zak.

27th **November 2009**
Subject: Weekend again!

Hi Maureen

I wonder how you are feeling? Be glad to get the next appointment over I should think. Don't forget if you have any down moments, which we all do sometimes, please feel you can say anything to me. I remember, only too well, those moments in the middle of the night. Still get them sometimes.

Well, Baby Darling arrived in approximately 3 hours! I have to get used to the name Zak yet. Mind you, I hadn't heard the name Lucas at first and now I couldn't imagine him being called anything else. Did you get the picture I sent by phone? If not, we can send one by email but it's not very good as we sent our phone picture to the computer and the quality is not all it should be. Lorna came home today. Hope she manages to get a bit of peace and quiet to settle in.

We are off to see "We Will Rock You" the Queen musical in Edinburgh tomorrow—a late night I shouldn't wonder. Threw a bit of a hairy canary myself this morning as I feel I have too many things on just now. Can't seem to cope like I did before. Keep doing stupid things. Still feel tired from last weekend really and from now until Christmas we have quite a full calendar. Oh well, one thing at a time eh? I'm going back to trying to think not too far ahead—drive myself mad! Still, Dave suggested we take Barney a nice walk this afternoon. It was cold but sunny and it was lovely along by the Forth further up the coast for a change. Blew away a few cobwebs.

Well, Maureen, hope you have a good weekend. Let me know when you hear about your appointment with the Oncologist. Can't believe it's another weekend and getting so close to Christmas. The Christmas Market opens in Edinburgh from tomorrow. It's really great—just like the German ones and we have a big wheel from which you can see all over Princes Street, the special skating rink and all in front of the castle. Lovely atmosphere. Hope to get over to that before long. You would enjoy it.

Anyway, speak soon. Lots of love and remember:-

Happiness keeps you sweet

Trials keep you strong

Sorrows keep you human

Failures keep you humble

Success keeps you glowing

But only Friends keep you going

Margaret xx

1st December 2009

Subject: Baby Gifts

Dear Maureen

We are just back from Chris & Lorna's and they were delighted with the little cardigan and bibs. You put me to shame as I don't knit now. What a lovely pattern and such a pretty lemon. Really snug too for this very cold weather. Zak was fast asleep in his crib. Looks so tiny. Lucas is great with him. I am exhausted having picked Lucas up from nursery this morning. Chris & Lorna didn't get home until about 4.45 p m but we took Barney for a nice walk round the front. Lucas was fascinated with the water. The tide was right up, splashing on the rocks. It was jolly cold down there though. When we arrived at the nursery all the children were fast asleep. They all looked like little pods lying side by side in rows. Can't believe they get them all off like that. Anyway they had to waken Lucas for us. Amazing!

It was lovely to speak to you this morning. It won't be long before you have another little grandperson. It really is a miracle when you see that little baby so perfect.

Well, I'm going to get my slippers on now and watch some TV. I feel another early night coming on. Still, tomorrow is free. Thursday I am getting my hair done. Friday will have to be shopping and housework as George and Issy will be coming over Saturday for the concert.

Hope to hear from you soon. Lots of love and thanks again for the lovely pressies. Margaret xx

8th December 2009

Subject: Re: Update

Dear Margaret

Lovely to hear from you as always. I must have sounded a bit vacant after just waking up. Liam let me sleep on as he knew I'd been awake at 4 a m. Having him at home is getting me in bad habits as I was always up and had most of my jobs done by 9 a m. That seems to have gone by the wayside at the moment but who cares.

Had a homeopathy appointment at 2.15 p m which was good to talk through how I was feeling about everything since the latest news. These meetings invariably push all my emotions to the surface but as Sally says it does me no good trying to bottle things up. Better to let them out and feel better for it. Am still quite tearful at times, doesn't have to be anything in particular that sets me off.

Am so glad you all enjoyed your concert on Saturday. Am doing my usual Thursday & Friday this week and having Ruby for a few hours so I expect the three of us will be off to the park, her favourite place at the moment weather permitting. Tracey & Grant both looked well, there is quite a large bump there from when I last saw her but of course they just want everything to be over before Christmas so we will have to wait and see. How is Zak? Is he getting into a little routine and sleeping well for them?

Pleased to get my hospital appointment for next Thursday at a different hospital this time, Queen Alexandra at Cosham which looks to be a little nearer at 2.15 p m. At least I will know what will be happening. As my bras from Nicola Jane are only 6 months old I bought some pockets to sew on the left side so hope my new prosthesis fits in them OK otherwise I shall have to get a new bra with 2 pockets, thought I'd try first as they are quite expensive just to be thrown in the bin.

Had a nice dry mild morning but the rain is back again now and getting quite dark. Just taking Mum shopping at Sainsbury's tomorrow morning she doesn't like the crowds this time of the year so will just take our time.

Hope you have a good week—how are you getting on with your shopping? Take care and lots of love as always. Maureen xxx

Maureen's next hospital appointment was 21ˢᵗ December. She had been waiting since 2ⁿᵈ December to hear this information and I was wishing it had been sooner.

11th December 2009
Subject: Hello again!

Hi Maureen

I expect you are out with Ruby. Good job you are not living here! It is so foggy and damp, you wouldn't send the dog out in it. Having said that, I did take Barney out this morning but it was not pleasant.

Maureen, where has this week gone? I am so sorry to have disturbed your lie-in which is quite justified when you have not had a good night. As you say, who cares anyway?

You sound as it you have a really good homeopathic person who is quite right in bringing things to the surface. Better to do it with someone than when you are on your own. I think this is a tearful time of the year. I had a job to sing some of the lovely Christmas songs in our concert they are so beautiful and also as I lost my mum on Christmas Day, it always brings up some sad memories. Still, I feel that once you have seen the Oncologist and get your treatment planned out it will straighten up your feelings also.

I have bought 3 bras from Nicola Jane now. I think they are fabulous. I have got an appointment to see the person who fits the prostheses next Friday so looking forward to maybe getting a better fit. My bras do have 2 pockets in. I am ashamed to say I didn't notice, until you mentioned it, that some have one and some have 2! I wanted a bra with a camisole top for V necks and I needed a black one to go under my choir black top so I now have both cream and black. They are superb but I don't want to wear them every day or they will wear out too quickly.

Have got Chris, Lorna & co coming for dinner Sunday. Zak seems to be a bit colicky and his crying time is from 1 a m onwards! They are both shattered. I have been cooking meals for them to try to help a bit as Chris said he gets in from work and has to cook the dinner and do everything as Lorna is occupied with Zak so much. It's a shame for them but I'm afraid that's what it's like isn't it.

Well, next week, I think there is something on every day. Please let me know how you get on Thursday and hope your cold is away now.

Have a lovely weekend.

Thinking about you and sending hugs as usual

Luv Margaret xxxx

P.S. Introducing Zak Darling (look at the big feet!) Hope you like the pics.

Maureen's new granddaughter, Sophie, put in an appearance on 16th December just 21 days after Zak. There were problems with Maureen's laptop at this point and she had been off-line for a couple of days but I was relieved to hear that her son-in-law had temporarily resolved the situation. Her mother was in hospital again, another worry for the family.

21st December 2009
Subject: Re: Update

Dear Margaret

Back online thank goodness. Gosh don't you miss it when you cannot use it.

Mum is comfortable again. Are now doing tests as they think it is bronchial as all other tests when she was in before were ok. Antibiotics and steroids are not doing her any good at all and she was getting a lot of side effects from them. Do hope they get her sorted this time.

Will let you know when I get the present. Won't be at the hospital till 3 p m. The weather here is still awful, main roads are fine but footpaths are so icy there has been no thaw at all. It has been dark and dreary all day.

Do hope things settle down now as I feel so stressed out at the moment. Do hope everything is ok with you. How is your weather?

Thanks for being there. Luv and hugs Maureen xxx

My memory is a little fuzzy at this time, but I believe it was at this appointment that, having said in the beginning it would not be necessary for Maureen to undergo a second mastectomy, she was told it was a good job she had the operation as the histology of the tissue removed showed cancer in the ducts of the breast. Presumably she would have had to go back for the second mastectomy in those circumstances. Maureen had given me details of her appointment by phone.

21st December 2009

Subject: Baa! Computers

Hi Maureen

Glad to know you are back in cyberspace! My, oh my. What a shame your mum having to go into hospital again. Still, she is in the best place and I do hope she will be better soon.

I wanted you to be able to take Sophie's present with you when you g to see her on 30th so decided to send it special post with guaranteed delivery tomorrow. I shall not be very happy if it does not arrive. I think having cancer has given me some kind of confidence, especially in the complaints department!! I am certainly not backward in saying what I think lately (if justified of course). I think "oh well, what the heck". Isn't that terrible. No, I do think we should speak up more when things are not right. I just didn't like to complain in the past.

Zak is still keeping Chris & Lorna awake at night. We looked after Lucas on Sunday whilst they went of to "Toys R Us" They took Zak with them. Lucas said "It's good fun at Gran's". We all went in the garden and threw snowballs. The snow was a bit too icy to make good snowballs but Dave dutifully let Lucas throw them at him to make him chuckle. I had Pat coming for dinner too. Luckily I had done most of my preparation Saturday evening otherwise I would have been at my wits' end! Pat travels south tomorrow. She is probably going to worse weather than we have. It sounds pretty bad in Kent and south east in general. As you say though, our paths are lethal as well and our side roads don't get gritted anymore—cutbacks? It does make it more difficult to get around though doesn't it.

I am trying to keep this week as low key as I can—you won't be able to unfortunately, with hospital visiting as well as everything else. You know everything will get done in the end but it takes some effort to keep going from one thing to the next. I have to keep checking my lists (of which I have about six) to remind myself of what there is to do. Still, I have no nights out or visitors now until Boxing Day. I spent all my Tesco vouchers last Thursday (£140). I save them up all year and get all the Christmas fare. I thoroughly enjoyed myself—it was like a trolley dash in slow motion! I have only to get my fresh stuff now so don't have too much shopping to do.

I know I will hear from you if the parcel doesn't arrive but I won't expect to hear from you for a while after that as I know you are so busy. You know I will still be thinking of you often and I wish you the best of Christmases. If you get the chance though, I would be pleased to know how your mum gets on. Get that camera ready for some Sophie pics. Perhaps she and Zak will meet up when they are about 18?? (Ha ha)

Lots more love winging your way. I look at my little bell on the tree and know you have yours on your tree also (I'm silly, I know, but it's a comfort)

Bye for now. Margaret xxx

22nd December 2009

Re: Update

Dear Margaret

Unfortunately you won't have to go down to the Post Office and berate them for non-delivery as you know your parcel arrived on schedule this morning. Re-kindles your faith in everything when it all goes right. Was laughing away to myself as can just picture you giving out!!

Mum seems a better, a bit confused at times and still has a bad cough but otherwise not too bad. Still getting tests done—think it could be bronchial. On a nebulizer so don't know at this stage when she will get home. Must have a word with the nurse or doctor tomorrow to find out a bit more.

Not sure when we will be going to see Sophie yet depends a lot on the weather but will keep you posted. I am sure I will have some photos for you then. Don't work too hard over xmas, have a lovely one with your family. From one old bell to another. Lots of luv Maureen xxx

I loved the reference to old bells, obviously with reference to our Christmas tree bells.

25th December 2009
Subject: Re: Baa! Computers

Happy Christmas and a peaceful and healthy New Year to you all I Scotland from us both. Thanks for the lovely pressies all put to use already! Luv Maureen & Liam xxx

Later, the same day:-

Subject: Re: Picture of Sophie

Dear Margaret,
Tracey has just sent us this picture of Sophie taken in hospital. She has just got her internet going again after moving house. Hope you had a lovely xmas dinner. Luv Maureen xxx

25th December 2009
Subject: Pressies etc

Dear Maureen
Thank you so much for my veggie chopper—I envied you yours! I can't wait to make my next batch of soup to try it out now. Really thoughtful.

AND what a lovely surprise—a photo of baby Sophie. Isn't she just gorgeous and so wide awake! I bet you can't wait to see her. I believe your weather has improved—we are getting it now although it hasn't snowed today. We went along to Chris & Lorna's this morning. Lucas was so excited and he hung his dummies (2) on the tree for Santa to take away and give to a baby! He loved the guitar we bought him (as you will see). The rest of the day has been lovely and relaxing. I shall be in full flow tomorrow getting a buffet on the table.

Did your mum manage to get home for Christmas? Hope she is feeling better now.

Well, off to beddybyes now. Night night, sleep tight . . .

Enjoy the rest of the Festive Season

Speak soon. Lots of love from Margaret xxx

27ᵗʰ December 2009

Subject: Re: Update

Dear Margaret,

Thanks for the lovely xmas photos you sent. Really good and all that snow. Thankfully our weather has been better and we can get out safely. I'm afraid Mum has been very poorly over xmas. We were quite worried about her yesterday but thankfully after seeing her today she is looking slightly better and talking a little. Got home at 4.30 p m. Hope you enjoyed your buffet yesterday we all had a nice day at Leisha's. Plenty of noise with the 4 grandchildren altogether but they have all been very good over xmas and have plenty of new toys to play with.

I shall be glad when things settle down again as it is a constant run to the hospital every day. Doesn't look as though Mum will be out for a while. Hope you are getting back to normal although Hogmanay is big with you so I expect you will be celebrating that and why not, now you are restored to full health. We weren't feeling so hot this time last year.

At least I am getting breakfast in bed albeit toast and tea but that's fine with me, a nice little treat. Take care and talk soon, luv Maureen

Remembering that my own mother died on Christmas Day 2005, I was so sad to receive a text message on 29ᵗʰ December to say that Maureen's Mum had passed away. Once again our circumstances are so similar.

30th December 2009
Subject: Re: Update

Dear Margaret,

Thank you for your text and kind words. Am feeling so unhappy at the moment, I'm going round in a daze. A blocked artery had been found so Mum was moved to the coronary ward where they were treating that. She was comfortable and stable when we left and felt sure everything was ok. We were not long home when the hospital rang to say she had taken a heart attack and to come back asap. Needless to say by the time we arrived she had gone. We sat with her until 11.30 p.m. and then came home. Got to bed I suppose about 1 a m

Didn't get to see Sophie yet but they will be down at the weekend weather permitting. Take my mind off things. We haven't a death certificate yet as there could be a problem with the cause of death and the coroner might have to be involved. My sister Marilyn is arriving from Newcastle tomorrow.

Was over at Mum's today sorting out her hospital bag and clothes she had took in. All her xmas presents are still sitting there unopened as she didn't want them in the hospital. Wanted to wait till she got home. What next I ask myself? At the moment am not in any hurry to start chemo, have not had any word from Portsmouth so might ring tomorrow. My gallstones have been playing up quite badly so hope to get a doctor's appointment tomorrow to get some tablets to help. Haven't been given anything so far and since I might have to wait several months before I get the op don't want to be in pain all the time. Hopefully there are some tablets out there which might help.

Talk soon. Luv Maureen xxx

My own mother's Christmas presents lay unopened and we had to get through Christmas Day as normally as we could. The Minister called in after morning service and said some prayers. The Undertaker also came on Christmas Day. My brother was up from Kent for Christmas and I was so relieved he was here to see Mum before she died. We have a toast to absent friends every Christmas morning but the happy day now always has a tinge of sadness. Life has a habit of throwing everything at us at once, I feel, but I just wished the hospital would get a move-on and get Maureen's treatment started, bearing in mind the lump had been found to be cancerous back in September (my thoughts, not Maureen's). The next e-mail produced news of even further delay.

1st January 2010
Subject: Re: Chat

Dear Margaret,

Happy New Year to you all. Just to let you know Portsmouth rang me yesterday and although I was down to start chemo on Tuesday this has had to be cancelled as the oncologist wants a ct scan done before I start treatment so they have something to compare as I go through chemo to see how my body was reacting. Obviously no lumps to measure this time so a different scenario. They had been in contact with Chichester and it didn't look as though there were any appointments available for 2 weeks so going to put me back a little bit but since I have a funeral to arrange yet, maybe its not a bad thing.

Mum's death has gone to the coroners office and we will know on Monday if there has to be a post mortem so things there are not moving too quickly either. It is freezing cold here but lovely and sunny and dry. Sophie will open her present from you today so will update you at the weekend. Hope your weather isn't too bad in Scotland and hope Zak and Lucas are both well.

Talk soon, thanks again for the bouquet. The flowers are looking gorgeous as I type this note . . . Lots of luv as always
Maureen xxx

1st January 2010
Subject: Stuff

Hi Maureen

Glad to hear from you and thanks for phoning yesterday.

I think sometimes things are planned out for us and that it will be best for you to get your mum's funeral arranged, and possibly over, before you can concentrate on yourself. I know you will want to get on with things as quickly as possible but it might be too much to cope with all at once if everything is going on at the same time. It makes sense to have a ct scan done, doesn't it, otherwise, yes, what do they have to compare. Anyway, Maureen, I always tell myself things happen for the best reasons and at least you can deal with first things first. I am sure a couple of weeks are no time at all in the run of things.

We are just back from a lovely walk—tricky underfoot but as we had another light snowfall it had covered the ice somewhat. Barney enjoyed it too and it clears the head (and hopefully gets rid of some of the excesses!) I hope your medication is helping your tummy. I was lucky I only had 3 really bad bouts of gall bladder pain before I was taken for surgery. Still, if it gets too bad, your GP should try to expedite your op for you. (Such a lot going on for you just now!) It is a rotten pain though and sometimes you feel as if it will never go away. I had to eat really low fat or I paid for it after.

Our weather is slowly improving I think but I am glad we weren't in Edinburgh for Hogmanay. It must have been freezing. We heard the fireworks going off from where we are, even though Edinburgh is across the water from us. Sounded like bombs going off! Very few locally I have to say and nobody was out and about. We went to bed just after the bells.

Lorna had Zak at the doctors 5 p m last night. They are at their wits end with his non-stop crying. They feel so sorry for him as something is bothering him. I think the doctor gave him some Gaviscon. They are getting no sleep and he is only quiet when Lorna is feeding him non-stop. He has put on weight so her milk seems to be OK. Lorna won't consider putting him on a bottle but I think I would try it, if it were me. They all have had a bit of a cold which I have now picked up as well (grandchildren hazard!). They are coming for dinner on Sunday so hope we will all be a bit better by then.

You must feel excited at seeing Sophie. Give her a lovely cuddle from her Aunty Margaret. Take care now. I am sure everything will work out gradually—one thing at a time. Best love and a Guid New Year to you all.

Margaret xxx

Though trying to reassure Maureen that everything would be all right, my heart was screaming out that I wished she were getting seen tomorrow! You cannot wait with cancer.

3rd January 2010
Subject: Re: Soup

Dear Margaret,
Glad to hear that you are making good use of your chopper, they really are a godsend when there are lots of veggies to chop for soups, a real time saver.

Well, we have had a lovely weekend with the family and Sophie is such a darling so quiet as long as she gets her bottle she is so content. At the moment she is nothing like Tracey a definite daddy's girl looking like Grant's family at the moment and quite fair. Tracey loved your outfit from Debenhams (so did I) and cannot wait to put it on her when she gets home. She said to say a big thank you from them all and I gave her an extra cuddle from her Auntie Margaret. Little babies do such silly things to you don't they but she has been a welcome relief to us all during this sad time, and it won't be too long before they are all back again.

Well fingers crossed we get the go ahead from the coroner tomorrow so we can get things moving forward. Still freezing cold here but no snow and at least we can get out without falling over. Had Peter my brother over for his dinner today, he has just gone back home to an empty house unfortunately. Obviously he is going to miss Mum most at first, as you know mums always do everything for the boys. Anyway he is off work to work in the morning so that should keep his mind occupied for a few hours.

I'm meeting up with Marilyn at Mum's for a while tomorrow to do a bit more sorting out. Other than that not much going on. Not a lot on the tele either, might get to bed a little earlier as we have had a lot of late nights.

Hope you all enjoyed your soup and your lunch today and do hope Zak is settling a bit better for Lorna & Chris. I'm sure Lucas has been a good boy as usual. Lots of luv to you all from Maureen xxx

It was at this time, a good fifteen months into our friendship that we found out we both had brothers named Peter who lived alone. I also felt, however, that it was such a shame that Maureen, on top

of everything else, was having to deal with her Mum's death, part of which was a post mortem.

4th January 2010
Subject: Nothing spectacular!

Hi Maureen

Glad Tracey liked Sophie's present. Judith was with me when we saw it and knew "that was it"!

Zak arrived in his lemon cardi yesterday which was lovely. He is still crying a lot so he is getting handed round to everyone to walk the floor. He did seem to enjoy looking at my dining room curtains (heavy regency pattern) but it's a shame. However, we all enjoyed our meal and yes, Lucas was as good as gold helping Gran get the dinner ready! (Personally, I don't know how it got on the table but he is such a little love).

Well, I can't remember you telling me you had a brother, Peter. Guess what??????!!!!!! My brother's name is Peter too. This is my brother in Kent who lives alone and had the heart attack last year. He has been diagnosed with some form of dementia which is very worrying. He phoned yesterday. He finds it hard to hold a conversation as he can't think of the proper words for things. I think it has something to do with his heart problem. I have always liked the name Peter. Is yours an older brother? Mine is six years older than me. We used to fight as children but I have become very close to him, especially since he got divorced a few years ago.

We have just taken down the Christmas decs—put the wee bell away for next year. Pat comes home tomorrow and we are meeting her from the station. She is a bit concerned what weather she is coming back to. We haven't had any more snow for a couple of days but it is still thick on the ground and not thawing at all. Haven't seen any snowdrops this year yet. My mum's funeral was 5 years ago today. I do hope you are soon able to arrange everything.

Well, Maureen, the soup was lovely—all the better for my chopper! Much easier on my sore arm. I don't think that arm will ever be quite the same again.

Keep me up-to-date with everything. I always look forward to hearing from you.

Lots of love, Margaret xxx

5th January 2010
Subject: Re: update

Dear Margaret, well my phone hasn't stopped all morning but at least we are getting somewhere now. The coroner's office rang—a post mortem was carried out this morning and cause of death a heart attack due to hardening of the arteries. Have to ring the Registrar later or tomorrow at midday to get an appointment to register the death and acquire death certificate. Mum's cremation has been arranged for Monday 11th January at 2.20 p m—the first available slot so we took it. We are meeting up with the undertaker tomorrow at noon so so far so good.

Leisha rang Chichester for me this morning and I will have my ct scan on Saturday 9th at 10.20 a m so have to be there for 9.20 a m to drink the bottle of white fluid again. I'm getting a dab hand at this. Then rang Portsmouth to inform them. They have just rang me back to book my first apptment to see the doctor at noon on Tuesday 19th January followed by chemo at 2 p m so up and running at last. Whooppee I must be mad saying that but I have to say I feel so different about everything now—bring it on—I must be getting this extra strength from my mum God bless her. I know she will look after me.

When here Grant set up my computer with Skype and said all I needed was a webcam as they have one. Anyway yesterday they rang me to click on and I saw them in their new house and watched Sophie in her Moses basket, it was lovely, such a lift. They are coming back down on Sunday. Little Ruby is 2 on Saturday so Leisha is having a little family party for her on Sunday which will be nice.

Yes, Peter is 3 years older than me and Marilyn is 18 months younger than me so I'm in the middle. He is really going to miss Mum as she did all for him. He will be 63 at the end of March so has 2 years to retirement. At least he has to get up and go to work which is keeping him focussed. What another coincidence. I do hope your brother will keep ok and not get any worse, it is so much harder when you are away from them.

Well Margaret I think that is the latest update for now. Glad all the family are well especially the little ones.

Talk soon, Luv Maureen xxx

6th January 2010

Subject: Getting going!!

Hi Maureen

So pleased to hear you have some dates to work on now. I just know that I would feel exactly the same as you—bring it on is absolutely the right sentiment! Strength, positivity and the old sense of humour—it will all be there again because that is YOU. Same as me, personality plays a big part in coping with life's traumas. We have to say "Don't let the b . . . ers get us down!!" and knock it right on the head.

I do hope the weather is kind to you for Monday. I believe the south are getting the snow again. We are not too bad here. Still getting showers and the ground is still covered and a bit dodgy walking out but we are lucky compared to some it would seem. I shall be with you all at 2.20 p m. I bet your mum will have a good old chinwag with my mum when they meet up upstairs! Wouldn't that be nice.

I shall be facing the music on Saturday. Think of me also at 10.20 a m getting on the dreaded scales at WW again! All the indulgences of the past two weeks will no doubt come to light.

We have booked our weekend in Inveraray. We go on 22nd January (Fri) and come back on the Monday. Friend Pat comes with us. We go to the Loch Fyne Hotel—you should look it up on the internet—it's really nice. We go with a company called Easybreaks and it is much cheaper than if you book direct with the hotel. We couldn't go last year because of my treatment but prior to that we had been 3 years running . . . It makes January seem a little less gloomy.

It is a shame for your brother. He will miss your mum but as you say at least he is still working. I hope you enjoy Ruby's 2nd birthday—I expect, like Lucas, she is getting to be a little chatterbox now. Zak is still unsettled but it can only get better for them soon, I hope.

Another friend Joan's daughter had a little girl two days ago. They live in France and have called her Abbi Joan. Joan & Bruce are moving to France this year. Her daughter and husband have been living in the house Joan & Bruce bought so they will all be living together for a while. The baby weighed in at 7 lb 7 oz—they all seem to be about the same don't they? Joan & Bruce live in our road and we will miss them when they move. I worked with Joan at the surgery for many years as she was our Practice Nurse.

Well, Maureen, I won't phone just now as you are so busy. Phone me if you get a minute but as I say, I'll be thinking about you as usual and let me know how everything goes. Best love again, Margaret xxx

10th **January 2010**

Subject: Weather etc

Dear Maureen

Thanks again for phoning. I hope everyone has managed to get to West Sussex for tomorrow and that everything goes as well as it can. Will be thinking of you all.

I took Barney out for a walk after lunch today. There is still a lot of snow but it is melting at the moment. As long as it doesn't freeze again tonight. There are no snowdrops out yet—just a few leaves beginning to poke their heads out of the ground. They are very late this year. It may be that yours will be out but with the weather being so cold it has probably delayed them. I remember one year we had a daffodil out on 14th February. That's pretty good going for Scotland. I keep hearing West Sussex being mentioned on TV news for more snow. Just hope it is not too bad. The wind is quite strong today and that makes it feel just as cold.

Glad your scan went OK—you can put that one behind you now.

Hope Sophie is still being a good baby. Zak goes 11 1b now so is thriving even if he does have a bit of colic. Not seen them this weekend as I have been busy reading all my papers for Tuesday's Research Ethics Committee meeting. I have had to look at some horrible pictures of bedsores and ulcers this time! I hope I never get one of them. Yuk.

Anyway, Maureen, as I say, I hope everything goes well for you all.

Lots of love as usual. Margaret xxx

12th January 2010
Subject: Re: good send off

Dear Margaret, thank goodness everything went well yesterday. We had no more snow although plenty lying about. The trip to the crematorium was through the country. The fields looked magnificent and mum would have truly loved it. The service was lovely, we had Susan Boyle a favourite of mum, I dreamed a dream on entering. Graham did a reading from the Bible, Sheena read a poem "Our Nan", the committal we had Vera Lynn We'll Meet Again and on leaving we had Sailing by Rod Stewart as mum's favourite charity was RNLI. I don't think we could have done any better. We all went off then for welcome soup and sandwiches and hot nibbles. I suppose we were home at 7 p m. The flowers were lovely all so different. Ours was a Mum in pink with white ribbons either side. No snowdrops here either yet. I shall be looking out for them. The burial of the ashes is now at noon on Thursday and that's it.

Hope your committee meeting goes well. Tracey & Grant are calling here in a minute on their way home so am busy typing away fast. Sophie has been as good as gold and got a blessing from Father Edward at the cremation. That was lovely.

Better close as see the car approaching. Hope you are all well and that your weather is improving.

Luv Maureen xxx

I thought Maureen sounded quite elated after her Mum's funeral. Two more coincidences came to light! As mentioned before, my own Mother was a pianist and although she suffered from an Alzheimer-type dementia, was able to play the piano up to a few weeks before her death. She used to entertain everyone in the nursing home by playing the piano in the lounge and some of the residents loved to hear her play "We'll Meet Again" amongst other wartime favourites and it became her signature tune. Therefore we too had this played at her funeral. Also, our favourite charity is also the RNLI as my husband's father was in the Navy and actually my husband had been rescued by the RNLI when a boat he and his friends were bringing round from Essex to Kent, got stuck on a sandbank. The rudder was lost and the boat was taking in water. Land could be seen from where they were but they had to set light to their scarves and bits of clothing to attract attention. They were also reported to the Coastguard because they were overdue to time they were expected to arrive back in Kent and out went the lifeboat. They were towed back, all safe and sound, thank goodness, although my husband had wished he got a ride in the helicopter that flew above them making sure they were all right. We had been married for four months. Maureen and I were both looking out for the first snowdrops to bloom. After my mother's funeral I felt quite emotional when I came across snowdrops in our woodland. I felt it was a sign of hope and new beginnings. I still look out for them each year in January as this holds a poignancy to me.

17th January 2010
Subject: Re: Weather etc

Dear Margaret, thanks for the photo of the snowdrops they look lovely. Haven't seen any here yet but then haven't been too far afield. We have lovely sunshine here today does the heart good just to see it. Yesterday it poured with rain all day and it was so dismal. Hopefully we will have a couple of good days strung together. My sister got back to Newcastle on Friday without any hitches. Having a quiet day today, back to the blood test tomorrow at the doctors and then off about 10.30 a m to the hospital. Don't expect to be back before 5.30 p m but you never know. At least the evenings will be getting longer as my treatment progresses.

Am trying to knit Sophie a little pink matinee jacket. Have got about halfway and have lost interest so must re-start or it won't fit the way I am going. Going through mum's things. Found her collection of Alan Titchmarch novels so at the moment I am on number 3 no wonder I'm not doing any knitting. They are very good and what I'd call an easy read. I'm on The Last Lighthouse Keeper now.

Hope you are all well especially the little ones and Barney.

Take care, lots of hugs Maureen xxx

18ᵗʰ January 2010
Subject: Hello

Hi Maureen

Thanks for your email. Haven't had a chance to get on computer for a couple of days and find there are 79 emails! These, as I said to you are mostly rubbish one wanting me to bet, buy medications, or get a Russian girlfriend! We try to block them out but it doesn't seem to make any difference.

Anyway, I enjoyed my walks with Barney—hence seeing the snowdrops down our woodland trail. I always feel they are "new beginnings", such sweet little flowers.

We too, had a lovely sunny day yesterday. Dave is still finishing off the utility room although it is looking good now. Must sort out the cupboards once he has finished so I was on Barney duty and we had a long walk after lunch before I got started on the dinner. Always makes you feel good, a walk. I have been worrying slightly about my sore arm. It never goes away. You wonder if anything going on in the bones. Maybe have to get some advice, or is it still the surgery?

Do you know, I am sitting here in my dressing gown (or goonie as I call it now). Not even dressed yet. Emptied the dishwasher, put away the cutlery and made myself a sugar free jelly. I sort of got caught up in pottering!

You have a busy week ahead Maureen. Sounds as if you had a nice weekend. Hope everything goes well today and tomorrow. Email me when you get a chance to let me know how you are doing. You know I shall be taking every step with you as we did before. It makes no difference that I am not having any treatment now.

More than lots of hugs to you. Bye for now. Love from Margaret xxx

The next email was the most distressing and devastating I had received so far. What a day for my dear friend.

19th January 2010
Subject: Re: Hello

Dear Margaret, got to see the doctor at 1 p m and took for chemo at 3.40 p m so quite a bit of waiting around again. Got the flush and steroid given and then came to the Taxotere which was out of date—18th January. No other supplies so have to go back to get it tomorrow at 10 a m as a priority so hope we are not waiting around too long as have solicitor's appointment back in Worthing for 2 p m but have that covered if I am held up.

Anyway, the ct scan is showing shadows on the liver so they are telling me it has spread to the liver now—what next? Will be doing another ct scan after 3 cycles and then another after 6. Might want to change the drug after 3 depending on what is happening. Also want a bone scan done as haven't had one since Sept 08, so on the ball at the moment seem to be doing everything possible.

Got home at 5.20 p m found a better route to the hospital that took us 35 mins to get there and 40 mins home so not too bad at least having the cycle tomorrow won't upset my next 3 week one. Has been dry today but getting cold this evening. Hope you are well up north.

Take care, bye for now, luv Maureen. xxx

Maureen must have been feeling devastated by this latest news but seemed to be keeping positive. However, my shock was obviously visible in my reply.

19th January 2010
Subject: Hospital

Dear Maureen

I can't believe your hospital had out of date Taxotere. How can that happen? It's stressful enough having to go for chemotherapy anyway, let alone things like that happening. All that travelling too. Still, we can't worry about things we can't do anything about so at least you will get it tomorrow (today, probably by the time you read this) and you will be on your way.

Your previous CT scan didn't show up anything on your liver did it? That must have only just happened. I keep forgetting to ask you how the gall bladder is behaving now? I suppose the gallstones couldn't be confused with the liver problem—they are very close together. It's going to be wall-to-wall hospitals then, Maureen, for a little while, getting all the scans again. Still that's the good thing that they can see things and nip anything in the bud.

Chris & Lorna had a phone call this tea time from the GP that saw Zak on Friday. She told them to collect a letter and go straight to the hospital there and then. They went off to the Victoria at Kirkcaldy, Ward 5 where they were expected and were seen by the consultant paediatrician straightaway—no waiting even! Anyway, the consultant has confirmed he has reflux and has prescribed Domperidon—would you believe what we had for nausea with our chemotherapy. I think they have had their minds put at rest and hopefully he will settle soon.

It has been much colder here today. I hope we don't get more snow before we go to Inveraray on Friday. Please keep in touch Maureen. I will text you whilst I am away to see how you are feeling. We will be back on Monday anyway. Take care. Thinking of you lots and lots. Know how you must be feeling but sleep tight. Best love. Margaret xxxx

20th January 2010
Subject: Re: Hospital

Dear Margaret, everything went well this morning, wasn't kept waiting too long on account of return visit. We got home at 1.35 p m so very good. The travelling is much better as long as there are no hold-ups. At least I am on my way now. Not much point worrying about anything else till the chemo is over. Then we can plan out where we go. Have Ruby to see tomorrow and then shopping tomorrow.

Hope I can sleep tonight as have been awake at 3 a m and 4 a m the last 2 mornings. Only to be expected I suppose

So pleased to hear that Zak has been seen and got his new medication same as mine. Do hope he will soon be a star baby for mum and dad.

Do enjoy your weekend away and hope you have reasonable weather. It has rained and drizzled all day here.

Take care and lots of hugs luv Maureen xxx

I sense a tone of resignation in Maureen's email and there are no upbeat positive feelings coming through. I was feeling the same and I was only too aware that this could also be me. I fully empathised with her. I replied only an hour or so later the same day and was desperate to help in some way. Maybe I could suggest something to help her dispel those awful, dark moments in the night or early hours when sleep eludes you. I had learned a relaxation technique known as Autogenic Training. One learns a mantra, going through arms being heavy, then warm, then legs and stomach. You repeat that your heart is beating strongly and your breathing is deep and regular. In between three repetitive chants, you tell yourself that you are perfectly calm and that noise does not bother you. The whole process takes about six minutes once learned by heart and it takes your head to a different place and it certainly helped me get to sleep throughout my chemotherapy. I have heard this discussed on the radio and it is said to be very self-healing. I personally revert to it sometimes if I have something on my mind but ideally one should get into the habit of doing it every day. After I had mastered the technique, I realised I had never before relaxed properly.

20ᵗʰ January 2010

Subject: Hospital again

Hi Maureen

Glad to know everything went OK today. I do hope you can get a good sleep. There is nothing worse, I know. Now you have started your chemo, things should settle down for a little while and you will be able to relax more. When we get back from Inveraray, I will send you details of something called Autogenic Training. It is a kind of relaxation programme. I was taught it by a speech therapist years ago. I found it so helpful when I couldn't sleep when I was first diagnosed and throughout the chemotherapy. It is worth learning. Whatever it does, it does send you to sleep! As I say, it takes a wee bit of learning to do it properly but once you have learned it, it only takes minutes to do. You can have a look and see what you think.

Well, better start thinking about getting some dinner ready. Jude gets in about 5.30 p m.

Yes, fingers crossed Zak will improve on the old "champagne". It was certainly good stuff for me too.

Take care and keep in touch.

Lots of luv again

Margaret x x x I am always so pleased to hear from you.

One of the anti-nausea drugs prescribed for chemotherapy users is Domperidone. I was not the first to compare the name to a brand of champagne. As several of us in the chemo-suite at Dunfermline said "I wish!" It didn't have quite the same effect, however, but gave us a smile nevertheless. I remember the chemo-suite so well. It came as a most unexpected surprise. Open-plan, comfortable chairs, big TV screen on the wall. As you attended on the same day of the week each time, you got to know familiar faces and struck up conversations. I was able to reassure a first-timer, who was not sure what reaction she was going to get to the chemotherapy, that it wasn't too bad, and one lady told me she had gone for a reconstruction and was delighted with the outcome. I retorted that I would have liked both my boobs off as then I could have had the 34As I had wished for all my life. This was speaking as a larger-bosomed lady, you understand. Camaraderie was in full swing and the visit to the chemo suite was never an unpleasant one.

21ˢᵗ **January 2010**
Re: Update

Dear Margaret, Yes I would love some info on autogenic training when you get back from your break. Sorry about no photo sent but I forgot to do it and only realised a few hours later. Silly me, head all over the place. Sophie is now 9 lbs 8 oz on Tuesday. Do have a lovely weekend and love as usual. Maureen.

PS Have just received the latest copy of Vita magazine. I do so enjoy all their articles—very interesting.

26ᵗʰ **January 2010**
Subject: Re: Update

Dear Margaret, I expect you have a mountain of e-mails to catch up on always the same when you are away for a few days. Your postcard arrived here this morning and the castle looks lovely. So glad you enjoyed your weekend.

Well to update you am feeling fine no adverse side effects this time. My food just tastes like nothing at the moment so will look forward to getting my taste buds back. My gall bladder is well behaving itself so that's a relief. Don't know if the previous CT scan showed any spots on the liver. We weren't told of any at the time but maybe they don't like to tell you everything. Don't know. Anyhow the girls have been doing some asking around and research and rung the Royal Marsden Cancer Hospital about an hour away from us. Obviously just deals in cancers. Thought they might give us a second opinion as my cancer is not straightforward at all. Told us to see my GP who would refer us on for a second opinion which everyone is entitled to. Did that this morning so he is sending it all off for me tomorrow. Cannot do any harm. Will still be continuing treatment at Portsmouth. Also am going for a wig fitting on Friday at 2.30 p m. Wasn't going to bother this time but since they phoned me thought I'd go ahead. Going for a short grey one this time. Obviously the last one isn't me any more since we decided to stay grey.

Got my bone scan through for Tuesday 2nd February 12.30 p m for injection and 3.30 p m for the scan. Everything is moving along nicely, then second chemo 9th February. Forgot to say am going to my hairdresser on Friday before wig fitting to get my hair cropped ready for it coming out, like we both did before. The wig fitting is at Queen Alexandra's Portsmouth. Quite a bit of news for you this time.

Also Sophie will be down at the weekend so I'm sure I'll notice a difference in her. She will be 6 weeks tomorrow. Do hope Zak is still progressing well and Lucas too.

All the grandchildren are well here busy with school, etc. Half term will soon be around next month I think. Had a lovely bright day today but wind cold. Don't mind as at least you can get out. Went into Littlehampton for an hour and then came home. Liam has been in his two sheds outside attempting to sort them out a bit and start having a spring clean and throw rubbish away, we will see.

Hopefully will give you a ring in the morning for a chat. Take care till then, luv Maureen xxx

I must say I felt very excited and delighted at Maureen's daughters taking charge and arranging a second opinion with the Royal Marsden. The comparisons between our treatments had been so blatantly obvious that I also had had concerns but would not voice them. I do understand that every patient has treatment plans according to his or her particular case but progress had seemed so slow and communication between hospitals apparently difficult that my alarm bells had been jangling helplessly away. Bravo Mandy, Sheena, Leisha and Tracey!

26th January 2010
Subject: Update

Hi Maureen
Just in case you go on line again before phoning in the morning. Just to say what a good idea to get a second opinion—and what wonderful daughters you have! There are a few things I thought I would have queried if I were you and this will give you more information, I am sure. I would have expected to have been told if there were any spots on the liver at the first scan and if so, I would have thought any treatment would have started sooner. But then we know nothing don't we. I don't think you can get better than the Royal Marsden anyway so here's to a second opinion.

I was going to email you this morning. Chris popped in (he is at the crane stage taking off next door's roof giving us all heart failure!) However, when I asked how Zak was getting on, he said last night was about all they could take. Lorna rang the GP but got short shrift because it was late in the day and was told they would have to wait until the next consultant's appointment on 19th February. He is constantly sick and crying. I said if I were them and they were at the end of their tether, they should just take him to the hospital through A & E. We know a consultant radiologist who does barium meals on babies with reflux so wondering why they are not going down that route. Zak is 8 weeks old now and should be settling down. Anyway, we had Lucas for the afternoon just to give Lorna five minutes and also Lucas, as it is hard for him with things so fraught at home. He is such a cheery little boy.

We did have a lovely weekend. Completely seamless from start to finish—a real treat. I'll attach a photo of me and Pat (with the same birthday as you) sitting on a bench in Tarbert. You can see how good the weather was. We had a wonderful walk round. There was a lovely harbour, art gallery and shop that sold lovely things but not too expensive.

I came home to another pile of reading for next week's Ethics meeting. It has come round really quickly this time. Still, keeps me out of mischief I suppose.

There was a lovely lot of news in your email and you are obviously getting into gear as before. I sometimes feel like wearing my wig again. I have sort of "gone off" my really short hair and don't know whether to try growing it again or what. I will put all your dates in my diary so I know when you are going for what.

Lovely to be in touch again Maureen.
Give us a ring if you can but don't worry if not.

Lots of love, Margaret xxxx

29th January 2010

Subject: Weekend again

Dear Maureen
Hope you are still feeling OK and looking forward to a nice weekend. The weather here is lovely, bright and sunny but oh so cold. There is a cold wind now.

I am sitting here having eaten far too much for lunch and feeling uncomfortable. A friend was having a coffee morning for RNLI this morning and of course there was lots of home baking. I decided to have a piece of fruitcake and a small pancake (Scottish). I thought I would make that my lunch but of course when I got home and made Dave a sandwich for lunch I wanted one too so I had a sandwich and an apple. I could just fall asleep now! Nothing doing this end for the weekend here unless the family come round on Sunday. I haven't quite finished my reading for the REC meeting on Tuesday so would like to get on with that.

Enjoy your weekend Maureen—speak soon.

Lots of love Margaret x x x zzzzzzzzzzzzz!!!!!

P.S. I'll never learn to eat less

30th January 2010
Subject: Re: Weekend update

Dear Margaret, First of all thanks for the autogenic training which arrived in the post this morning. I am going to give it a go today so do hope I manage it, I'm sure I will, if it works for you then hopefully I will achieve some benefit. My sleeping has improved somewhat but still wake several times in the night. Today could be best day yet as my taste buds are returning and everything doesn't taste like cardboard! I do so hate not being able to taste my food.

Funny you mentioned a coffee morning for RNLI. They were out collecting in Littlehampton this morning. It was Mum's chosen charity which brought a tear to the eye again. Never mind, feeling good and positive once again.

Got my hair chopped yesterday morning and then went off to get a wig fitting. Having light silver platinum in Jasmine style which is short. Unfortunately she hadn't my colour so would order me one which should arrive sometime next week.

The Royal Marsden got in touch and had booked me in for Tuesday 2nd February. This is, of course, my bone scan day. Tuesday is clinic day, 9th is my next chemo so now have an appointment for Tues 16th February at 2 p m. Will be sending a letter in the post. Don't mind waiting 2 weeks as my treatment is ongoing at Portsmouth.

Hope you have managed to get all your reading up to date for your next committee meeting. Very cold here also today but the sun is shining so that is ok with me. Hope you will be seeing Zak and Lucas over the weekend. Sophie is due here in the next hour. Have been washing and ironing this morning so on top of everything. Mandy is doing dinner for us all tomorrow so that will be nice.

Do have a lovely weekend and will catch up soon. Take care lots of luv as always Maureen xxx

1ˢᵗ February 2010
Subject: Weekend update

Dear Maureen

It took me a while to learn the Autogenic Training—kept having to open an eye to see what was coming next! However, once I knew it, I did find it beneficial. Hope you do.

RNLI is our chosen charity as well. I didn't mention it before but Dave was actually rescued by the lifeboat four months after we had been married in 1967. He and two other friends went round to Maldon in Essex to bring a barge back to Medway. Dave, being a shipwright by trade, always had his own boat for years—until we got a house anyway! His pal had his own barges and travelled across the channel and back for his business. Anyway, a storm blew up unexpectedly and the barge landed on a sandbank. They couldn't get off and it bounced up and down. They lost the propeller and rudder—by now were off Clacton and could see land and lights. They ended up setting fire to their scarves and other bits of clothing to attract attention. Eventually the helicopter came (Coastguard had been in touch with me and friend's wife as they had been reported as overdue). Poor Dave thought he was going to get a ride in the helicopter but they held out a notice "Are you all right?" They gave the thumbs up. The lifeboat came then from Clacton and they all got a ride. They had self-heating soup and Dave arrived back in WRVS clothing. It was all on TV and local radio at the time—his little bit of fame. Dave's father, also having been in the Navy, made a big donation to the RNLI then and we have kept it up ever since at Christmastime and also when our fish man comes on a Saturday, all our change goes in his RNLI tin. So there we are too—another coincidence really.

I am afraid Dave had to wait until his 50th birthday to get a ride in a helicopter (my present to him) to appease his previous disappointment.

Your wig colour sounds fabulous (glamour puss!) You must send me a photo when you start wearing it. What a shame the Royal Marsden appt. didn't come through for Wednesday! Still, I, like you, would be quite comfortable knowing I was having treatment whilst you are waiting. They certainly responded jolly quickly—great. Let me know how the bone scan goes. If I remember correctly, I had to go round for a chest x-ray after it and then they told me both were OK whilst I was still at the hospital so you maybe will get the results straightaway.

Chris, Lorna & Co came round for dinner. I was extra adventurous and did us all a mixed grill (whew). My oven is a grill as well and it is always difficult if you need the oven as well as the grill. Still, we got there in the end and it was all enjoyed. Zak was very good, although needed holding all the time or he would cry. I had a good cuddle whilst Chris & Lorna had their desserts and a chat with Dave & Judith. The weather is really cold but sunny. I hope to get out for a good walk with Barney later. Am just about to go over my reading again to refresh my memory for tomorrow. Dave's birthday is 8th February—haven't a clue yet what to get him. I think men get more difficult as they get older (in more ways than one?!!)

Well, Maureen, hope all goes well tomorrow and wait to hear from you soon.
Lots of love to you
Margaret x x x

3rd February 2010
Subject: Re: update

Dear Margaret, lovely to talk to you this morning. How are you getting on with Dave's birthday present—any more ideas yet? I know how difficult it is to buy for the other half!
It has been a damp, dull and drizzly day here today but not cold. Tracey got back to Nottingham about 2 pm and went and had Sophie weighed. Now 10 lbs 14 oz so doing well. Has a little sticky eye but has drops which seem to be helping. Don't know if an infection or blocked tear duct but we will see.
Forgot to tell you Sheena had her operation on her hand yesterday to cut and re-sew tendon in her thumb. Had it done last year but it wasn't a success so has had it re-done. Is now in plaster for 3 weeks. It is her left hand but she is left handed so a bit of a pain. She wasn't supposed to get it done till 8th but had a cancellation. It was her birthday yesterday, not a good way to spend it, but never mind.
Am enjoying doing the autogenic training. Think I have got the hang of it. I say it when I'm having a quiet moment on my own in the daytime and then when I'm in bed awake. Forgot

to ask you is that what you do? How many times a day can you do it, as few or as many times as you want?

Do hope Chris and Lorna get little Zak sorted. He is having a rough time of it and of course so are they. We went off did the shopping and had lunch out so didn't have to cook. Got washing and drying done when I came back. It is so nice to be able to taste my food again.

Off to help with Ruby tomorrow whilst Leisha goes to work for a few hours. She and Matt have a wedding in London on Friday coming back Saturday so Ruby is going to her 2 cousins who are 12 and 10 for the weekend so she should enjoy their company. She is a very sociable little girl.

Just watching tele tonight nothing special. Hope Dave finished the utility floor for you. I'm sure it is good.

Anyway take care and lots of luv from this end as always Maureen xx

4th February 2010
Subject: Autogenic Training

Hi Maureen

When I first learned AT, the speech therapist who taught me said I was to do it twice a day which I did religiously to help the problem I had with my throat (I had sung through a bad cough and cold and strained my throat so I had a croaky voice all the time). I was working at the time but I took myself off into one of the surgeries, sat on a chair and went through the routine. As it says, once you know it, it only takes about 6 minutes. I always did it last thing at night as well and that is mainly what I do now. There was a discussion on it on radio a few years ago and it was suggested we should all do this, whether we have a health problem or not, as it is so beneficial. I phoned in to the radio station at the time to say that I had learned it etc etc. I had to be honest and say I didn't do it every day then because I was lazy! Now, if ever I am worrying about anything, have difficulty sleeping or generally feel I really want to relax, I always fall back on it. I am doing it more now, probably because I got into the routine again with treatment etc. If you sit on a chair, the speech therapist called the position to sit in as knock kneed, pigeon toed—knees together, toes pointing inwards. I think it is best on a dining room chair rather than armchair as you can dangle your arms but now I always do it when I'm lying in bed. Still, we should really do it twice a day as routine I think. I am going to start again properly.

You will probably think I'm daft but when I was first diagnosed I did the autogenic at night and once I was in the fully relaxed state, I then went on to some visualisation. I told myself, mentally, to go into my left breast and have a look. All I could see (obviously in my mind's eye) was a big royal blue blob. I invented a little creature with big sharp teeth and imagined it munching into the blue blob. The strangest thing was that much later on I decided to "have another look" (after I had chemo) and there was no royal blue blob??? Please don't stop emailing me because you think I am loopy!! We all have our ways of coping with things and that was probably one of mine. But the autogenic training certainly puts you in a very relaxed state which has to be good for you.

I would just do it twice a day and make the second just before you go to bed. I was told the breathing part was important. Nobody breathes properly apparently. Deep breathing is very good for you and AT also promotes proper breathing. However, it does not matter how many times a day you do it if you want to.

The floor is almost finished. I can't wait to get my new cupboards sorted out so I know where things are. We had more snow last night but there's just a sprinkling left this morning.

Sophie is doing well (no pictures coming through for some reason). I expect she is smiling well. I have only managed to get a smile out of Zak once (what a shame) but he has Lorna's dimples in his cheeks.

Sheena will find being in plaster very difficult. Hope the op is successful. 3 weeks will soon pass I expect. I had a carpal tunnel op about seven years ago (typist's occupational hazard). I was amazed how much I couldn't do with one wrist out of action.

Anyway, had better get dressed—still in my goonie. Might get up the town today to have a look for—yes, you've guessed—a birthday present for you-know-who!

Lots of love as usual and I just love our chats.

Margaret xxx

Having never actually met Maureen, I still trod very carefully when introducing another part of myself that I thought she might regard as a bit eccentric. I genuinely thought she might let the friendship peter out, such was my uncertainty of what she might think of me and my visualisation. How wrong I was!

4th February 2010
Subject: Autogenic Training

Dear Margaret

Thanks for the advice on the autogenic training. I do find the bed the most peaceful and relaxing place to do it so will do it twice a day probably morning and evening. I understand completely what you say about visualisation. This time I'm imagining the cancer being eaten by the chemo inside me. I feel so much more relaxed about the chemo this time. I want it so much to get better, much more than last time. I think I was always fighting it in some way last time but not now.

Am sending the photos again to you so hope they land this time. Good luck with the present hunting. Hope your snow has gone it was wet first thing again but has been a nice dry afternoon. Love our chats also. I'd be lost without you!!

Take care and lots of luv as always Maureen xxx

5th February 2010
Subject: Sophie etc

Hi Maureen

What lovely photos. Sophie looks a real sweetheart and I just love the bootees. Thanks for them.

I am glad to hear how you feel about your chemotherapy. I know I felt quite bereft when mine finished—it was like a safety net. Some regard it as a poison but it isn't to us. It's more like nectar! I am pleased to hear you do some visualisation too. We do have so much in common. What colour is your chemo when you see it eating the cancer away? I would make it red, I think, or a nice bright yellow!! Have you to go to the hospital the day before for steroids again? I disliked taking all the pills but only because I was afraid I was going to miss some or take some at the wrong time as some were 3 times a day, some were morning only and some with meals, some before meals . . . whew. The hospital gave me a good chart to follow. They do look after us.

Hope you have a good weekend. We still didn't manage to get Dave anything for his birthday. We looked at casual jackets but he wasn't keen on any. We'll have another look later and I'll get him a nice big bar of chocolate as a treat (he doesn't put any weight on, not fair).

Damp here today but I had a good walk with Barney. Hope I've lost a bit of weight tomorrow when I go to WW. Have really worked at it this week. I am still about 12 lbs over what is healthy for my height so I have to keep at it.

Lorna & Chris undecided whether to let Lucas have the swine flu vac. Is Ruby having it? I'm glad I don't have all these decisions now, although it was the whooping cough was that was suspect when Chris was a baby if I remember. There's always something, I suppose. Oh, here comes a nice up of green tea for me, very refreshing.

Keep at the AT, the longer you do it, the better you feel.

Bye for now. Hope all goes well on Tuesday—let me know if you get your bone scan results and look forward to speaking to you again soon.

Lots of love

Margaret x x x

7th February 2010
Subject: Re: update

Dear Margaret, lovely to hear from you as always. Yes, I'm doing my AT when I go to bed at night and when I wake up in the morning whatever time. At the moment it has been around 6 a.m. so not too bad. Do seem to relax and doze off for a couple of hours. Liam has been bringing me tea and toast in bed for breakfast and I haven't been getting up till 10 a.m. No rush is there. I have green tea all the time my favourite although I do like an odd cup of Birds mild coffee with soya milk. I am totally dairy free now.

Do hope you see a little loss when you get weighed as it will spur you on to keep going. You are doing so well. At the moment I don't have that problem as I'm down to 8st 4lb now and don't want to lose any more. I have been that weight now for the last month so hopefully all the stress of the last couple of months has passed. My appetite is very good. We had roast chicken, roasties, cabbage and leeks today, lovely. I don't eat many puddings although soya custard is nice as is soya yoghurt and the sugar free jellies.

Liam is so like Dave—loves his bar of chocolate and never gains any weight either. Glad you liked the photos of Sophie. Matt and Leisha decided against Ruby having the swine flu vaccine, so you will have to let me know if Lucas has it. Do hope Chris and Lorna had a better weekend with Zak.

Good weekend weather wise quite spring like but it is supposed to be turning wintry again as the week goes on so I suppose we will have to wait and see.

Do hope I get on all right on Tuesday. It will be great to have another one behind me but naturally feeling a little apprehensive as the day approaches again. Will let you know of course how I get on.

Anyway do hope your weekend was good also. Happy birthday present hunting and Happy Birthday of course to Dave for tomorrow. Take care both of you and lots of luv from Maureen x x x

Maureen's hospital visits were becoming more frequent but nevertheless cracks in her treatment constantly appear. Having been promised the results of her bone scan at her next visit, I was disappointed to hear differently. I really think I must have been extra lucky that throughout all my appointments and treatment, everything happened as and when I was told it would which made me more confident that everything was under control.

9th February 2010
Subject: Re: chemo update

Dear Margaret, Just to let you know didn't get bone scan results as not back from Chichester. Should get them at my next chemo so no news is good news. No point in worrying about something I have 3 weeks to wait for the results.

Didn't get home till 6.30 p.m. left here at 10.30 a.m. so another long day. Anyway another one completed. We have just had dinner and I have taken 4steroid tabs. Will be taking my anti-sickness at bedtime. Have been waking at 4 a.m. but at least I'm getting a few hours. Do my AT when I go to bed and when I wake up whatever time. It is getting easier to remember.

How are you? Will give you a quick ring in the morning if that is OK.

Talk soon. Lots of luv Maureen

11th February 2010
Subject: Things

Hi Maureen

Hope you are feeling OK after your 2nd chemo. Mine used to sometimes really kick in on day 2 but anyway, whatever, it won't be for long.

It was lovely to talk to you yesterday. It's almost a year since we first actually spoke on the phone—when you were having your surgery in March. I felt really nervous when the nurse said she would put me through to the phone beside your bed. See how quickly the time goes without us realising it.

I had a nice lunch with my former colleague yesterday. We went to a place in Dunfermline called Abbot House—right by the Abbey (of course). It is a coffee shop and museum. Lovely old building and peacocks roam in the garden. We had a delicious bowl of carrot and coriander soup and we noticed on the way out that the place is in the Good Soup Guide—didn't know there was one! Anyway always nice to meet and catch up with all the news.

I am just about to get ready for a 4 mile walk with the Dalgety Bay Roamers. I've got the thermal vest out as it is very cold and frosty but it should be lovely if the sun stays out. I have not been to the area called Fordell Firs so I'm looking forward to it. Have you got any snow? The news this morning said Kent and Essex had it quite bad again. Didn't mention Sussex so perhaps you have missed it (hopefully).

Well, better go and get ready. Just thought I would let you know I'm thinking about you—keep taking the tablets!!

Speak soon,

Lots of love as always

Margaret xxx

I am as anxious as Maureen must be in anticipation of her first consultation at the Royal Marsden on 16th February. Our next couple of emails just ramble on about everything and nothing and what I really wanted to say was that I hope she was going to be OK in London. I suppose I was thinking we would be getting down to the nitty gritty soon, facing reality and I was hoping the Marsden would be able to offer some really effective treatment for what sounded like a very difficult cancer to manage.

13th February 2010
Subject: Re: chitchat

Dear Margaret, thankfully we did not get any snow on Thursday morning but the wind is so bitter cold. Is there no let up to this cold weather? Giving more snow showers here for Tuesday so we will have to wait and see I suppose as to what we get. Had a quiet Friday did a bit of pampering had a shower washed my hair—yes I still have a decent covering cannot quite believe that. Did feel tired and feel tired again today but otherwise cannot complain at all. Mandy is doing us dinner tomorrow so won't have to cook. We usually have egg, chips and beans on Saturday—one of my favourites and so handy, no preparation.

How did your 4 mile walk go. I'm sure you enjoyed it as long as you are well wrapped. Oh, to have your energy. Yes, cannot believe it's coming up to a year since my first operation—time certainly does fly. I shall be so pleased to see May!

Sent for a camisole bra from Nicola Jane but the cups are not a good fit for new prosthesis so have returned it for a 34B instead of a 34C. It was the lacy one in champagne. If still not a good fit I think I will have to go for the dearer one at £42 which has a smoother cup but will let you know, thought it would be nice under summer tops. Did you get one? Remember you mentioning you might. At the moment am waiting for a wash to finish can then pop it in the dryer. Do hope you both have a lovely weekend and will catch up with you next week. Take care and lots of love as always. Maureen xxx

16th February 2010
Subject: Stuff

Dear Maureen

I am thinking about you and wondering how you are getting on. I do hope your journey was not too tiring for you and that you get some satisfaction from your consultation. It's a long time since I went to London. Even when we visit Kent, we never seem to get round to doing things other than visiting people although that really is the purpose of the visit.

Yes, I did enjoy the walk on Thursday. However, I DID feel as if I needed hip and knee replacements when I got back! That was certainly my limit and there is not another one until the 2nd Thurs in March so perhaps I will have recovered enough by then to go on that one. I am registering for the Race for Life again. Ours is on 20th June.

Poor Lorna woke up on Sunday with a migraine. I must have second sense as I text Chris to see if we could take Lucas to feed the ducks if they were not busy. So, we collected him at about 10.15 and had him for the day. Made things a bit easier for them. The ducks were quite happy to be fed—there were lots of 3 year olds doing the same, all clutching their bags of bread. I was exhausted by the time we took him home at about 4.30 but had the evening to recover.

Only 2 weeks to the Easter concert and we feel nowhere near ready (as usual). We are doing Zadok the Priest among other things—lovely Easter music. We have also got our new lilac coloured waistcoats to wear over black so the choir will be very smart this year.

I am rambling on a bit again. Still, only emailing to say hope you are getting on ok in London. Let me know (I know you will anyway).

Take care—hope you are sleeping better.

Bye for now

Lots of love and another big hug

Margaret xxx

Maureen phoned me to let me know how delighted she was with her consultation in London. She was astounded that she spent 40 minutes with the Consultant. He offered to take over treatment of her "tricky" cancer and all she had to do was to see her GP who would arrange it for her. I felt she was doing the right thing and she obviously did too. After some deliberation she went off to see her doctor.

17th February 2010
Subject: Bras (!)

Dear Maureen

It was really great to hear of your Royal Marsden experience. Thanks for letting me know.

I forgot to mention in my email about the Nicola Jane bras. I have 2—one is the lacy one in champagne and I got a black one (hussy!)—no it was to wear under my V neck black top for choir concerts. Even though I had my prosthesis changed just before Christmas, it still doesn't sit against my skin in an ordinary bra. I think the camisole bras are lovely. I really want to wear them all the time but then think I will spoil them for when I really need one under a lower top. I know Nicola Jane are a bit more expensive but they are beautiful. I did also buy an everyday pretty bra from them which I am very pleased with. My other ones are a bit matronly and "sturdy" and I do like pretty undies and the camisole ones definitely come into that category. I don't think I would go anywhere else for my bras now. Just got a new catalogue arrived and they have some lovely swimwear also. If I manage to lose the weight before we go away in the summer, I will probably need a new swimsuit so I am already choosing it in anticipation! Mind you, stayed the same last Saturday and was fed up because I had done everything by the book. I know I was told it would be difficult to lose weight after treatment, so I expect that's why. Being only 5foot tall, a few pounds too many makes me puff and blow very easily.

We have a very heavy frost here this morning with fog to boot. I don't think Barney was very keen to go with Dave to get the paper this morning. Pat's heating has broken down so she is in a freezing house waiting for people to come. She thinks she will have to have a new boiler. What an expense that will be.

Well, Maureen, I'm still in my goonie. Must go for a shower. You will be off to your GP this morning to get things sorted.

Speak soon. Extra lots of love again

Margaret xxx

17th February 2010
Subject: Re: Bras (update)!

Dear Margaret,

Yes went off to my GP this morning and he will do the necessary to activate my treatment at The Marsden. Considering my difficult cancer he thought I was doing the right thing. I just have to sit back and wait now for things to develop. Have been sleeping much better but didn't have a good night last night, probably too much on my mind. Hopefully tonight will be better.

I sent my camisole bra back on Saturday as cup was too big and re-ordered a B cup. This arrived this morning and as you say, it is gorgeous. Put it on to try for size and haven't taken it off yet so comfortable. Must have the same as you as mine's champagne also. Should be perfect for the summer. Yes I received a catalogue as well—the swimsuits are lovely aren't they.

Liam had his scooter serviced today. Needed a new battery so is up and running again. Did shopping and had lunch out just the usual. We had beautiful sunshine all day such a treat as it poured all day yesterday. Taste buds still not perfect but not too bad. Off to Ruby tomorrow and Sheena will be over with her lot as it is half term. Plenty of fun and games and noise no doubt.

Am definitely tired now so it looks like an early night for me. So glad you are getting geared up for your concert. I'm sure everything will sound lovely. Great to talk things through with you. I do so value your thoughts on things. Glad Lucas enjoyed feeding the ducks. Take care and lots of luv as always. Luv Maureen. xxx

19th February 2010
Subject: Weekend again!

Dear, dear Maureen
Lovely email from you—thank you. When you said about Liam's scooter, I was flung back to my teens when I considered myself a "mod". I went dancing one Saturday all dolled up and my brother (Peter) said to me "If you go out like that, you will come home on a scooter". Well, he was right! I did. And Jude had one for a while for nipping round the town.

We have a lovely spring-like day here although the temperature on the car thermometer was registering minus 2 when we went to Tescos so it is pretty chilly. I hope you are enjoying some sunshine today. You seem to have more energy this time with the old chemo. Still giving an eye to Ruby and shopping etc. I remember feeling pretty whacked—and what about those wobbly legs? Still get them this time? Wait until you get your platinum chemo. Platinum eh? Only the best for the best but what about the diamonds to go with it—that has to be next Christmas' pressie! (Poor Liam). What with that and arthritis being treated with gold injections, how many of us are walking treasure chests. You are a walking treasure that's for sure! Even

I can't wait to get you started on your new treatment. I feel it's me again.

After WW tomorrow a group of us are going to the nearby park to try out Nordic walking (ha ha). See me and my co-ordination. Well, you have two poles apparently and it exercises the upper body as well as the lower which ordinary walking does. A man is coming down from Kinross to put us through our paces—an hour for £2.50. I said I would give it a shot. I expect he will be looking for business but we should have a laugh if nothing else. Our WW group are good fun. I hope I have lost a bit this week after staying the same last week. I get fed up with having to do it but still don't want that 3 stone I lost to go back on.

Well, Maureen. Have a lovely weekend. Just going to get some lunch and then a walk with Barney and a bit of housework I suppose (endless).

Take care—onward and upward!

Best love, Margaret xxx

21st February 2010
Subject: Re: update

Dear Margaret,

Lovely to hear from you as always and all the gossip. Glad to hear about your experience with a scooter! Liam has a nice yellow and black one only 2 years old. It means he can scoot off to Arundel to watch his racing if I'm not about. I do have a photo which I will send to you at the end of this email if I don't forget. Good luck with the walking with sticks. I have seen it on the telly and as you say is a brilliant exercise. When I was in the ICA in Ireland we used to learn lots of different skills. I made a rug which Mandy still has and it washes up lovely in the washing machine. I did patchwork and made rag dolls which I thoroughly enjoyed.

Tiredness not too bad as I do rest lots on the days I stay home. I feel I have to. A little bit of jelly legs at times but not too bad.

Had a call from the Royal Marsden on Friday saying I have to have this next ct scan at St Richards on the same scanner so they can compare everything exactly. Will be trying to sort this out on Monday which should be interesting as you know how slow they are. Will keep you in touch with progress or lack of it.

Keep up the good work with WW you are doing so well. Hopefully something will come off this week. Sophie and Tracey will be down next weekend so looking forward to seeing how she has changed. Apparently she went to bed at 11.30 p m and didn't wake till 8 a.m this morning. Tracey kept waking to check on her every few hours—had to laugh. I told her to enjoy these extra hours.

Hope you all enjoyed your weekend sunny and cold yesterday but miserable rain back here today. Off to Leisha for a roast at 2 p.m so should be nice. Forgot to say we have had no tele since Friday. No signal problems with aerial. Came to look yesterday to confirm box on aerial giving problems so will be back on Monday to fix I hope. Have a dvd player in tele so we have been watching all our dvds haven't had time to watch before.

Catchup with you next week. Take care till then. Luv Maureen xxx

Maureen has evidently become a little ironic about her previous treatment, obviously in the light of experience.

22nd **February 2010**

Subject: All sorts

Hiya Maureen

Hope by now you have sorted out an appointment for your scan at St Richards. Let's hope they come up with the goods pronto this time.

We had a busy weekend. I lost 1½ lbs at WW this week so I am pleased it is going down. Still got 9 lbs to go to get back to what I was before chemo. I would like to get shot of that before my niece's son's wedding beginning of May. We will be travelling to Stafford on 30th April but only staying until 3rd May. We haven't been to that part of the country before. Bit of a drive for Dave. The Nordic pole walking was great. I can feel I have exercised, especially back and shoulders. We had some fun anyway.

We had friends round for lunch today and on Friday I decided to make some scones. What a disaster! Must be losing my touch. First of all the whole egg shot in when I wanted to keep some back to brush the tops. My recipe said ¼ pint milk so I flung that in, put my hands in and . . . it was like glue. No way would that knead together or roll out. Of course I started adding extra flour blah blah blah. I was determined to not waste the mixture and finally managed to get some on to a baking sheet (as well as on the bag of flour, the worktops, the taps, my nose, etc etc). Anyway, they amazingly rose and were edible but not for anyone else so on Saturday I decided to make an old favourite farmhouse fruit loaf. Thank goodness that came out all right! I do little baking these days. My mum would have had a good laugh seeing me making the scones—she was a brilliant baker. Did your mum go into domestic service when she left school by any chance? My mum had no choice apparently, but it did make her a good cook. She worked for 2 schoolteachers—how times change. You wouldn't get that now.

Friends have not long gone home after a nice lunch together. It's a glorious day but very, very cold. My friend Carol, who came to lunch moved up to Scotland when we did. Her husband, Les, worked at Portsmouth Dockyard which also closed and he and Dave met whilst working in Rosyth Dockyard and waiting to get organised to move us all up. Anyway, Carol, before she moved was a Radiotherapist at Portsmouth hospital. I was telling her about your experience. She said she has a friend who still works there who says the service doesn't seem as good as it used to be. I feel sure you have done the right thing going to the Marsden.

Thanks for the picture of the scooter. Jude & I thought it looked like a wasp or a bee. Lovely bright yellow. Jude said she wished she still had hers.

We ended up looking after Lucas best part of yesterday. I was trying to get some housework done but apparently he was asking for Barney Gran (what he calls me). We took him for a lovely walk down through the sailing club so he could see the boats. You have to pass a pond that was frozen solid so we threw stones so he could see they wouldn't go into the water. We went on the beach and picked up shells. He had a great time. However, when we got back home, his silly side took over and he started throwing his toys all over the place! (Terrible 2's). He has started drinking from a cup without a lid now but Chris said he deliberately tipped it up this morning! Happy days.

Well, I'm rambling again. Speak soon and let me know when you have got your scan organised. So look forward to all your news too.

Lots of love. Keep warm!

Love from Margaret xxx

Maureen telephoned to let me know her scan was booked for 24th February.

24th February 2010

Subject: Brrr . . .

Hello again Maureen

Well . . . we are in the throes of more snow falling. It has been snowing all day. We had to go to Dunfermline for a funeral this afternoon and it was really thick there. We are not quite so bad as we are near the water. Of course, I had my smart shoes on and needed to hang on to Dave for dear life in case I slipped over! Will winter never leave us. Dave used to work with Hugh in the dockyard and I know his wife well. They are neighbours also. It was a nice service.

Just writing to say I hope your scan went OK. Here we are Thursday again tomorrow already. It's our local paper day and I am expecting there to be a lot in it about Queen Margaret Hospital where I had my treatment and op. It was on TV news that the Inspectors had been in and found a mattress that had been passed for use but was really badly soiled. They also said their sharps boxes were overflowing and the high dependency unit had hygiene problems. I don't know! It doesn't seem to matter which hospital you go to now. Things are just not like they used to be—or is it that we hear more about the bad things. I couldn't fault the hospital when I was there.

Well, I'm just off to do my crossword and have a cuppa—hope you are doing similar.

Speak soon, take care, big hug . . . xxx

Lots of love
Margaret xx

25th **February 2010**
Subject: Re: update

Dear Margaret.

Sorry to hear you are having more snow and still very cold. Do hope by today it has started to disappear. Things are not much better here really as although it has gone quite mild we are having loads of heavy rain everyday. Raining again now and giving till tomorrow morning and then to brighten a little. Saturday is fine and then more heavy rain and gales for Sunday. Horrible.

Yes, ct scan went ok yesterday. Was home just after 4.30 pm. We were not kept waiting around too long. Waiting now for Tuesday when we will get the results and what my future treatment will be. Interesting. Should get the bone scan also.

Am feeling fine this week but of course on countdown till Tuesday but I must not think like that and enjoy my good days not worry about the bad ones.

Most hospitals seem to be falling down somewhere down the line. Did you see Stafford on the news at all? Terrible reports from there about more elderly patients being left in soiled beds for days and not being fed and getting drinks. It is so sad.

Anyway thanks for your emails love to read them and onward and upwards for next week.

Take care lots of luv as always Maureen xxx

I was so concerned for her and would have given anything to be with her to give her a real hug instead of one by email. How helpless I felt. Maureen had a wonderful family round her. However, we still felt a special bond because we had been through the illness together from the start.

26th February 2010
Subject: Weekend ahead

Hi Maureen

Here we go, another weekend looming. Gosh, how the time is flying by. Our weather has been absolutely atrocious all week and I don't think tomorrow is to be any better. We haven't got the snow that they have further north but my goodness, what rain! And wind. Uggggh. I feel as if I am coming down with a cold maybe.

I would be saying "Roll on Tuesday" if I were you! I feel Tuesday will be the day when you find out exactly what treatment is for you and you can get your head round anything new (platinum?) It will be good to hear that your bone scan is fine, which I am sure it will be. Your CT scans will be in place for the future and you will sail through your chemos just as you did before.

Take care

Lots of love

Margaret x x x

26th February 2010
Subject: Re: good day!

Dear Margaret,

Thanks for your email. Just could not wait till next week. We heard from The Marsden today as they had seen my ct scan from Wednesday and to let me know as I was responding very well to Taxotere there would be no change to my next chemo on Tuesday at Portsmouth and I'll be hearing from them to book me in there for number 4. Such good news or what. Obviously I should hear more detail and bone scan results on Tuesday but this has given me such a lift. They also said if things were not responding and I needed to change they were going to book me in with them on 9th March to start new treatment so either way I was not going to miss out on anything. I think I have been a bit depressed of late so hopefully can fight that side of things now.

So sorry to hear you think you have a cold coming and feel a bit under the weather. The wind and rain doesn't help. Hope you perk up soon. Will be back in touch next week. Have a lovely weekend.

Luv & hugs Maureen xxx

26th **February 2010**
Subject: Wow!

Dear Maureen

Just had to reply to your latest email. This is really exciting and proves the Marsden are completely in control of the situation. How great that they even phoned you will the good news. It is quite understandable that you may have been a bit depressed lately although you are very good at disguising it! With everything up in the air as it was, you haven't known whether you were coming or going and the uncertainty of it all. This is such good news and I am so excited for you. It reminds me how the heat had gone out of my breast after 2 chemos. I didn't dare think things could improve as quickly as that but they had and now it is happening to you.

You won't mind having the next chemo on Tuesday knowing what good it is doing. I think you deserve a little brandy over the weekend, that is 1) if you like brandy (which I don't) and 2) your taste lets you enjoy it. This is purely for medicinal purposes you understand!! Relax and enjoy your good news—I am grinning like a Cheshire cat whilst I am typing this.

Luv and hugs back

Margaret xxx

Once again, as I said before, I felt it was me.

1ˢᵗ **March 2010**
Subject: Weekend

Hi Maureen

Brrrrr . . . we are still freezing up here but at least today it is beautifully sunny. I took Barney out this morning at about 7.15 as Monday is my "stand-up pill day". I must have told you that on top of everything else, when I had the dexa bone scan they came up with me having the start of osteoporosis, so I have to take a tablet once a week on an empty stomach, with a full glass of water, and not sit down, lay down or anything down for at least half an hour. Hence me doing the first morning walk with Barns. It was gorgeous looking across the water that early but the cold just bit me.

I hope you had a nice weekend with the family and are now ready for no. 3 tomorrow. Pat came round for dinner yesterday. Her new boiler has a problem now and the engineers have to come and check for a leak somewhere. So no heating for her again. She enjoyed her meal anyway and had a good warm (she and Dave even had a wee whisky and lemonade after dinner (yuk from me—don't like whisky). In fact, I have never regained my taste for wine or anything alcoholic since my chemo. I do sometimes have a glass of wine but I don't enjoy it the same as before.

It was the big rehearsal also yesterday, with the orchestra and I swithered over whether I should go with this cold or not. However, I couldn't really miss it so I used my Sinex decongestant and surprisingly I still have a voice (of sorts) and it was fabulous. So thrilling and uplifting. We are doing Zadok the Priest which you will have heard, the Vivaldi Gloria which pretty well takes the roof off and something more sad in Latin for Easter. Beautiful music. I don't know what I would do without my music sometimes. Anyway I had made a Hungarian Goulash in the morning and put it in the slow cooker. It stayed there from 10 a.m. until 5 p.m. and was delicious and the meat lovely and tender.

I must have another look through my papers today for tomorrow's meeting, just to refresh my memory and on Wednesday we are going over to Edinburgh. Our friends Agnes and James are coming to Edinburgh from Glasgow and we are meeting for a bit of lunch. We are not sure where to take them as we don't know Edinburgh that well but I think we may walk down the Royal Mile (plenty of places to eat there) and we may end up in the new Scottish Parliament building which I don't think they will have seen. Otherwise, there is the Museum of Childhood with lots of things that make you say "Oh, I had one of those when I was little". They even had a Mettoy typewriter where you twisted a wheel and pressed something to make the letters come out. Needless to say I had one of those. Hope you are still on a high Maureen but don't forget you have been through a lot since September with your mum and everything. It's bound to affect you sometimes. I just felt I wanted my mum's arms round me to tell me everything was going to be all right. It seems we always want our mums whoever and whatever age we are. It will be nice to get out in the garden soon, hopefully. The lighter evenings are not far away now. You enjoy your garden too. Oh, I forgot to ask you about your cat. Dave had told me you were taking her to the vet. Everything OK?

Lots of love (won't send the sneezes).

Bye for now and look forward to hearing from you soon.

Margaret xxx

2nd **March 2010**
Subject: Re: good update

Dear Margaret.

Just a quick email to let you know that my bone scan was clear and the tumour in my liver reduced from 43 mm to 26 mm how about that. Also have a tumour under left arm lymph node shrunk by half. Also 3 tumours around neck and collarbone and those have shrunk by half as well. Won't bore you with exact measurements but much smaller around 9, 11 and 13 mm I think. We got home at 5.05 p m so much better than last time only running about 1 and a half hours late.

Boomerang *(the cat)* is fine. Forgot to tell you just went for her yearly checkup and injections. Still a little overweight has to lose about 3 lbs but we should achieve that over the summer as she always gains in the winter. A lazy cat doesn't go out much just thinks of her belly all day!

Weather beautiful the last few days gorgeous sunshine looking forward to getting into the garden as you say. Am starting to feel so much better. It's great I have you urging me on. Roll on the Marsden now on March 23rd.

Talk soon. Lots of luv Maureen xxx

We were both truly on a high now. Were things really going to be OK? It sounded good.

6th **March 2010**
Subject: Hope u ok!

Hi Maureen

How are you? Hope the old chemo not making you feel too bad but if it is, it must be working away.

What a busy time I have been having. We took Lucas yesterday as Lorna was going to get her hair done. Her mum came to sit with Zak (who seems to be settling a bit more now) and we had Lucas. We went for a lovely long walk. He is a really good little walker for his age. We ended up on the beach throwing stones in the rock pools. We had to clamber over a few rocks to get on the beach and we both went flying. I only had my ordinary shoes on and they are not great grippers. Still, plenty of padding (!) plus well wrapped up so neither of us came to any harm other than covered in sand and feeling a bit foolish. No one around though. We had a laugh about it. Also the day before, I had ordered him a Noddy train and car set from Amazon. It actually came whilst Lucas was with us. I saw the postie van drive up and I said to Lucas "Here comes Postman Pat". So we both went to the door. I whispered to the postie he was Postman Pat and I asked him where Jessie, the cat, was. He said "She's at home, I'm just going to find her". I said "you know more about it than I do". He said "I'm only guessing!" Anyway Lucas thought he was Postman Pat. He just loved the train set as everything was just the same as in the DVD. You also get a Noddy, Big Ears, Mr Plod and the teddy bear figures and it was easy to put everything on the tracks or road. The car plays the Noddy theme as it goes around. I don't know who enjoyed it most—Lucas or me.

Well, today is the concert. I didn't make rehearsal on Monday with my cold but have to be in our places today by 1.30 p m for big rehearsal with soloists etc. Concert itself is 7.30 p m. Have just stood and prepared all my veggies for tomorrow's dinner as I am out this evening. Family coming for roast tomorrow. I do like to get ahead of myself if I can. Anyway, I'm looking forward to the concert and it's not too long. Choir then finishes until end of August so I'm looking forward to the break as much as I look forward to going. Needless to say Dave took the cold after me and is really suffering. Still, over the worst now, I should think.

I hope you will be having a restful weekend. The weather here seems quite settled at the moment. Still a bit chilly, but dry and brightish.

I had better go and get my shower now and try to make myself presentable for tonight. We will be standing for quite a while so had better just wear my comfy shoes. They are nearly worn out as wear them so much. No-one will see them under the long skirt.

Take care and once again hope you are not feeling too many side effects this time.

Best love

Margaret xxx

11th March 2010
Subject: All sorts

Hi Maureen

Hope you had a good couple of days away and the jelly legs haven't got the better of you. We have had some glorious weather here last few days. I did my 4 mile walk this morning—that's 4 weeks ago I did the last one. It was really good although I had to make the effort to go out in the first place. You get talking to different people all the time which suits my busy jaws.

Dave has been helping Chris with Pat's kitchen so have been listening to one of my favourite CDs. It's the sort of music we sing at choral union but all by a composer called John Rutter. He composes absolutely beautiful music. A friend of mine gave it to me when I was in the middle of treatment and said "sit back, relax and let the music wash over you". Well, Maureen, it does. I would love to send you a copy because it helped me when I was feeling a little bit out of sorts. I *will* send you a copy. If it's not your cup of tea, never mind but see what you think.

Well, we are almost at another weekend. Can't believe how the time flies. I'll be back to WW this Saturday. Hope a little bit more of me has disappeared (the bit round my middle certainly doesn't want to disappear!).

Look forward to hearing how you are and all about Tracey's house, etc.

Speak soon,

Lots of luv as usual. Take care

Margaret xxx

18th March 2010
Subject: Re: Update

Dear Margaret,

Received your photo of Barney after being clipped. Such a handsome feller. Definitely the same colouring as Fern. Such a pity he hates going. I'm getting there with the cold but haven't shook it off completely yet. Have had a quiet week as the old legs aren't as good as they should be at the moment. Leisha is calling for me in the morning to go into Worthing to M & S to spend some of my Mother's Day money if I see anything. We are then going to have lunch at the Fish Factory. Haven't been there since Sheena got married so am looking forward to that.

Weather still lovely and quite mild. Still waiting for my first daffodil but my neighbour's have started to open so mine should not be too long now.

Am sending a couple of photos which were took when Tracey was down here. Hope Zak has settled once again poor little mite. Cannot believe another week has nearly gone by and it's the weekend again. Busy week for me next week getting used to new people and new surroundings but am sure things will be fine.

Hope you all have a lovely weekend. Lots of luv Maureen xxx

I had been contacted by my Breast Nurse who asked me to chair a talk with 5 medical students—baby doctors who were straight out of medical school and apparently wouldn't even know what a mammogram was. They were in the Breast Unit to learn about patient experience and communication. I had told Maureen by phone that this was coming up and my next email goes into detail about it. I really enjoy this kind of experience. Actually, only have to go into a hospital and want to work there! I would have loved to have been a hands-on medical person, given the opportunity but it is much too late now.

19ᵗʰ March 2010
Subject: What a stunner!

Hi Maureen

Now, who do you think I am talking about? Ruby? Sophie? Tracey? Of course, that goes without saying but it's YOU! You look really fantastic in your new wig. I think it is virtually the same style as mine was, perhaps a little shorter but the way it goes across the top and with the fringe. Really stunning.

Yesterday was my talk with the 5 medical students so back up to the hospital. I really enjoyed it (making my mouth go, you see). No. There were 4 of us patients, each with a different breast cancer experience so we all had a good time getting to know each other whilst waiting for the students to arrive. There was a younger woman who had just had 3 FEC (chemo that I was on) but next time starts Taxotere. She just found a lump under her arm which her GP didn't think was anything sinister but sent her up anyway. She had been very shocked when she was told what was going on. Another lady had just finished her treatment having had a double mastectomy. She was down to have her right breast off but was found cancer was through both. She has had reconstruction. Another one had a lumpectomy and had just had her first radiotherapy, not needing any chemo. Anyway, I started the ball rolling when the students arrived and asked each lady what their reaction had been when the Consultant told them the news initially (I felt I wanted the students to realise how important communication was between doctor and patient). As it does, one thing leads to another and before long the students were all joining in asking us things, which is what was wanted. One student had been allowed to go up to theatre. She came back down after and was absolutely beside herself with excitement at the experience. She saw a mastectomy and full lymph node clearance. I asked her what lymph nodes looked like. She said "Very red, and like the seaweed you pop, all sort of joined up". I think we have a budding surgeon there. The students all agreed they get more from one of these sessions than they ever get from a 3 hour lecture with slides. Anyway, we didn't finish until about 5 p.m. and I had been at the hospital since 1.30 p m. I was really tired but it was girls' night as well so went but to be honest I was too tired to enjoy it as I normally would.

Back to your photos. You have beautiful daughters and Ruby, well, isn't she delightful. I hope she marries Lucas (ha ha). Poor Chris called in this morning and said they had literally no sleep last night and he said "I mean NO sleep". Lucas was awake from 11-2 and then Zak the rest of the night. I was telling the girls and we all agreed (in the light of old age and experience) that he must be hungry. Was it Farex we used to put in the bottle last thing at night? Just to bulk it up a bit They can't go on like this, that's for sure.

It is very blowy here today but lovely and sunny. Am just about to take Barney up the shops. Apart from the big shop which we will do later on, I haven't anything particular to do today. I should do some housework but . . . . naah!

Cheltenham Gold Cup today. I think of you and Liam when the important races are on. I expect you have been following it all. Let's hope you get your legs back soon. Enjoy M & S. Chris & Lorna gave me a voucher for the salon so I'll get my legs waxed and eyebrows done before our holiday. That was the up side of chemo—no waxing necessary! Thanks again for the lovely photos—I keep looking at them.

Take care now. I shall be waiting to hear how you get on next week. My, how the time flies.

Lots of love and hugs (big ones). Chin up, old bean (sorry about the old)

Margaret xxx

23rd March 2010

Subject: Re: What a stunner!

Dear Margaret,

Just a quick email as have just had something to eat as we didn't get home until 6.30 p m as lost our way a bit coming home—no tom tom but we eventually got back on track but lost about half an hour. Everything went well, have to be back there at 11.30 a m for chemo tomorrow. You get a bleeper when you book in so we can go off and have a sandwich and not miss being called.

Booked my next ct scan for 12th April at 9.25 a m and then hopefully 5th chemo on Wednesday 14th April. I have to be there for 11 a m that day where bloods will be done, be seen by the doctor and get ct results and then go on for chemo.

Wednesday is my chemo day now. Probably a longish day but I bet we still get home before we did at Portsmouth. I feel so much happier in myself already so that cannot be bad!!

Will be back in touch tomorrow after I get home. Do hope you are all well. Lots of luv from your bosomless buddy Maureen!!! xxxx

It was reassuring to get such an upbeat email from Maureen. The Marsden were certainly moving things on for her and I see her old sense of humour is back. Telephone calls became the norm for a while as Maureen was feeling the effects of her chemotherapy and didn't always feel up to emailing. I continued to email though as I knew she was always pleased to receive all my news.

26th March 2010

Subject: Mamma mia!

Hi Maureen

I expect the chemo is beginning to kick-in again. Still, let it chomp away (I'm remembering my visualisation). Hope you are not feeling too bad anyway and can have a nice, relaxing weekend. It was lovely to hear from you on Wednesday and very reassuring (for me too) that the Marsden seem so much better at everything.

We are off to Glasgow about 10.30 this morning to meet up with Agnes & James. I am still so tired. We had a good "Abba" practice yesterday but was there from 12 noon until about 4.30. You have to concentrate and consequently, I was ready for bed about 9 p m. Managed to hang on till 10 though. My stomach is churning a bit thinking it could be an utter disaster, but I'm sure it won't be really.

Our other friends George & Issy had their Ruby Wedding last week and we are taking them for a meal tomorrow evening. I am hoping to get a Ruby Wedding balloon. Dave will take it along to the restaurant in the afternoon so that it is on one of the chairs when we get there. Just a little surprise for them.

Well, it's pouring rain here today at the moment. Dave has taken Barney to get the paper. Barney has his coat on also as he doesn't like the rain. He is going to be on his own for a wee while today whilst we are in Glasgow. Pat has an 80th birthday lunch to go to but she is going to pop round after to let him out. Dogs are such a tie at times and I do worry about leaving him for too long on his own.

Well, I had better get washed and brushed up. Think about you often. Speak soon.

Lots of love to my dear bosomless buddie.

Margaret xxx

I had explained to Maureen on the phone that one of the GPs I used to work for was retiring. Some of us former employees decided to do an act at his leaving party, and we had started practising the Abba song "Mamma Mia" but to different words, applicable to that GP, composed by myself,. It was really good on the night, as we had watched Abba videos to learn some of their movements. We became perfection! I wore a beaded headdress, one of the other girls wore a trouser suit and a moustache, and a former nurse wore Ugg boots as a parody of the long white platforms that became the Abba trademark . . . What a laugh we had. All wore wigs and the fact that we were not in the flush of youth made the performance even more hilarious. All the hard work was rewarded by the applause we received and the delight on the GP's face at our efforts.

29th March 2010
Subject: Yawn, yawn

Hi Maureen

I don't know about you, but I am really missing the hour we lost over the weekend. We had a lovely meal out on Saturday. We treated our friends to celebrate their Ruby Wedding. They came back to our house after the meal and didn't go until about midnight which meant it was really 1 a.m. I couldn't get to sleep then as I was still going through the evening so did the autogenic training which helped. Felt just like I was on chemo all day yesterday and went straight to bed after the Dancing on Ice final at 9 p m. Still feel tired this morning but know I have been overdoing things. We went to Glasgow on Friday and we were late getting back as the traffic was horrendous. This week is quieter at the moment although I have a load of Ethics Committee papers to read ready for next Tuesday. My, these meetings come round really quickly!

Not very nice here today at the moment. It is snowing in Stirling, I believe—only 40 mins up the road from here) and we have been promised some tomorrow. I'm still in the polo necks. Haven't seen Chris and Lorna over the weekend. Hope they were able to relax a bit. We have booked tickets for July to take Lucas to see the Gruffalo which is on at the Edinburgh Playhouse. I hope he won't be scared though! He loves the book and the DVD. It will be his first experience of the theatre.

I hope you are not feeling too bad after the chemo, although I suspect these are the worst days at the moment.

Well, Maureen, I'm just going to get stuck into the reading I have to do. Hope it's interesting or I'll be falling asleep.

I'll give you a ring in the morning if you are OK for that.

Lots of warm love from a cold, dreary, Dalgety Bay.

Margaret xxx

4th **April 2010**
Subject: Update

Hi Maureen

I hope you are having an enjoyable Easter. I'm glad you have got over the worst of your side effects again. The coffee sounded great!

I am not feeling well. As I said to you, I feel as if I am on chemotherapy again but I am so tired I don't know what to do with myself. I will leave it another week and if no better will see GP in case anything going on. I expect I am panicking a bit with everything that is coming up and I have certainly been doing far too much. I have been cancelling a few things to make life a bit simpler. I am frustrated to think I can't do everything the way I used to but c'est la vie. I am sleeping OK but don't feel as if it is doing me much good. Got no energy. Still, enough of my moans and groans.

Got Zak a new outfit for Easter. He's into little jeans and shirts now. I put some money in Lucas' Trust Fund but also found him a toy cash register. He just loves playing shops and I have saved a lot of cardboard boxes of everyday things (toothpaste, porridge, rice, tissues, etc) and we stand them all on the coffee table. He is the shopkeeper and I have to come in with my bag, buy everything (!) and he puts things in the bag. He will just love having a till to go with it for his pennies.

We had a lot of violent winds with the snow during the week. It has left our shoreline pretty devastated. The beach has been washed up over where the paths were and where there was turf, it has been ripped up and fallen away and a few trees down. The high tides coincided with the winds—always a bad thing. The esplanade at Kirkcaldy was closed as water all over the road and a caravan site just a little way up the road had a landslide leaving some of the caravans hanging over the edge. The water here came up into some people's gardens. Just imagine what a tsunami must be like.

Well, I prepared my veggies and set the table last night to save time today. Just remembered, I haven't got the prawns out of the freezer! Better go and do that. My brain not working properly again. Never mind.

Hope you enjoy your meal with your brother. Speak soon.

Lots of love from us all,

Margaret xx

Unfortunately, it seems that once you have cancer, the fear of recurrence is never far away. What ailments you would normally shrug off without another thought become cause for concern. Always, always, it is in the back of one's mind that the dreaded big C is rearing its ugly head again. This seems to be the legacy you are left with and although most of the time you can remain optimistic, you still have those dark, miserable moments of gloom and despair. Maureen cheered herself up with a soya latte after her infusion of chemotherapy. I so fancied one of these coffees after she had described it so enticingly.

10th April 2010

Subject: Weekend again!

Hi Maureen

Just going off to WW in a minute. We had a lovely meal out on Thursday. The restaurant had only 9 tables, all bearing lovely fat candles. Lovely atmosphere. We both had soup which was courgette with parmesan, mint and all sorts—delicious. Dave had his favourite steak and I had sea bass on a confit (!) of petit pois, potato, bacon, baby shrimps with a red wine jus (very posh). Again, very tasty. Everything on the menu was very different and cooked whilst you wait so very fresh. Really enjoyed it. However, have woken today feeling exhausted. It makes me miserable and not wanting to do anything. I'll be OK once I get out and about, I'm sure.

Hope you have a lovely weekend. The weather is very promising. Have asked Chris & Lorna if they want to come for dinner tomorrow—no pressure. When Lucas came on the phone to wish me happy birthday, he kept saying "Gran, want to come to your house" so even if they don't come, perhaps we can have Lucas for a little while.

Hope you have a flutter on the Grand National. I expect Liam could give us a few tips! Hope there aren't any casualties.

Well, Maureen, had better go and see how much weight I have put on (pessimistic me).

Hope to hear from you soon. Be with you whilst you are having your scan xxx

Big hug

Lots of love

Margaret xxx

Maureen's CT scan was fast approaching. Her appointment was on 12ᵗʰ April. I was to get a phone call from her after the scan but as she wouldn't be getting the results the same day, we would all be anxiously awaiting the results.

13ᵗʰ April 2010
Subject: Re Update

Hi Maureen

Lovely to hear from you as always. Kept looking at my clock yesterday, wondering how you were getting on. Glad to know everything went OK. Yes, you will be on tenterhooks until you get your results. After last time being so successful, you will be hoping for similar this time. We all will!

I went shopping this morning. Jude and my friend Agnes both gave me an M&S gift card and I managed to get a lovely pair of cropped trousers in a gorgeous cornflower blue, a t-shirt, white with a thin blue stripe to match the trousers. It was on a model in the shop and caught my eye. I also got a new bag. I treated myself to a nice top from Debenhams. It was half-price—a Jasper Conran. I managed to get a couple of birthday pressies (??!!) as well—just what I was looking for. Let's hope you have finished your treatment, or almost, if you have to have some radio this time, by your birthday (and Pat's). What a celebration that will be for you and the family, especially as it is, dare I say, a special one this year.

Well, we did have a mini heatwave, but it's gone as quick as it came and it is cold again today, but bright. The 2 lovely days we had brought the garden on very quickly. We have two different types of magnolia trees and they are both about to burst into flower now—usually much earlier. Dave has been scarifying the lawn and I have been doing nothing (in the garden, that is).

Just going to have a cuppa—is it soya and 2 sugars for you Maureen? (Ha ha).

Will be anxious to hear from you next time but look forward to it.

Best love and hope your chemo goes OK tomorrow.

Margaret xxx

15th April 2010
Subject: Phonecall

Dear Maureen

Even though we spoke on the phone last night, I still wanted to email you to say again how well you are doing. I still think that positive attitude sees us through—plus the best treatment of course. It is a wonderful feeling when you are told your tumour(s) have shrunk. I feel the Oncologists involved are also genuinely thrilled for us too. Great job satisfaction for them! Keep working hard, Maureen—I know you will anyway. Pamper yourself as much as you can.

Got a shock when I looked in the mirror this morning, seeing the different coloured hair! Have got to get used to it. The hairdresser always manages to do it better than I can so will have a go later on and see how I can handle it. She has left it longer than I have had it up to now—a bit more like it was before it fell out. It's the girls' night tonight so see what they think. I am feeling less tired at the moment but will be glad when Saturday is over (Abba here we go). We are calling ourselves "Blabba" (load of nonsense). Went to see the venue yesterday to work out where we can put our props etc (oh dear). Will let you know how it goes. Hope to get some photos.

I have got an eye test today.

Pat was expecting her friend up from Worthing today. She was flying British Airways. Now all the Scottish airports are shut for the foreseeable future because of the Icelandic volcano! Don't know when she will be able to travel now. No-one knows how long it will take for the ash cloud to shift but it's moving south apparently so LOOK OUT!! We will have to get the shovels out (ha ha). Shame though for anyone travelling today. Even worse for the Icelandics, I should imagine. You just never know what is round every corner. That's for sure.

Well, the sun is out here—no volcanic ash there then.

Once again, Maureen, delighted to hear of your great progress. Let me have dates of your next appointments so I can work with you.

Lots of love

Your now blonde-haired bosom buddie

Margaret xxx

16th April 2010
Subject: Re: Update

Dear Margaret (my new blonde-haired bosom buddy!) what a mouthful. Glad you like your hair it sounds lovely for the summer and for the wedding also. Sorry I'm late in replying but so much has been happening since Wednesday. Liam's brother and wife came to see us yesterday. Didn't like to put them off so found that quite tiring. Also, because of finding out about my next treatments, has led me to decide to go to Liam's nephews wedding in Ireland on July 3rd. Have known about it for a while but obviously will finish on 16th June so have took the plunge and decided to go. Will fly out on Fri 2nd July and come back on Mon 5th July. Sheena and Tracey will be coming with us so a nice foursome.

Only one problem. I go to get passport, driving licence etc so the girls can book tickets online before they get too dear and cannot find them. I know I have them all together when getting Liam's retirement sorted out and council tax etc but where I put them I don't know—not where they should be. My head has been all over the place this last few months so hopefully I didn't throw anything away. Anyway to cut the story short, phoned DVLA this morning and they gave us numbers needed to book the tickets and will be issuing new licence. Sheena has booked our flights to Belfast International from Gatwick and also a hire care for 4 days, and I rang the lady in Ireland an hour ago who we always stay with when we go over, she runs a lovely homely B&B and we are booked in there for 3 nights. Do hope I haven't bitten off too much but feel I need something to focus on now.

Yes, so pleased with all my results. I have been on a high but am back down with a bump today as chemo is kicking in but never mind. Found a receipt whilst looking for other things and we stayed at the Tillington Hotel in Stafford for Tracey's wedding, just thought I'd mention it since you will be going soon. I cannot believe all this disruption with the airports. Terrible isn't it but like you, we have some sunshine. Weekend is looking great with warm sunshine so hope to sit in the garden and enjoy. Glad you managed to get some nice things in M & S and Debenhams. Just went for a soya Costa coffee this morning (no sugar) for my little treat.

Think I've bored you enough with all my little problems this week. Oh yes, appointments before I go. Because it is Bank Holiday, next chemo will have bloods and Doctor on Wed 5th May at 11 a.m. and chemo no. 6 on Thurs 6th May at 11 a m so 2 visits again that week but that is fine. Anyway, will say cheerio or you will definitely be yawning by now.

Lots of luv and hugs from Maureen (your baldie buddie for now) xxx

We had made arrangements to go to my nephew's wedding in Stafford at the beginning of May and it appears that one of Maureen's daughters had married in Stafford, hence the reference to a hotel in Stafford. I was glad Maureen felt able to look ahead enough to arrange to go to a family wedding in Ireland in July. I thought in her last email she was feeling a bit chemo-weary. It has been a long haul but hopefully completion of treatment is not far away. I felt so much on Maureen's wavelength that I was uneasy one day that she wasn't feeling too good. She beat me to the phone.

19th April 2010
Subject: Weekend

Dear Jelly Legs

Almost rang *you* this morning as I thought "I bet Maureen's feeling a bit ropey". You always sound cheerful in your emails but I know it is just a case of hoping the next two or three days hurry up and pass so you feel back to your old self.

What a weekend! Quiet Sunday?????????? Oh No! Didn't go near the computer yesterday.

You will be pleased to hear Blabba was a great success. The song was really good. I hope to see some video footage and photos in the near future. Other members of staff did "turns" also. The nurses at one surgery called themselves Dr Taylor's Sugar Lump Fairies and they did a dance from "Swine Lake" (!) They tutu'd in complete with pig snouts and ears and did a really good ballet dance—lot of work. The other nurses all sang words to "My Favourite Things" (Sound of Music) only the words changed. Some were a bit rude, like "giving out bottles for patients to sh . . . t in. These are a few of our least favouring things"!! Very funny anyway. Dr Taylor himself dressed up as Elvis and sang words he made up and he also introduced Elvis' sister, Elvina, who was one of the other GPs who apart from the Elvis wig was every inch a woman, even though he isn't. Hilarious and very medical school.

There was a lovely buffet and the bar was free. I am still on my Slimline Tonics (still off alcohol since chemo) but some took full advantage of it!!

Glad you were able to sit in the garden. Ours is looking a lot brighter now. The two magnolias are bursting and lots more green leaves in sight. We are enjoying the spring flowers now and the rhubarb won't be long before I can pull some.

I couldn't sleep after Saturday night with everything going through my mind and then we had Lucas yesterday from 10 a.m. as Chris & Lorna were going shopping for shoes for Chris to wear at Lorna's brother's wedding next week. It was raining in the morning so we took him (Lucas) to the Play Planet in Dalgety Bay. There are masses of soft playthings to climb on, slide on, climb through, run round. I had a ball! Lucas wanted me to do everything with him of course. Still, it was indoors and he loved it. We took Barney out after some lunch and had a good viewing of Postman Pat and then Lorna, Chris & Zak came for dinner. I finally got to sit down about 8 p.m. but I felt everything had gone well so I felt content.

Well, Maureen, I'll look forward to a phone call tomorrow. Will probably walk Barney up the shops first thing but if you would like to phone about 10 a.m. that is if it is not interrupting a nice breakfast in bed. That would be lovely.

Do hope you are not feeling too bad now. My own GP was there on Saturday night. She said I looked good and she liked my hair—I had a bit more than when she last saw me. The wood pigeons are chasing each other down the path—tut tut. They must know spring has arrived.

Bye for now

Love Margaret x x x

The volcanic ash situation in Scotland is causing a good deal of concern. One day airports closed, next day open. Would we get away on holiday? We were hoping to fly to Turkey with our friends, Agnes and James. All the uncertainty made me wish it would be cancelled and then we would know where we stood. The last thing I wanted was to get stranded in Turkey, not able to get home.

22nd April 2010

Subject: Hello

Hi Maureen

I hope by now you are feeling stronger day by day and looking forward to a pleasant weekend.

Just had to stop this email. Jaffa is in front of the monitor, looking for a big fuss. He is a very affectionate cat and will not be put off! I have been combing him as he is moulting (all three cats are!) He also goes mad for anything mint and because I have just cleaned my teeth, he won't go away. Keeps rubbing round my hands and I can't type properly—or see the monitor. Anyway, have lifted him off now. He is a lovely cat.

Went up the town after to get all my holiday stuff from Boots. Make sure when you turn 60 to get a Boots Advantage Card because you get 10% discount on all Boots products. If you already have a card, ask at your Boots about the scheme. You just have to fill in a form. I bought sun cream, Boots beauty serum (ha ha that's a joke). No, I do believe in looking after my skin, paracetamol and a small first aid kit to pop in the case. All Boots brand and I saved quite a bit. So, turning 60 does have SOME benefits.

I am going to count up my tablets today to see what I have to order to make sure I have enough of everything until we get back at end of May. It does look as if we will get away now. We were having our doubts up until yesterday when the planes started flying again. However, what will be will be. Nothing seems as important now as things were before the big C.

It was lovely to talk to you on Tuesday. Hope you enjoyed the rest of your day. I expect my Nicola Jane pockets will come today. That will give me something to do, sewing them into my swimsuit. I used to do such a lot of sewing—all

Jude's little dresses when she was wee. I've got my Gran's sewing machine which my mum said she remembered when she was a little girl. It is a museum piece but still works. It has attachments for making ruffles and a bobbin, not a spool. Still, I think I will have to do the pockets by hand as a bit fiddly.

The time is whizzing by. Think how far you have come again. You are doing so well. Take care and I hope you feel all the love winging its way down the country to you. All my friends ask after you each time I see them. They all have your welfare at heart as well.

Speak soon,

Lots of luv again

Margaret xxx

I can see now that I am re-reading these emails, what an extraordinary friendship this had become without even meeting. I genuinely felt the love of friendship for this person who was no longer a stranger, but was at the same time.

23rd April 2010
Re: Weekend

Dear Margaret,

Lovely to speak to you and re emails as well. Am sitting on my own as Liam is off to Mandy's again. What started as one room has turned into nearly the whole house but at least she is getting a spring clean at the same time. The weather has been ideal to throw windows and doors open whilst work is going on. He will be back there again next week to finish up but keeps him out of trouble for a few days. I was sitting in the garden for a while this morning but the breeze is still chilly so came in.

Do hope your Nicola Jane parcel arrived. They don't usually take too long to arrive and you have had the sewing needle out. Had to laugh at your Jaffa's antics. Boomerang is exactly the same and won't take no for an answer. Tracey is trying to arrange Sophie's christening for 25th July or 1st August which won't be long in coming round. Have been feeling fine since Tuesday just haven't much stamina for doing things. Trying to do a little spring cleaning of cupboards but only manage one at a time. I expect you will try and have a quiet weekend before you both head off to Stafford for your wedding. Will be having a quiet one myself. Will just try and get to Petworth mass on Saturday evening as I missed last week not feeling too great.

Anyway Margaret, have a good one and will catch up with you next week. Do envy you your lovely blonde locks. From your baldie buddie, luv Maureen xxx

29th April 2010
Subject: Packing

Hi Maureen

Thought I would send a quick email before we go tomorrow, just to wish you a good weekend.

I have just packed my bag for the weekend—do I really need all that? My wedding clothes I am going to hang in the car rather than put in the bag. Feeling more up to going now. I think you get out of the way of it all and it is definitely more of an effort to go places. Keep hearing bad news reports for M6. We come off at Junction 13 and all the reports seem to be around 15 and 16. Hope we don't get stuck anyway.

Dave has just gone up to our big Asda to get some money out of the cash machine. It is the only one we know that gives you English notes. Some shops in England still don't like taking Scottish money although with us using it all the time we can't understand why. He's filling the car up with petrol as well (some price that is too!!)

Well, you should be back to your old self, near as, by now and hopefully getting your taste back. That was horrible for me, who loves her food. Still, the human body is a wonderful thing and it recovers exceedingly well, thank goodness.

I'll look forward to speaking to you on Tuesday.

Take care, relax and enjoy.

Best love,

Margaret

I said a prayer for you today
And know God must have heard—
I felt the answer in my heart
Although He spoke no word!
I didn't ask for wealth or fame
(I knew you wouldn't mind)
I asked Him to send treasures
Of a far more lasting kind!
I asked that He'd be near you
At the start of each new day
To grant you health and blessings
And friends to share your way!
I asked for happiness for you
In all things great and small—
But it was for His loving care
I prayed the most of all!!

xxxxx

We were off to Stafford for my nephew's wedding on 1ˢᵗ May. It was a lovely family occasion and we met up with my sister, nieces all their families. I had not seen any of them for about four years and so obviously not since my cancer diagnosis. It was an emotional time but I felt well and happy. We met a couple who were also going to the wedding, who were staying in the same hotel as us, Irene and Derek. We hit it off instantly and actually travelled to the wedding venue with them. This was a big relief to my husband as we are both hopeless navigators and had already been lost driving in the town. Derek easily took us with the aid of his Tom Tom satnav and this led, us, on our return, straight to the nearest Halford's to buy one ourselves.

3rd May 2010
Re: Weekend Wedding

Dear Margaret,

Do hope when you read this you are home and have had a lovely weekend in Stafford. I think the weather was ok for you. It poured with rain here Sunday but Saturday and today have been ok. It has turned so cold again like winter. We went for roast dinner to Leisha yesterday. It was lamb, my favourite, and apple pie and custard. Yes, back on form this week, I don't seem to be as tired this week so maybe supplements are taking some effects. I can actually taste my toast at the moment. It always tastes horrible.

Will obviously update you after Wednesday's visit to the doctor before chemo on Thursday to see what they are going to do with me next.

I look forward to hearing from you tomorrow and hearing all about the wedding. Will be going to Chichester with Leisha tomorrow after our chat to have a look for an outfit for myself. Might need my winter coat again at this rate. Anyway everything fine here have been busy baking cakes this morning and a little bit of spring cleaning.

Look forward to tomorrow. Hope you are not too exhausted.
Luv Maureen xxx

4th May 2010
Subject: Re: shopping and photos

Dear Margaret,

Lovely to talk to you this morning and so glad that you had a fabulous wedding weekend apart from the cold weather. Had a good look around Chichester. Got a multi-coloured skirt in M&S and a purple blouse in Dorothy Perkins which look very good together. Liam has a grey jacket and dark trousers with a blue shirt and tie so both of us are now sorted. Just hope the volcanic ash decides to move somewhere else in the next few weeks.

Have sent you 2 photos of Ruby taken on Monday. A proper little jockey. She was saying "giddy up Denis", to the pony!

Will update you after my visit tomorrow, till then bye and lots of luv from Maureen xxx

5th May 2010
Subject: Beautiful Ruby

Well Maureen!

How gorgeous is that wee granddaughter of yours. And looking so pleased with herself. Denis (!!) is gorgeous too. Thankyou so much for the lovely photos.

We are settling back in—just in time to be getting ready to go to Turkey on Monday. However, Glasgow airport is closed today, so I feel it is debatable whether we go to Turkey at all. We'll see.

Hope the blood test etc went OK today. Look forward to hearing from you when you have been to the Marsden.

Going up town now so BYEEEEEE

Lots of love

Margaret xxx

PS A few photos of the wedding. Steve (bridegroom) looked like Mr D'Arcy with his pony tail and frock coat! I loved the decorations in the marquee.

8th May 2010
Subject: Re: Bon Voyage

Dear Margaret, I trust you are packing again and are all set for your departure on Monday morning. Looks like you will get away ok. Just to let you know that a familiar box was delivered by the postman this morning so have popped it into the cupboard ready for the 29th. Seems a long way away but will soon come round.

Not feeling too bad today. Have been awake since 3 a.m. so a little tired this evening. Enjoyed my egg and chips so that says it all really. Very dull here today nothing exciting going on. Planted my runner beans in pots so will see how they do this year. Just chilling tonight in front of the television. The election was a bit abysmal with no positive result so will have to see how things evolve over the next few days. All could be a lot different by the time you return in 2 weeks.

Anyway Margaret have a lovely holiday with your friends and enjoy the good weather. It will be a lovely time to chill and re-charge the batteries and gain a tan at the same time. Will catch up with all your news when you get back.

Lots of luv for now, Maureen xxx

9th May 2010
Subject: Packing again

Dear Maureen

Yes, packing again and stomach churning. 6 Scottish airports closed again today (up the top though Inverness etc) because

229

cloud over Europe but likely more tomorrow. I wish someone would just phone and say it's cancelled as I really don't want to be stuck in Turkey neither can I face hours of hanging about at airports. Not being very positive am I? Anyway, the family are coming round later but I am not cooking today. We are having a take-away (or carry out as they call them in Scotland) from the local Cantonese shop.

I hope you are not feeling too bad, although this is probably the worst few days just now. I hated the not sleeping bit. Strange, isn't it how it does this to us. Still, I used to use that time for my visualisation and the autogenic training to at least relax, even if you don't sleep.

I shall miss our chats for a couple of weeks. Glad to hear the box arrived safely. We get back on 24th May (early hours 25th actually) so I thought there might not be time for it to get to you then. Celebrations all round then. I feel confident the Marsden will sort you out (good and proper!!) That will be the best birthday present ever.

I shall text you now and then on holiday. I am away to get on with the packing—how do we need so much stuff? It's unbelievable. Went to the salon yesterday to get legs waxed and eyebrows done and under one arm (don't grow anything under the radiotherapy side!). Amazing how much money I saved when hairless with the chemo—one plus point.

Take care, Maureen and text me if you want to for any reason.

Missing you already!

Lots of love and great big hugs to you.

Margaret xxx

Maureen's birthday, I mentioned before, was the same day as my closest friend's in Scotland—29th May. I was doing a meal for our friend here and Maureen was going out for a lovely lunch. This was her 60th birthday. The ash cloud had done its worst whilst we were away. People arrived at our hotel on the Tuesday who had been travelling since Sunday. They had not been able to fly from Liverpool and were bussed to Manchester. The situation was the same there and so they went on to London and flew from there. There were people with small children and it must have been exhausting for them all. Our friends with us in Turkey were only staying for one week—we had booked two. It looked as though they would not get home, until it was announced that Glasgow Airport was the only British airport open. I wanted to go home there and then and forego the other week but the tour operator persuaded me that there was nothing to worry about. Should we be delayed, we would all be well looked after. And so, our friends went, leaving us to see if we would get home the following week. Some interesting things were going on just now—and we did make it home. I always liked to pass on newsy bits to Maureen as well as talking about the illness.

28th May 2010
Subject: Weekend

Dear Maureen

Well, I feel as if I need another holiday now. The ironing is still piled to the ceiling and I have not had a minute somehow to get everything sorted out.

I hope you are looking forward to tomorrow. We will raise a glass of wine to your good health when Pat comes for her birthday meal tomorrow. I am doing melon with parma ham, mixed grill, and meringue nest with strawberries and cream. Let me know how your lunch goes. I am sure you must be looking forward to it.

Still chilly here but bright and sunny. Did the Tesco shop this morning and thought I had better do some housework. Dave is cleaning the windows. We had two big pigeon marks on two of the windows. They sometimes fly into the windows. Luckily no dead bodies anywhere!

Chris had to go up to A&E Wednesday night as his eye was playing up again. Don't know if you remember he had an ulcer on his cornea before. This is the other eye. He was told that was what it was and he had to go to Eye Clinic yesterday. Dave took him up as with drops etc he wouldn't be able to drive. He has to go back next week. He has cream to put in his eye 5 times a day. Lucas thinks it funny because he is wearing a big patch over his eye. They are all coming for Sunday dinner.

Met up with the girls last night. My friend Eileen's daughter is at the Eurovision Song Contest. She reports for Kingdom FM (local radio station) but gets herself involved in all sorts as well. Mum said she was meeting Graham Norton (again!!) last night and has been on TV four times. I still don't think I can watch it all just in case I see her. It's nice to know what she is up to. Her auntie made her a special evening dress with sash, all tartan silk, and she managed to get to wear it at a very posh "do" and got to go on the red carpet.

Well, enough of my chatter. I will give you a ring in the morning.

Byeeee and lots of love from

Margaret xxxx

28th May 2010

Subject: Re: update

Dear Margaret,

Hope you have managed to plough your way through your ironing by now. Holidays are lethal for making so much more work. Went for our usual soya latte this morning. Littlehampton has a market on now on a Friday so had a little meander round and bought some more plants and a hanging basket. Thought I'd better make a little effort as expecting visitors tomorrow. Also sat on a stool and tidied up all my daffodil foliage. It was looking so tatty lying everywhere and the sun did come out. Forecast rain tomorrow morning so won't be in the garden!

Shall be thinking of you all at lunchtime tomorrow as you tuck in. All sounds lovely. Happy birthday Pat. Hope Chris will be better by next week. Anything to do with the eyes is always quite painful. I can see why Lucas enjoys looking at his Daddy with an eye patch on.

Look forward to hearing from you in the morning. I shall be up bright and early to open my pressies. Oh, nearly forgot. Thank you so much for the gorgeous trinket box and Turkish delight from Turkey. My earrings are already installed inside and the Turkish delight will be ceremoniously opened tomorrow as the visitors start calling. I am so pleased I shall be able to taste my meal and enjoy everyone's company so much more on Sunday. Just have to try and get my strength and energy levels up a bit more now.

Take care and lots of love as always Maureen xxx

I sent Maureen a Harris Tweed purse for her birthday—something really Scottish. I had one for my birthday and simply loved it. I have been buying them for friends' special birthdays ever since.

31st May 2010
Re: Birthday

Dear Margaret,

Having a quiet 5 mins so thought I'd better start on my emails. Had a lovely weekend with the family. Unfortunately, as I predicted, it poured with rain on Saturday so I had a houseful coming and going all day. Yesterday was much better with some sunshine and we had a lovely carvery, with balloon decorations. We went back to Leisha's where I had a 60 cake with sparklers on and a lovely cup of tea. Such a nice weekend and I did so well with presents. Flowers, choccies, champagne, smellies, clothes and quite a bit of money to go out and spend in due course. No hurry.

Had loads of phone calls from my friends so nice to unwind today. Hope Pat had a nice day also. Went along the beach this morning for an hour for a walk before the legs gave out. Had a rest halfway but feel I am progressing. It is dull today but dry. Just come in from the garden sorting out the plants I was given and re-potting some tomato seedlings I have been growing, quite shattered now.

What have you been up to today? A nice walk with barney no doubt. It was so nice to enjoy my food. I even had some ice cream! Have sent a couple of photos. Hope you like them. Take care and thank you again for my lovely purse and toilet bag. Went out with my purse yesterday in my new handbag. Lots of hugs. Maureen xxx

31ˢᵗ May 2010
Subject: Birthdays

Hi Maureen

Lovely to see you looking so good in your birthday photos. It sounds as if you had a really lovely day and, well, balloons as well—what can I say!

We had a super evening with Pat. She came round about 4.30 p m and she opened her pressie—I got her a purse as well. Not the same as yours but a small brown leather one. Coincidentally, she said she had been looking at purses smaller than the one she has been using so it fitted the bill very well. We had a gin and tonic (!) and I started getting our meal about

6 p.m. I got some birthday confetti and scattered it over the table and I bought party napkins (covered in balloons) just for a giggle. She was delighted.

The mixed grill went down very well. So did the red wine!! I think we all had a bit more than usual but we had a really good laugh. We also raised a glass to you and yours for your birthday. Sunday we walked Barney to the shops and saw just about everyone we knew for a chat. Chris & Lorna and the boys were coming for dinner so I had a lot to do but it all went very well. The evening came out really beautiful so when we had cleared up (they went about 7 p.m. for baths and bed) we walked Barney round the shore and it was gorgeous. The tide was up and the evening sun shone on everything.

I was very tired after a hectic weekend but enjoyed every moment.

I have been reading today as it is my Ethics Committee meeting again tomorrow but I also ironed from 6.30 p.m. to 9 p.m. I am still dealing with the holiday washing!

What a lovely photo of Sophie—Zak is now lifting his head and shoulders when he is on his tummy on the floor. It doesn't look as if he will be long in pulling himself around. What an appetite. We blended everything we had for him (roast lamb. Jersey Royal, broccoli, sprouts, carrots with a little gravy) and he couldn't get it down fast enough. I think that was what was wrong with him earlier when he couldn't settle. Still, he is fine now.

A couple of photos of our holiday—the cats always seem to find me. This pretty little one was mewing at our window so I let her in to make a fuss of her.

Will speak soon,

Going to bed now—God Bless—sleep tight—don't let the bugs bite xxx

    Lots of love

    Margaret xxx

4th June 2010
Re: Weekend again

Hi Maureen

We must have had the same idea! Your email came through just as I was reading another one before sending one to you—if that makes sense. Just back from a walk with Barney—only a short one as it is too hot for him to go far. It's fantastic weather. I got all my housework done this morning so quite pleased with myself.

It's Judith's birthday today. Funny how you go over the day they were born all over again. I remember Dave's mum had taken Christopher out in the pushchair whilst I went off for my ante natal appointment. I had gone beyond my date. In those days, you had an examination if you were 10 days overdue and when the doctor examined me he said "Whatever arrangements you have made, put them into action!" I was in labour without knowing. We had to go and find Dave's mum to tell her and then get off to the hospital. You never forget. It will be a bit like that with our treatment I expect. I am already thinking two years ago we were in Kos and that was the first inkling I had something wrong.

I got Jude's vouchers for the salon and likewise got 20% off in the card shop. I bought a few things and got the benefit of a "goody bag" with Yankee candles and air fresheners. It doesn't take much to excite me!

I am making Jude a special meal for her birthday—steak—her choice, and all the trimmings. Dave is off to the Gardening Club tonight so we'll have it at the usual time when she gets in from work.

Hope you have a lovely weekend and that this weather holds out for us all. Look forward to talking to you next week.

Lots of love Margaret xxx

4th June 2010

Subject: Re: weekend again

Dear Margaret, cannot believe another week has gone by. The weather is so warm—nearly too warm for comfort but mustn't complain. We went off early this morning for a walk along the beach before it got too warm and ended up with my Costa coffee—lovely. Dorothy Perkins had 20% today so bought a purple cardigan with birthday money. As I feel the cold, thought it would be of most use. Also got some earplugs for the plane journey as I always seen to suffer with my ears when I fly—do you at all?

Tracey & Sophie will be down again tomorrow making the most of her time off before she goes back to work at the end of September. Sophie is just starting on vegetables and seems to have got the hang of the spoon now—didn't like it at first. Glad Zak is thriving now and loves his blended food.

The photos of the holiday were great especially the little cat. Funny how they seek you out. The scenery is also stunning. What a lovely place you stayed in. Hope your committee meeting went ok and you have now caught up with your holiday ironing and enjoying the good weather as well.

Watching the racing at Epsom whilst typing this. The fashion is lovely there today. Shaun, Kieran and Ruby had lunch with me yesterday whilst their mums slipped off to do other things. After the two boys had stopped dabbing one another, they were very well behaved. Ruby watched their antics from my lap and when things settled down joined in with their games. Sensible girl!

Will be enjoying the good weather I hope this weekend. What about you? Glad to have put my summer duvet on the bed. Hope you are well and topping up your holiday tan. Take care. Lots of luv as always Maureen xxx

11th June 2010

Subject: Another week gone!

Hi Maureen

It was nice to talk to you on Tuesday. Here we are, Friday again already.

I do so wish the weather would improve—it is just so cold. However, I am making good use of the comfort blanket my sister made me. I feel like a real little old lady with it across my knees in the evenings but I can feel the difference.

We are babysitting tomorrow evening whilst Chris & Lorna go out for a meal together. It will be the first time we have sat for Zak so I hope he behaves himself. Lucas will be excited so I don't suppose bed will be on the agenda for a good while.

I am off to WeightWatchers again tomorrow. I had only put on 3 lb over the holiday but that went on in two weeks. It will probably take me a lot longer to lose it again. Still, I was pleased it wasn't more.

Just about to go to Tesco shopping (yawn yawn). As I said to you, things have really quietened down now. It's nice though. Actually got round to cleaning the oven AND hob yesterday (about time too!) Job well done anyway.

So, Maureen, have a nice weekend and I won't begrudge you the nice weather (if you get any sunshine). I am back in polo neck jumpers! Not to worry.

Let me know how Ruby got on at the doctors. Hope she is ok again now.

Lots of love as usual

Enjoy your weekend

Margaret xxx

11th June 2010

Subject: Re: Another week gone!

Dear Margaret, like you cannot believe another week has passed by already. Ruby is doing ok now. They brought 2 doctors in to look at her on Tuesday as her glands were so swollen. She also had an ear infection so was given antibiotics and told to come back on Monday if not any better. She is in a lot better form and her glands are well down now. Tracey & Sophie brought Liam home yesterday afternoon. The weather hadn't been great in Nottingham but Liam managed to get most jobs done for her. Tracey is going back home this evening after Sophie's last feed.

My school friend Pauline and husband Richard arrived this morning, luckily after the rain had cleared away as like you it rained all night here. We went into Arundel had a coffee and toasted teacake and then went for a walk into Arundel and out to the lake to see the ducks and swans and their babies. They were all gorgeous so a good morning. We are forecast a good weekend so hope that is right. The local church has their summer fayre on tomorrow so we are off to that with my brother Peter. Will let you know how we got on there next week. Other than that nothing else happening.

Glad you are still well chilled and enjoying your cooker cleaning!!! Hope Zak is good and you eventually get Lucas to bed—good luck with that one. Anyhow have a great weekend till we next speak. Lots of luv Maureen xxx

Our emails are full of general chitchat and we both know Maureen is just getting on with her fresh lot of treatment.

18th June 2010
Subject: Hello

Hi Maureen

Just finished the housework and thought I would do an email before I go for my shower (sorry I am not very clean!) Watched a bit of Ascot on Ladies Day too. Some lovely hats. Shame the Queen's horse just missed winning. It was so close. My leg is still sore. I'll see how I get on after the Race for Life. I have been walking more to make sure I am up for Sunday and it is not too bad. Just wonder what it is. I certainly don't remember pulling a muscle.

The day your Boomerang caught the starling, Dave found a dead sparrow on Judith's bedroom floor. We don't know who was the guilty culprit but more than likely Billy or Jaffa as Josh is far too fat to be quick enough to catch anything. Billy is a hunter as he was feral when Jude got him but we have rescued birds from Jaffa's mouth before now so it could have been him. It's the time of year when all the young birds make easy catches for the cats. Shame though.

Have got the family all coming for dinner (tea time) Sunday. I cheerfully said I would work round the Race for Life. I thought I'd make a big shepherd's pie tomorrow and it can just go in the oven on Sunday. Zak and Lucas will both eat that as well so it will be easy. Lucas went to the nursery attached to the school yesterday for a taster session before he starts every day in August. He loved it, so no probs there.

The lovely weather is holding at present—what a pleasure to be able to go out without a jacket and not feel freezing all the time in the house. Barney is feeling the heat so we have to take him out later in the day when it has cooled down a bit. Not complaining though.

Well, better go and have my shower—hope for a wee sit down before I start preparing dinner. I could do with 40 winks—not sleeping too well just now.

Have a lovely weekend, Maureen. Take it easy and think of me doing that Race for Life. Hope it's not too hot for it. And I'll be carrying you on my back!!

Lots of love as usual

Margaret xxx

Maureen always managed to make me feel better when I was a bit down. This time in June was no exception as our son was experiencing problems with his business and it didn't look as though there was going to be a quick resolution.

20th June 2010

Subject: Re: Hello!

Dear Margaret,

Hope everything went well at your Race for Life today and that I wasn't too heavy to be carried around! We were thinking of you. Try not to worry too much about Chris' dilemma. Hopefully things will sort themselves out. Hope you all had a lovely Shepherds pie, one of my favourite dishes. We went off to The Black Rabbit at Arundel for a lovely lunch. Must be a year since we were there. Sat outside as we had the dog with us but it was lovely and warm, then went for a walk along the river. Liam has had a good day so hope Dave was spoiled also.

Will be minding Ruby tomorrow whilst Leisha works but will catch up with you hopefully on Tuesday. Trust your aches and pains are ok too. Wimbledon next week so am looking forward to watching some of that as the football was a total disaster on Friday evening. It cannot get any worse so hopefully Wednesday will bring something better.

Talk soon and keep that lovely chin up. Thinking of you, hugs and kisses Maureen xxx

We tend to think of ourselves as being the only ones who suffer setbacks in life but when you see the number of people doing the Race for Life, reading the moving tributes on their backs and talking to people along the way, you realise that's just life.

21ˢᵗ June 2010

Subject: Race for Life

Dear, dear Maureen

You are a love. You have always managed to make me feel better since I've got to know you and no matter what the problem.

We had a heart to heart with Chris. Lorna was on her hen weekend and we all went down to Burntisland with the boys—Jude as well. We went for what the Scottish call the shows which is a funfair in England. Lucas just loved it. He went on everything he was able to and hooked a duck (remember when we were little?) Anyway we went back to Chris' house after and both boys went to sleep. We had a cuppa in the garden and Jude was telling Chris what she does for her boss, e.g. he has Terms & Conditions attached to all his estimates etc. drawn up legally. Chris found what she had to say very helpful. The Race for Life went very well again. I walked with a woman (another Margaret) about my age who goes to the Wednesday WW class. I didn't know her but I do now! We chatted all the way round and it went in no time. She has a grandson aged 2 who lives in Middlesborough.

He has a heart murmur and is going to Newcastle soon for a procedure. He will then be on Warfarin for the rest of his life. So many people have to face difficulties in life it seems. I said that probably because he will grow up with it, it will become second nature to him. It's like diabetic children who just accept they inject themselves and know when they have to eat and what not to eat. Shame though. We walked the 5km in just under the hour which was a bit slower than last year but that didn't matter. I will have about £70 sponsor money. They announced over the tannoy system there was a little girl of 7 there who by herself had collected over £1,000. Amazing. Anyway, pictures enclosed. My T-shirt was the stretchy kind, showing all my lumps and bumps! Never mind.

We all sat in the garden when the family came round. Zak was on a rug, sitting up now and playing with things. Jude blew him some bubbles which he was totally engrossed in. Lucas didn't want his dinner but has been a bit off colour. He fancied a few strawberries. He was lively enough anyway. After everyone had gone and we had cleared up, we sat in the garden again and I had a glass of wine. I really enjoyed it. It was so peaceful after a busy day.

Well, my bosomless buddie, I'll look forward to a phone call tomorrow. I have a nice quiet week apart from a Barney haircut on Thursday. Hope the sunshine lasts—it's wonderful.

Lots of love

Margaret xx

The photograph I sent Maureen was the sign on my back stating that I was doing it for her " . . . still battling. Go for it Girl!" It obviously hit a spot as she mentioned in our phone call that she had shed a tear.

25th June 2010

Subject: It's me

Hi Maureen

I know you must still be emotional about things concerning cancer and I am sorry if I made you shed a tear. I also still feel very vulnerable and at the moment I am again mentally going through all the tests leading up to that diagnosis on 31st July 2008. Had just got back from Kos (mid June) and realised there was something not right. I saw my GP at end of June and got an appointment at the Breast Clinic within 2 weeks and then it was the biopsies, ultrasounds, etc etc. I remember only too well how that felt and now I am feeling it for you having to go through more scans and uncertainty. I know you have every confidence in your consultant and everyone, and I would too. I am sure they know just how to deal with you—I would pick you up, turn you upside down and shake you—I wonder if they have thought of that? Sorry, I don't mean to be facetious. I wish that was all we had to do, don't you?

I should have a fairly quiet weekend this week. I am looking after my friend Joan's cat from this afternoon until Sunday. They are going down to Essex to a relative's Ruby Wedding celebration. Also we are looking after another neighbour's dog, Solo, a cocker spaniel just for tomorrow as Joan is being taken to the theatre for her birthday (think I told you). Anyway, hope the cat doesn't run away and Solo doesn't mind me going into the house. I'm going down at 4 p.m. today to get my instructions.

Jude is in the process of booking a late holiday with her friend Claire and her two boys (Kieran & Aaron) It looks as if they are going where we went but in different accommodation. If it gets confirmed they go on 13th July. It will be very, very hot at that time. Still, they will have a nice swimming pool to dip into. She is quite excited anyway.

It's good you enjoy getting out for some walks. It will be ages before your stamina is back to how it was—I don't think mine is even now, but we have to persevere to get back to normal.

No sunshine today but still very warm. Dave is putting some new roofing felt on the shed. Our strawberries are nearly ripe and quite big now so looking forward to getting a taste of home-grown. We are growing some beetroot as well for the first time.

Barney was a very good boy for his hair cut (meaning he didn't bite the groomer this time!). She managed to give him a lovely cut and he has been like a Spring lamb ever since. He must feel good.

Glad Andy got through yesterday—things will hotten up next week so hope I am not too busy. My reading for the next Ethics Committee arrived yesterday so I have an excuse to sit. I am sure I can read and watch the tennis at the same time??

Well, Maureen, have a lovely weekend—Kieran is going to love his bubble-blowing pistol, I know.

Lots of love from Margaret (hope you haven't still got your feet in that bowl of water—be cold now!) Lovely jubbly.

Maureen was off to a family wedding in Ireland. I am so glad she had decided to go. These occasions are a complete diversion from what is going on with ourselves and our illness. I remember our grandson's first birthday party was a couple of days after my first chemotherapy. I was afraid I wouldn't be able to enjoy it but then completely forgot everything that was going on with me. One becomes self-centred, quite understandably, without even realising.

1st July 2010
Subject: Scan

Hi Maureen

Just a little note to say I hope the scan went according to plan and you weren't delayed or anything.

I expect you are now getting ready to go away having got the scan out of the way. What a nice change it will be for you and I know you will enjoy every minute.

I have got one more project to read for next Tuesday's meeting so am up to speed. I am hoping the family will come for dinner on Sunday and I am afraid they will have to put up with the tennis being on screen instead of Cbeebies. Great to see Andy going through although Friday will be a real challenge for him I expect.

Well, just going to Tescos again—second home! It's pouring rain so going in the car. Barney can stay home today.

Look forward to hearing all about the wedding when you phone on Tuesday evening.

Best love and hugs

Margaret

X x x x x

1st July 2010
Subject: re: packing

Dear Margaret,

Just had my shower and have at last got round to doing some packing. Tracey won't be down till quite late so will be waiting for her before we go to bed and then up at 4.30 a m. Disappointed to be missing Andy but might get to see a telly when we are on our ceilidhs. He is doing so well and has a good chance. No rain here yet but a little cooler which is most welcome.

Scan went well. No hanging around at all. Just have weak veins now which makes the cannula rather painful but survived that ordeal. Can forget everything now for a few days. Do hope I don't forget anything important I need to take.

Will be in touch when I get back and after my results on Tuesday. Have a lovely weekend with the family.

Take care till next week. Luv Maureen xxx

Tuesday's scan results were not as good as hoped. The chemotherapy was not shrinking the tumours as much as it should and it was suggested that the way forward was to go into clinical trials with several drugs to see if that had any effect. It was at this time that Maureen was told her cancer was terminal but she was given hope that the new drugs would control the cancer, if not cure it.

We had arranged to take Lucas to see The Gruffalo at Edinburgh Playhouse, his first experience of live theatre. Chris then phoned to say they had booked a short break in Aberfoyle, about one and a half hours from home. This coincided with the theatre trip! I panicked and was annoyed as we had had the tickets for months. Chris was very laid back about it and said there would be no problem. He would just drive back for it. We had to get a bus at 9.30 a m and if we missed it, we would miss the performance. I wish I could cope with unexpected changes in arrangements!

8th July 2010
Subject: Edinburgh Playhouse etc

Hi Maureen

It was lovely to talk to you on Tuesday. Of course, I am as concerned as you will be about your results but I have faith and I am sure God will give you a safe landing, even if you are not having a calm passage. There are quite a few clinical trials going on with the drugs that you mention (as I expect you have looked up as well). It all looks very promising. If it was me, I couldn't wait to get started.

Well, we got to the Gruffalo yesterday, in spite of everything! Chris arrived with Lucas about 8 a.m. having driven for one and a half hours. Lucas hadn't had any breakfast, said he would have some Weetabix and then didn't want it. Still, we got the bus which he loved. The show itself was great and all the children loved it. We didn't realise you could pick up booster seats or cushions in the theatre so that the small ones could see properly, but someone behind us had brought both down for their little girl. She decided on the cushion so they gave the booster seat to Lucas which was perfect. The show only lasted an hour and we all had a good shout and roar—panto style. We went for some lunch after but again, Lucas only had a little bit of pizza. We got home about 2.15 p m. Lorna's mum came to collect him as she was driving him up to Stirling, meeting Chris who was driving the rest of the way back to the hotel. Whew! Still, at least Lucas got to see The Gruffalo. I don't know!

I am hoping for a relatively quiet weekend. Going out with the girls tonight and have had quite a busy week. Judith goes on holiday Monday evening so she will be busy packing.

I am not going to WW this Saturday so will not have to dash about. However, as I think I said, we have been seconded to cleaning one of Chris' extension houses. The people come back off holiday on Sunday and he wants it to be really pristine when they walk in! Hopefully it will only take the one day.

I went to the Abbey last Sunday and it was a lovely service (as usual). There was a talk from one member of the congregation who was back in Scotland on holiday but who had decided he was called to go to work in Israel teaching chemistry in a school. He said there were Jews, Muslims and Christians attending the school and one day two boys were late for class. When they arrived he said he was about to ask them where they had been but they produced a tray of cakes for the Jewish children and this was traditional for a Jewish religious festival that was on that day. These boys were Muslims. They did not eat the cakes themselves as it was Ramadan. What he was saying was that these children all respect each other's religions and festivals over and above their own. I had to admire the work he is doing in an area with so many problems. If only the world could look at things in the same way. Whenever I go to the Abbey, I always come out with food for thought.

Let me know your dates again Maureen so I can keep up with you. I wrote down your drug names but not when you are due to start.

Take care, keep calm and relax. You are in good hands.

Lots of love from Margaret xxx

P.S. Hope to see a photo of the wedding.

I received a lovely gift of an oven glove and pot stand from Ireland, Maureen having been to her family wedding. I particularly like the art of Thomas Joseph and his famous sheep and there were sheep all over these gifts, which gave me added pleasure. Maureen looked the picture of health in the photographs she sent of the wedding. Everyone looked wonderful. I returned some photographs of my son's wedding a while ago as the church in Ireland reminded me very much of Dunfermline Abbey where Chris & Lorna got married.

9th July 2010

Subject: Lovely surprise!

Dear Maureen

Thank you so much for my lovely gift from Ireland. How did you know my favourite (well one of them) animals is the sheep. I couldn't phone you to thank you though as I was rather touched by your comments. We have such a special friendship.

The wedding photographs are lovely. You look absolutely fabulous in your outfit and I just loved the fascinator. Just the right finishing touch. What a beautiful church too. It put me very much in mind of Chris & Lorna's wedding at the Abbey. The bridesmaids looked beautiful. I hope the tiredness is settling down again. I know Dr Duncan told me to "keep life simple." That's easier said than done sometimes but hopefully you will have a quiet weekend to recuperate.

We went out with our friends George & Issy last Saturday and the subject of Zante came up. We had to say we wouldn't be going this year. We don't feel up to the flights plus we want to wait and see if we have to help Chris financially at all. They have gone ahead and booked for themselves, but the flight out, is overnight. I couldn't do that at the moment. I need a "beam me up Scotty" machine I think!

Have attached one of Chris & Lorna's wedding photographs. They had a piper outside the church and also one to pipe them into the reception. Look at Dave in the kilt! I would have liked to send you one of inside the Abbey but we only have the official photographs on a DVD. This was 2005 by the way.

Have a nice weekend and take care my friend. My oven glove and pot stand are in place already.

Lots of luv—big hug

Margaret x x x

12ᵗʰ July 2010
Subject: Re: Update

Dear Margaret,

Such a lovely wedding photo of you all from 2005. The kilts were fabulous and Judith looks so like you!! Poor girl!! No you all look fabulous cannot believe this was 5 years ago before we had any inkling of troubles ahead. Hope you had a good weekend. It was so hot again all weekend but has cooled down today thank goodness and bearable. No rain yet.

We all met up on Saturday, went to feed the ducks had a swing in the park and then 7 of us went on the miniature train ride £2 return up and down Littlehampton seafront. Just about survived that as it was so hot but you always get a breeze along the sea. Just went to mass Saturday evening and had a bag of chips for a treat. We never went out Sunday just too hot, so sat in the shade book reading.

Looked after Ruby today so am just catching up with my emails. Should be leaving around 11.30 a m tomorrow morning. Will be in touch when I get home of course. Glad you liked your wee pressie. Like you am trying to get a little less emotional but it is not easy, quite a battle but maybe one day, anyhow not feeling too bad at the moment. Quite expectant as to what might happen tomorrow, whatever will be will be. At least I will be getting some kind of treatment, which I need, so all positive on that front.

As I said, will be in touch tomorrow. Till then take care, hugs and kisses luv Maureen xxx

16th July 2010
Subject: Weekend

Dear Maureen

Glad to hear the day went well, albeit a long one for you. I do believe you get the best of everything when you are in a drug trial so be prepared to get pampered. Are you getting travelling expenses? That is always one of the points brought up at the Ethics Committee meetings. Would you let me know the name of the company again? I didn't manage to write it down before. I believe you said it was French.

Monday will be fine! Don't be nervous. It will be no different from what you have been doing so far. Don't be afraid to ask any questions you may have (sure you will ask anyway). I will be waiting to hear how you get on. I wish I could hold your hand there. I will be, in spirit.

Well, you have rain and wind. GOOD! (Ha ha). Ours has never stopped yet! I expect you have seen some reports on the Open at St Andrews. Well, as we are not far from St Andrews, what you see there is what we are getting as well. Poor old Barney. He's fed up with getting towelled down every time he goes out. Jude is enjoying lovely sunshine in Ibiza. She says their apartment is lovely and everything is good.

Lucas has a proper boy's haircut now (re Ruby at hairdressers). He looks lovely but completely different and grown up. Must phone my brother this weekend. Haven't heard from him for a while but I know some of his friends were taking him to—yes—Newcastle (!) to see another old friend. Are you sure we don't have the same brother?

Have a lovely weekend then, Maureen and keep thinking "onwards and upwards" and take every day as it comes.

Best love as always

Margaret x x x

17th July 2010
Subject: Re: Flowers

Dear Margaret, what can I say only a very big thank you for my lovely flowers which arrived this morning with the postman—what a lovely surprise. I am afraid more tears surfaced as you are so supportive and have enough on your own plate at the moment with your own family. My actual research study is being run by a Dr Mary O'Brien and the anti-cancer drug Vinflunine has been developed by Pierre

Fabre Medicament who is sponsoring the study. The cost of reasonable travel expenses will be reimbursed to me.

Off to the graveyard now as Mum's headstone has just been erected so have to check it out to make sure it is what we ordered. Lovely day, just a bit breezy again. At least Scotland looks as though it is drying up now. Glad Judith is enjoying the sunshine lucky girl.

Will definitely phone after treatment on Monday with an update. Lots of hugs, luv Maureen. xxx

Would be lost without you!!!

17th July 2010
Subject: Flowers

Dear Maureen

I am glad you liked the flowers—I had asked them to arrive Monday for the start of your treatment. Still, as you have such an early start, it's probably better receiving them today. See, someone is looking after us! It is out of our hands.

Wind still blowing here and getting some heavy showers. Stayed the same at WW. I think it is my activity level—not what it was. I am just going to look at a website regarding something called Zumba which is a form of dance exercise that is all the rage here. I need to jump around a bit, I think.

Look forward to hearing from you on Monday.

Lots of Love

Margaret x x x

I was now hatching an idea that I would like to visit Maureen. I knew that her clinical trials were only clinical trials and that things looked more than serious, especially with the tumour in her liver not responding to the previous lot of chemotherapy. I felt

that if we were ever to meet, it should be sooner rather than later. I therefore decided to phone Liam (Maureen's husband) whilst Maureen was at the hospital with her daughters. Liam didn't go to the hospital with Maureen as their girls, he said, could remember more of what was said than he could and could ask any necessary questions. I wanted to test the water.

Liam leapt at the opportunity for me to visit and said there would be no problem about where I would stay—either one of the daughters would put me up (or put up with me!) I didn't think it would be wise to leave it as a surprise for Maureen although asked Liam not to mention it until I had spoken to Maureen myself.

When Maureen phoned me to tell me how she had got on at the hospital, I asked her how would she like a visitor? She was surprised and delighted and so the seeds were sown. My friend Pat, here in Scotland, had a friend who lived in Worthing—just a couple of train stops away from where Maureen lived. I asked Pat what the journey entailed and she told me she was visiting her friend in September. So, it was decided we should travel down together. I was to travel back alone as I wouldn't be staying as long as Pat.

21st July 2010
Subject: Visit, etc

Hi Maureen

I do hope it was not too much of a shock that I would be paying you a visit. I just want to say that if ever you don't feel up to it, please don't be afraid to say and we can make it later on. I know I can change my tickets or cancel if necessary. I don't want you to feel under any pressure whatsoever.

I am meeting my friend Liz (I used to work with at the dental surgery) for lunch today in Dunfermline. Usually we go to Abbot House, in the grounds of the Abbey, and have our lunch in the gardens if it's dry. There are peacocks in the garden and last time one was parading his feathers right in front of us. Beautiful. However, we have been promised heavy rain again today so don't reckon much on our chances this time.

Let me know how you are feeling on your new tablets. I wonder if you will get the wobbly legs? Still, once again Maureen, if you feel extra tired or anything when I am down to see you, you must just do what you would normally do and I can sit and read quite happily and give you peace.

Well, I must phone Agnes now (we went to Turkey with Agnes & James). It is James' birthday today and they have just been down to visit relatives in Folkestone, Kent so I am interested to hear how they got on.

Hope to hear from you soon.

Lots of love (and real hug soon!)

Margaret x x x

P.S. Just had a phone call from Liz to say she can't make it for lunch after all as she can't get away from work. What a shame. We are going to make it next week now. Poor Liz—I'm glad I'm not working now. I'm all dressed up and nowhere to go!

22nd July 2010
Re: Update

Dear Margaret,

Yes I think I'm over the shock that soon we are to meet but I feel I know you so well already it will be lovely. Can't wait!! We have several options to explore as to where you will be staying so there won't be a problem. Of course being down here we will do the touristy bits for you so if there is anywhere special you want to see let me know. I have to say today is my best day yet since starting the tablets on Monday. Just have felt a bit under the weather and have been very burpy stomach wise so don't know if that was excessive acid but everything seems to have settled down nicely today.

We actually had a heavy shower today which lasted nearly an hour and quite heavy. I'm sure the grass enjoyed the drink as it is looking quite sorry for itself at the moment but doesn't take long to bounce back again.

Well Margaret, what can I say, only thank you for caring enough to come and see me especially as we live the other end of the country to each other. I have to say Liam is also looking forward to meeting you as are the rest of the family including Boomie and Fern. Luckily my energy levels are not too bad at the moment so hope that will continue. Hope you are seeing plenty of sunshine between the showers.

Lots of luv to you as always, Maureen xxx

23rd July 2010
Subject: Weekend

Hi Maureen

Just to say I hope you have a lovely, restful weekend. It sounded from your email you may not be getting too many side effects with the new tablet. That will be a bonus if so.

Judith arrived home from Ibiza very bronzed. They had a lovely time—no holiday romances though! (I am ever hopeful of getting her married off!) No, not really, but as she is 33 now it would be nice for her to settle down with someone nice.

The weather has been wonderful today. I walked Barney round the shore this evening and it was like being abroad and the scenery was magnificent. I never get tired of seeing the Pentland Hills, either in the late sun or even in mist and cloud. They always look beautiful to me. There were lots of little boats out from the local sailing club. Barney enjoyed his walk.

He didn't want to go far at lunch time as it was a bit hot but he thoroughly enjoyed himself tonight. I gave him a shower this afternoon. He's always like a spring lamb after a shower—bit like myself! (More like mutton—ha ha).

I hope this weather holds for the big day tomorrow. Lorna has gone up to St Andrews tonight, staying over. Chris is getting himself and the boys ready and going up tomorrow. So, a quiet weekend for us. Someone in Dalgety Bay has a garden party tomorrow for Marie Curie nurses. She does this every year and has entertainment and a cake stall. She has a lovely garden too. We may pop round if it's nice. She books the church hall as well, in case of rain. The line dancers usually do a demonstration—I used to go before diagnosis. I keep meaning to start up again but haven't got round to it. The last time we went to her garden party, I was waiting for all the results of my biopsies etc.

Take care then. I will give you a ring on Tuesday if that's OK. Lots of love as always,

Margaret x x x

Our optimism was short-lived and side effects of her new drugs started affecting Maureen's hands and feet to the extent that she had to contact the hospital for advice.

27th July 2010

Re: Sore feet, itchy body

Dear Margaret,

Just to let you know I telephoned The Marsden after coming back from my homeopath. They wanted to see me either today or tomorrow. Mandy was at a loose end so we decided to head off getting up there at 2.45 p.m. We were seen practically straight away. To have the rash as well as the sore feet and hands is very unusual (trust me). Anyway, I have had to stop the last 6 days of tablets so that the symptoms clear up. I got anti-histamine tablets for the rash, and can take usual painkillers for feet. Also to carry on moisturising them so they do not crack or peel (heaven forbid). I then keep my next appointment on 10th August where they will reduce the dose as I am on the strongest dose at the moment. All being well with little side effects I carry on. If side effects still bad will reduce the dose once more and monitor again. If this is unsuccessful I will then have to come off these tablets and be reviewed again but that is the worst scenario. I just cannot describe the pain I have been in so hope I feel better tomorrow.

Liam's brother & wife called at 8 p m. They have just left so thought I'd email you. So glad I have got myself sorted. Do hope you have had a good day. Off to take my anti-histamine tablet now and bed. Catch up with you soon. Take care, luv Maureen xxx

This is becoming a nightmare for Maureen, I feel. I must try and keep upbeat with our conversations.

28th July 2010

Subject Re: Sore feet, itchy body

Dear Maureen

I am so glad you got seen so quickly with the side effects you were getting. I thought you might have to have some anti-histamine for the rash. Yes, trust you getting the hands and feet as well as the rash! You don't do things by half measures that's for sure. Let's hope they have got you sorted out now. You should get some of those special socks you can get for night time moisturising of feet. I don't know if the Body Shop does them but you put the cream on and then the socks when you got to bed so that the cream works whilst you are asleep. I bought my sister a set of foot care things from Boots (I think it was called Gorgeous Feet) but it included the socks for night time.

She gets very sore feet but was told by the chiropodist that as we get older (!!!) the skin on the soles of our feet gets thinner and that is why a lot of older folk get sore feet (oh joy—what else eh?) Anyway, hope painkillers will suffice in this case.

Don't forget to let me have Tracey's address so that I can send a card for the Christening.

Have been up to Dunfermline today to meet up with Liz for lunch—we were supposed to meet last Wednesday but she couldn't get away from work. We were able to sit outside for our lunch in the gardens of Abbot House and it was lovely—no peacocks this time though. I took Judith's boots in to get the heels repaired. He said they needed soles as well and the bill came to £18.95. I think the boots were only about £25 to begin with. I think he saw me coming (as usual).

Dave is still painting our corridor where the bedrooms lead off. It's very dark and he is painting it white to see if it makes any difference.

Well, hope you don't get any more pain in those old footsies. It must have been agony for you.

Take care—love to hear from you.

Lots of love Margaret x x x

28th July 2010
Subject: Re: Address

Dear Margaret,

Thanks for your email and sorry I forgot Tracey's address. My concentration seems to have gone down the pan at the moment. Went shopping this morning with a list and still came back with several things missing. What it is to be getting old. Thanks for reminding me about the socks—had a pair hiding in the drawer that I bought off Avon for a rainy day and here we are!! Glad you got to lunch with your friend after missing out last week and the weather was kind to you.

Talk soon, luv

Maureen xxx

30ᵗʰ July 2010
Subject: Side effects

Dear Maureen

I am writing this, hoping that your side effects have subsided completely or at least are not as bad as they were. Sounded awful for you. I remember having an itch all over my body just after I had Christopher back in 1973. It was urticaria and it put me in hospital as my lips all swelled up as well (not a pretty sight!) Nobody could tell me the cause but I can still remember the agony of the itch—I think I made myself bleed with scratching.

I expect you are looking forward to Sophie's Christening. I hope the weather stays fair for you all. I wonder if she will sleep though everything. Zak doesn't sleep much during the day now, I believe. We are babysitting this evening whilst Chris & Lorna go out with her mum and dad and last week's bride's mum and dad. They make the most of going out when Lorna's dad is home. He goes back to Nigeria next Wednesday. Have now got a few photos of the wedding that Chris took on his phone so I shall still look forward to seeing the professional ones in the church etc. The wee soul (Lucas) must have been really hot in all the regalia but he didn't complain apparently, maybe because he made £80 with guests putting money in his sporran! I have put a photo on here for you, plus 2 nice ones of Zak, coming on nicely now.

Well, Maureen, will be thinking of you all tomorrow and, as I said, hope your feet are not too sore now.

I look forward to hearing all about the Christening and how you are after the weekend. We haven't much on again this weekend on. I ought to be tidying out cupboards really but . . . well, we'll see (ha ha).

Lots of love to you and yours,

Speak soon. Margaret x x

30ᵗʰ July 2010
Subject: Re: Side effects

Dear Margaret,

Just come in out of the garden to watch some of glorious Goodwood before I jump into the shower. Firstly the photos are lovely and Zak is certainly thriving now such a lovely little boy. Lucas is certainly so much more grownup now he is approaching 3 years of age. He looked absolutely adorable in his outfit.

My feet are still painful but nowhere near as bad as Tuesday and the rash is doing really well, not bothering me at all now. Wednesday I took a more sore than usual mouth and my tongue was terrible yesterday. Could only eat soup and my bottom lip inside is red raw. I also had diarrhoea yesterday so what is left? Talk about less side effects. I have had everything going now. I must say the lesion I have on my sternum outside has definitely got smaller and has dried up quite a bit so at least there is something positive out of all this. I know things will be fine when they get the right dose for me.

Looking forward to tomorrow very much so will be in touch again after the weekend. Enjoy your weekend both of you. Talk soon. Luv always Maureen xxx
PS Will send Tracey the latest photos so she can see how the boys are growing.

The lesion Maureen speaks of has been really troublesome, weeping and open. The previous hospital she attended put it down to the effects of her radiotherapy but when a swab was taken at The Marsden, it too, was found to be cancerous. Every day, I realise just how lucky I have been. This disease is wicked and evil.

2nd August 2010
Subject: Re: update christening

Dear Margaret,
We had a lovely day on Saturday, weather good, journey good and baby good!! Everything went very well. We arrived home at 10.30 p m so not too bad. Have attached some photos for you. Will give you a ring in the morning if that's ok. Hope you all had a good weekend. Talk soon. Luv Marueen xxx
PS Feeling much better thank goodness.

I received the photographs of Sophie's Christening—three times!

5th August 2010
Subject: Update

Dear Margaret,
Lovely to talk to you as usual. Cannot believe 3 sets of photos arrived, I must stop clicking too many times, so impatient I suppose. As you say, seems to take forever to send. Anyway

when you are down here you can see a better view of Graham's pictures on my laptop. My fingers on my left hand have started to peel big lumps of dead skin just falling off but not painful. Am just creaming away with E45 cream, feet as well. I cannot believe how well I feel today. Looked after Ruby for a while and had the 2 boys as well and no tiredness. Must be a first. Hope this continues, as I hate the thought of going downhill again. It is lovely to feel this way.

We had thunder yesterday for about an hour, real black skies with some rain but passed over after about an hour. Had a coffee with my hairdresser in between customers and caught up with things. Liam's brother & wife came for us yesterday at 6 pm and took us for a carvery which was lovely. A bit late eating for me but I avoided the Yorkshire pudding (unfortunately) and the roast potatoes and was fine last night. No indigestion. We were not home too late.

I do seem to have a good colour but mostly am sitting in the shade as cannot cope with the sun too much now. I have a nice head of baby fluff now so think about another couple of weeks and I won't need my headscarf any more. Won't be bothering when I go back to hospital on Tuesday. Shall be pleased to start back on the tablets at a lower dose as cannot believe how well the lesion on my chest has responded. Shrunk quite a bit and dried up a lot. So much more comfortable than before.

Do hope you have had a good week so far with not too much rain. I think we have more tomorrow. Anyway, take care. Lots of luv as always Maureen xxx

6th August 2010
Subject: Weekend

Hi Maureen

Thanks for your email. Not very nice for you having lumps of dead skin falling off (I'd probably be helping it on its way!) I like E45 though. I first used it when I broke my wrist a few years ago and the skin got very dry under the plaster (stookies, we call them in Scotland). We even take some out to our friend Angela in Zante when we go because she loves it but can't get it in Greece. What with your hands and feet—you will be so creamy you will be sliding everywhere! Nice to hear you are feeling so well though.

The carvery sounded very nice (that's where we used to take my Aunty Doll in Haywards Heath, to one called the Priory). Loads of lovely veg if you didn't want the Yorkshire etc. We are picking Pat and her friend Joan, who is also our neighbour a few doors down, up from Rosyth port on Sunday morning when they get back off their cruise. I am going to invite them both for Sunday roast to save them worrying about cooking a meal straightaway. I have got a lovely strawberry cheesecake recipe I want to try out and they have lovely strawberries at our garden centre. Ours from the garden have all finished now. So, I shall be busy tomorrow when I get back from the town. I see that our Rosyth ferry was involved in a collision with a fishing boat of f Berwick yesterday. They are still searching for one of the young men on board the fishing vessel. We have been to Bruges on that ferry and can't imagine how it could have happened. It has been on all the national news bulletins, along with that terrible story of the 3 children stabbed in Edinburgh, looks like by their mother, so I expect you have heard about it.

It is really good news that your lesion has dried up a lot. What a nuisance this was for you. Hopefully it will go altogether when you have had a few more tablets, albeit a lower dose.

Our weather is still dull and showery. Not going to complain about rain with what they are all suffering in Pakistan. Poor things. Must be horrendous.

I expect you received your copy of Vita. I have read mine from cover to cover. I found it hilarious that there is an article telling you how to be careful when you meet someone you have been chatting to on the Internet, for the first time! We had both better bear it in mind (ha ha ha). I am so looking forward to meeting you and Liam. It will be two years November when we first "met". Time flies. It's a great little magazine though and you can relate to so much in it.

Well, Maureen, have a lovely weekend and build yourself up for Tuesday. I won't phone. Perhaps you could phone me when you get back just to let me know how you got on.

On, I nearly forgot! I wasn't expecting to hear anything from Tracey & Grant but I was so pleased to get such lovely photos of Sophie in all her Christening finery. She is absolutely gorgeous and is now sitting on my unit shelf beside her Nanna Maureen. Much appreciated.

Lots of love to you and yours

Byeeeeeee

Margaret x x x x

13th August 2010

Subject: Hello, hello, hello

Hiya Maureen

Lovely to know you are feeling fine—hope you still are and can stay on this dose. Happy creaming, etc! Speaking of creaming, we had Lucas on Wednesday afternoon. It was not nice enough to go out and was quite happy playing with the toys we have here. Then we (me) decided we would bake. He was very good at that sort of creaming. I got him using the wooden spoon and then I let him hold the mixer (with me) and switch it on and off. I let him break an egg (!!) I had some funny face decorations so he had a ball sticking them into the icing on the tops but went home proudly carrying his little box with cakes for everyone.

I love to see photos of your grandchildren. They are all beautiful children (I am sure you agree). Look forward to hearing more about them when I come down.

My, only 4 weeks until we meet. Please, please don't go to any trouble. I feel we should go with the flow—and maybe I will get to try one of your Soya lattes? Or go to your church? Whatever you think. I am not looking for lots of outings or anything—just to meet you all and have a proper good old chinwag.

No, my tablets weren't changed. Although the nurse said everything was "up", it wasn't by much apparently so didn't need any action except to maybe get a bit more exercise. She said my kidneys were fine. My blood pressure was very good. Cholesterol was 5.8 and it is usually 5 or under. Might be a bit of stress. Dave's cholesterol was up at 6.8 (he eats lots of ice cream!) and his blood pressure was a bit high so he has to go back at end of August for another BP check. His dad had heart disease so he does have a family history and maybe he will have to be checked up to make sure he is OK.

Our evenings are drawing in as well—it's getting dark about 9.45 pm especially if it's cloudy. It was 11 p m or later not so long ago.

We have Lucas' birthday party on Sunday. I am sandwich-maker in chief and have to make 70 triangles (2 per child). It is a Fireman Sam birthday party. Chris knows someone to do with the Fire Service and he is going to try to bring a fire engine along for ½ hour. This is at our local leisure centre. What happened to 2 or 3 children to the house and playing pass the parcel? Everything is on such a grand scale these days. However, it will be wonderful for the children if the fire engine can come along—as long as nobody thinks there is a fire and evacuates the whole place!!

I'll let you know how it goes and see if we get any nice photos. It doesn't seem five minutes I was sending you pictures of his second birthday last August, does it?

Well, Maureen, have a good weekend. Take it easy and don't go getting any nasty side effects (sure you won't this time). Barney has the vet on Tuesday for his booster and a haircut on Thursday. We are off to Glasgow Wednesday to meet up with Agnes & James (we went to Turkey with) but I'll give you a ring on Tuesday morning if that's OK. Barney's appointment not till 11.40. I'll ring about 9.30. Hope that's not too early.

Lots of love again

Margaret x x x

When we next spoke, Maureen told me that both the things I mentioned I would like to do when I visited, namely, try a soya latte or go to her church, were the very two things she would have suggested. Same wavelength again, I believe.

15th August 2010

Subject: Re: chat

Dear Margaret,

Do hope all went well at the birthday party for Lucas, it sounds as though it was a very special day. I am sure he enjoyed Fireman Sam and hopefully the fire engine. As you say it doesn't seem long since he was two. Time is flying by so quickly. Will catch up on Tuesday, 9.30 a m will be fine for a chat.

Still ok today. Do hope things continue. I will be so pleased to have very few side effects this time and they have the dose right. Mandy & Graham had a day in London today so left Fern with us. Took her along the beach at Littlehampton and had a little paddle. Finished with fish & chips & ice cream. She should be collected around 9.30 p m so a long day here. Boomie *(the cat)* has sulked all day as doesn't like dogs and has been in the bedroom.

Liam is like Dave, likes his ice cream. We have never had our cholesterol tested might be interesting! Gets dark here around 9 p m now at least you are a bit later than us.

Hope you all had a good party and look forward to speaking on Tuesday. Forgot to mention enjoyed my copy of Vita also. A good magazine. We are still getting juicy cherries from Kent and lovely strawberries from Fife! Take care, lots of luv, Maureen xxx

19th August 2010
Re: Tired update!

Dear Margaret,

What a day, lovely but oh so busy with so many people coming and going and 4 grandchildren. It has been bedlam. I'm shattered this evening but never mind can chill and stay in bed tomorrow. Got some lovely photos of Marilyn and her daughter Joanne, also Sophie and Kieran but alas left my camera at Leisha's. Won't see her now till Sunday so will send you some then. Tracey went back to Mandy's. She stays there when she comes down so they are already used as a B & B. It will be lovely for you to meet the family. Anyway Tracey left her steriliser behind and her camera as well. It is so chaotic when the children all get together but we had a nice lunch of sandwiches, crisps, lemon muffins & jaffa cakes which all went down well. Then we had a Waitrose Victoria sponge for afternoon tea. Will definitely have to go on a diet! The weather turned out lovely and warm so we ended up in the garden. Am going out with Peter & Marilyn on Saturday to Littlehampton for some lunch and take Marilyn to see Mum's headstone.

Am feeling fine today. Feet & hands a little red and tight but otherwise ok thank goodness. Seems this dose will be ok. Apparently there is an enquiry going on in the pharmacy now as was recorded that I was given 84 tablets (I only got 76). At the end of the day 8 tablets were left unaccounted for so must have been mine. Anyway have been given the go ahead from the doctors to finish this cycle minus 8 tablets so am happy with that. Next visit I will be counting them before I leave the hospital.

Do hope Barney got his injections and his haircut today. Got my Autumn/Winter catalogue from Nicola Jane today. Has your arrived? Lovely underwear as usual. Do hope you all have a lovely weekend, will ring you Tuesday if convenient, between 9.30-10.00 a m. You can let me know if this is ok. Take care as always, luv Maureen xxx

20ᵗʰ August 2010

Subject: Yawn Yawn!

Dear Maureen
Hope you are still in bed after your marathon day yesterday. It sounded lovely though. Lovely lunch!!
Maureen, you are going to have to forgive me. I have been going back through all your old emails—I have kept them back to 17.10.2008. I thought I had all your daughters and their respective children sorted out but I now realise I may have

not! How silly of me after all this time. I thought Ruby was Mandy's but something I read now tells me Ruby is Leisha's. So—Shaun and Keiran are Mandy's (along with the horse and Fern)? I know for definite that Sophie is Tracey's as obviously I was in at the birth (ha ha) etc. I re-read that Sheena had her hand op. Who belongs to Sheena? You must think I am daft. Please put me right.

It made fascinating reading I must say, going back that far—it's like a diary. I have kept all the photos (you all at the Isle of Wight, first one of Sophie etc etc). I can't bring myself to delete them as it shows exactly how our friendship has grown. Dave wondered what I was doing as I was down in the room where the computer is for over an hour just reading them all!

Poor old Barns. I told the Vet I was concerned about his sight. He shone lights in his eyes and was very puzzled as he said normally you can see the back of the eye, cornea etc but he couldn't see anything at all. He then put fluorescent dye in his eyes (he looked like an alien dog with glowing green eyes!) but it made no difference. He said he was going away to look it up as it was very unusual—like Barney has shields over the front of both eyes. He is not totally blind but I fear the condition will get worse. He has had a nice haircut. It must be a relief to him.

What a carry on with your tablets. Yes, I would count them before leaving the hospital as well. Still, 8 tabs respite.

Hope you enjoy your trip to Littlehampton on Saturday. Well, Maureen enjoy the rest of your sister's visit, take it easy and I look forward to a phone call on Tuesday.

Lots of love and don't get over-tired (Say "Yes, mum")!

Margaret x x x

I didn't realise then, when I mention re-reading all Maureen's old emails, that I would be recording everything in this account of our quite unique friendship. I am really hoping that others will appreciate how close we became. I felt I could say anything to Maureen and likewise she could to me.

23rd August 2010
Subject: Re: Update

Dear Margaret alias Mum.

Had a laugh when I read you had been going through past emails trying to sort out who belonged to who. Obviously, I'm not very good at explaining things. Yes, you do have it wrong. We will start with Mandy & Graham who have Fern & Holly and no children. Then there is Leisha & Matt who have Ruby. Then there is Sheena & Loz who have Shaun & Kieran. Amy is from a previous relationship Sheena had before she was married. Then there is Tracey & Grant who have Sophie and as you say that is the easy one as you were at the birth—well nearly!! Hope that sorts you out now, that's the trouble having 4 daughters. I get quite muddled myself with their ages and birthdays.

Had a lovely day with my sister on Saturday but obviously did too much as my feet were sore before I went out. Paid for it on Sunday. Was in agony again couldn't do anything except sit in the corner feeling sorry for myself. Took my last tablet this morning and thankfully the pain in the feet has eased although cannot walk too far yet. Should be on the mend by the time I talk to you tomorrow morning.

Hope you enjoy choir tonight and had a good weekend with the family. Poor Barney. Do feel sorry for him and you. Do hope things don't get too bad too soon but he is getting on—something we all cannot escape from unfortunately. Won't say any more. Look forward to our chat in the morning, had plenty of rain here over the weekend. Lots of luv from Maureen xxx

25th August 2010
Subject: Re: Update with photos

Dear Margaret,

Lovely to talk to you yesterday as always. Collected my camera this morning on way to hospital so will attach some photos at the end. Everything went well and we left the hospital after one and a half hours. On the way home we collected Fern from the vet. She has had diarrhoea and had been vomiting so wanted her in for an x-ray of the stomach. The lining of her stomach is inflamed so is on a strong anti-biotic just for 2 days and has to go back on Friday for further investigation. She was so pleased to see her Mum as like Barney does not like the vets. Mandy asked which wine you drink, red or white. I wasn't sure? Only you will be having a takeaway of some sort after church on Saturday and they always participate with a glass. They drink red themselves but will have white for you if that is what you prefer. Do hope my feet behave whilst you are here. That is my only concern. I think Leisha is doing Sunday lunch for us so you will see Ruby and hopefully if Sheena is not working, she will bring the boys over to say hello. The other days depending on the weather we have Arundel—the Cathedral, the castle and Littlehampton—Costa coffee, the beach, Mandy & Graham have a super coffee machine so lots of lattes there as well. They use ordinary milk as well as soya so you will be spoilt for choice.

Raining here at the moment although it did start out dry, just catching up with emails this afternoon, how about yourself? Fingers crossed for Tuesday although feeling quite positive, just need to get the feet sorted out a little bit and I will be quite happy.

Hope you like the photos. I'm sure you will know who is who, let me know. Glad you got your tickets sorted out—what a shock for you. Take care, luv Maureen. Sorry I'm still a bit baldy but don't mind myself, don't really wear my wig now gone into storage. Byeeeeee.

Despite Maureen's sore feet, plans are being made for my visit. It sounds as if everyone is getting quite excited now. The ticket saga had given me a fright. My friend Pat, with whom I would be travelling and I went along to our local railway station together to book our tickets, she to Worthing and me to Littlehampton. She was returning after me, so we had different dates for travelling back. We had to have tickets to London and then onwards to Sussex. Whether this was all too confusing for the booking clerk, I don't know, but it was a few days after we had our tickets, I was perusing them and realised the ticket was dated 9th August for travelling down and not 9th September as requested. I dreaded the thought of having not noticed this and being on the train and challenged to the validity of the ticket—and possibly having to pay the full price of another! I will cut a long story short by saying that we eventually got it all sorted out but the system leaves much to be desired. I enjoyed the photographs that arrived of Maureen with her sister. I wanted to take gifts down for Maureen's daughter Mandy with whom I would be staying and had asked her to find out the name of her favourite perfume. I had bought wee things for the children—a Toy Story watch for Kieran, a small bear dressed as a Scottish piper for Ruby and some colouring books for Shaun. I took Maureen some crystals and will explain this more later. For Liam I took some Scottish tablet as he had a sweet tooth. I hoped they may not know what tablet was as it was not an English confectionary.

25th August 2010

Subject: Photos, etc

Dear Maureen

Thank you so much for the email. Your photos are lovely, although I do think you should be getting a haircut by now!! You and your sister are very alike. My hair is like your sister's now, but I don't know whether to have it cut really short again as I did like the convenience. Look at Sophie. She is an absolute baby doll—such blue eyes. Kieran is so blond too—a handsome little boy.

Glad everything went OK at the hospital and no hold ups anywhere. Yes, everything crossed for next week.

A glass of red would be lovely. Since my chemo I sort of went off wine but I do take a glass at the weekends so I will look forward to that. In fact, I am really looking forward to everything. Now listen you! We will certainly not overdo anything walking-wise to make sure your feet don't suffer. It will be lovely to go to Arundel of course, but you must be honest and not just say you are OK when you are not just because of me. I know you—you will put up with things and not say. I wouldn't want your feet to suffer any more than they have to. Also, if you are tired from your chemo or ANYTHING, you must rest or it will be a slap (like you sent me in one of your emails I have just re-read).

Keep working on Mandy for me (hee hee)

I have changed my WeightWatchers day to Wednesday morning as everything nice seems to happen on a Saturday and I want to keep my Saturdays free to do other things. I went along this morning and ended up giving out the cards. Gave me a chance to meet all the Wednesday members but a few knew me already from Race for Life or because they came to the Saturday class occasionally. I am going on a short walk this evening. We have something called Bums off Seats (if you'll pardon the expression). The walks are not strenuous but very social—plenty of chatting—and aimed at the over 60s. It's been a nice day so hope the rain stays away. I will probably be out for about an hour as it starts to get dark fairly early now—earlier than I said last week now. Aye, the nights are fair closing in (as they say in the Scottish accent that I can't copy).

Well, Maureen, getting excited now and yes, I don't want any more panics with tickets now. I had a fit of the vapours.

Best love,

Margaret x x

27th August 2010
Subject: Weekend

Hiya Maureen

I am a bit late writing this weekend—been rushed off my feet getting prepared for tomorrow's meal. Why do I put myself through this I ask myself? I know I will enjoy it once George and Issy are here. I still have some cooking to do tomorrow but the main course is made and some Greek butter shortbread biscuits to have with our coffee. I have found a Greek recipe for baked apples. They are stuffed with walnuts, raisins, cinnamon and a coffee cup of brandy! I thought that would be nice for dessert after a casserole. The recipe says to serve cold. I have always had baked apples warm. I hope the juices don't caramelise and go rock hard, knowing my luck.

We are having some wonderful weather. Bit dull first thing and chilly but really warm and sunny the rest of the day. Hope it stays for a while.

Haven't heard yet how Lucas got on at "big" nursery. He started Wednesday and will go every afternoon now until he starts school. The nursery is attached to the primary school. Dave has been helping Chris this week and I think he has quite enjoyed it. It felt quite normal to me with him going off to work like he used to and I could get on in the house etc. Did mean I had to do all the Barney walks but I don't mind that. More exercise for me.

Hope you are still feeling OK and the feet are not playing up now. Will you still be starting your course of tablets the Monday before I travel down? I think that was how it worked out originally but it may have changed slightly.

Don't worry if you can't find out Mandy's perfume. I have one or two other ideas. I am taking myself over to Edinburgh one day next week as I haven't been for some time. I will have some reading to do for the Ethics Committee meeting which is on the Tuesday before I come down to see you. The following Tuesday is a Training Day. It is being held at the Hotel where Chris & Lorna had their wedding reception so I will probably be distracted with memories. It's a lovely hotel though and it will be nice to see it again. The only thing is Dave will have to drive me there for 9.30 a m and come back for me at 4 pm. It will mean 4 trips for him and it's quite a way. He doesn't mind, thank goodness.

Well, that's Barney just in from his last round the block until tomorrow. He will be looking for a treat.

Hope you have a lovely weekend (oops just remembered it's Bank Holiday your way). Even better then—there might be some different things going on for you to go to.

Anyway, will give you a ring on Tuesday—same time, same Bat channel, if that's OK

Lots and lots of love and . . . . see you soon!!!

Margaret x x x

29th August 2010

Subject: Tuesday phonecall!!

Dear Maureen

Wasn't until I was walking Barney up the shops this morning, thinking, as you do, I realised I said I would phone you Tuesday but of course you will be at the hospital. How could that slip my mind, even for a minute? Anyway, perhaps you could give me a ring later when you get back. I will be keeping everything crossed for you.

My Greek meal went very well. Thank goodness after all the angst of preparation and hoping it would all turn out as it should. George and Issy pretended they were the judges on Masterchef, describing my pastry as "melt in the mouth" etc. Flatterers. All good fun. Totally exhausted today but have got an easy day and some reading for the Ethics Committee Meeting on 7th September. Lovely feeling I can just sit down and relax today. Hope you are doing the same.

Bye for now

Lots of love as always

Margaret x x x

1st September 2010

Subject: Today

Dear Maureen

I hope you had a lovely sleep last night and feel full of energy today!

Dave has to go for an ECG at the hospital—it's only because from now on with a raised cholesterol level he will have to attend the Vascular Clinic at our surgery and an ECG is part of the protocol. We have an open access clinic at Queen Margaret so he can pop up any day between 9 a m and 4 p m to get it done. I think he's going up tomorrow to get it over with (not that it is anything, as well we know). His blood pressure was better this time. He has to go back to the surgery beginning of October for another blood test.

I am gradually getting my reading done for next Tuesday's Ethics Cttee meeting. Been up the town today and got a few things. Free day tomorrow (our 43rd wedding anniversary). I think we are going to have a Chinese takeaway so Judith can join in. Shall look forward to that. Friday I'm getting my hair cut. It's driving me silly! Saturday, if all goes well, I think we are cleaning the house where Chris (and Dave) have been working this past 2 weeks as owners get back Sunday morning from their holiday.

I have another small walk this evening 1.8 miles. Might as well go though, as at least I am not sitting in the armchair. I expect I will only be gone about half hour.

Everyone I tell that we are going to meet thinks it's great. _So_ looking forward to it.

Barney is fast asleep at my feet (snoring). We had quite a long walk after lunch so he was ready for a sleep—me too, given half the chance!

Better get on with the reading then.

Take care—and don't go overdoing things.

Lots of love as usual.

Margaret x x x

1st September 2010
Subject: Re: Update

Dear Margaret,

Congratulations for your anniversary tomorrow. Do hope you both have a lovely day. I presume you are going short with the hair again as it is so much easier to keep. Not that I know anything about this problem due to a lack of hair but it is coming along nicely albeit very slow. I'll probably be cursing my unruly hair in due course.

Yes, everyone I have told is thrilled we are meeting up. Will we recognise each other they ask—what a silly question? Another nice day here with plenty of sunshine. Just been food shopping again. Feel quite flat today I suppose after the highs of yesterday, back to reality and more tablets. Had an iffy stomach yesterday and still doesn't feel right. No appetite at the moment but hopefully will pass.

Ordered a book for Ruby for her birthday from Amazon. The packaging duly arrived this morning but no book inside! Caught up with the postie who took the packaging back with him to the post office saying he will look into things for me. Oh well, can but try. At least I have till January to get another one. Don't work too hard at your house cleaning on Saturday but I'm sure everything will look lovely.

Looking after Ruby tomorrow along with Shaun and Kieran so will probably be exhausted by the time I get home. Never mind, back to school next week. Anyhow have a great weekend both of you, doing a countdown—8 days to go.

Lots of luv, Maureen xxx

Maureen's "highs" were because the hospital visit and results of a recent scan showed good results on the liver tumour and those in her neck, all having shrunk almost by half. Alleluia to that . . .

3rd September 2010

Subject: Weekend again!

Hi Maureen

Here we are again . . . happy as can be (la la la) Weekend already. My, I have been so busy. We went shopping last evening (after our lovely Chinese meal) instead of this morning as Dave still off helping Chris. I spent the morning taking Barney for his walk and then making a shepherd's pie for tomorrow as we might be busy all day cleaning the house ready for people coming back off their holiday Sunday. I then prepared all the veg for today's dinner. By then it was time to make Dave a sandwich for his lunch and one for me. After lunch it was time for another Barney walk and I am off to the hairdresser's for 3.15 p m. Still not sure what to have done!

It's another glorious day here and we are just lapping it up whilst it lasts. It is cool in the mornings and evenings and believe it or not, the leaves on the trees are already changing colour. Autumn is well and truly on the way.

Chris, Lorna and co are coming for Sunday dinner as they didn't come last week and won't be coming next Sunday (!!) I'm keeping it nice and easy with a roast. I had already made some of the famous lentil and bacon soup and it's in the freezer so I'll get that out. I have bought a dessert, although I should have made something with all the apples George & Issy brought over last weekend off their tree. We are getting a lovely lot of plums this year off our Victoria plum tree. They are delicious.

Well, I hope you are all set for a nice weekend and that you are not getting any rotten side effects yet. We are discussing some research on leukaemia on Tuesday regarding the chemotherapy that you can give people before they get a bone marrow transplant. It was very interesting. Not the chemo either of us has been on but the side effects for it were so like what you describe (sore feet and hands and very sore mouth) I had to do a double take to see if it WAS the one you are on. This is also a clinical trial. Until we are affected by illness, we have no idea what research is going on in the background to help us. These people are just so clever. Anyway, I didn't fall asleep reading that project!

Hope your weather is as good as ours. I am on countdown now—no not THAT Countdown—does it still come on TV? Pat is instructing me what to take for the train etc. I am glad I am travelling at least one way with her so I get to know what I am doing. Still, I have a tongue in my head—stoppit! I know I talk too much sometimes. Am going to look out some photos before I come down.

Take care. Sending a big hug and lots love

Margaret x x x

5th September 2010

Subject: Re: update

Dear Margaret,

Hope you all had a good weekend and you enjoyed your roast today. We have had a good sunny week. Leisha rang to say she was doing a last Barbie for the year so we all went round there and the food was lovely. Home for 6 o'clock. The feet are quite sore and red again so plastering them in cream so will see how they will go over the next few days otherwise everything OK. How did the haircut go on Friday? Will I recognise you? Ha Ha!

Trying to get everything sorted this end but Mandy seems to have everything in hand. Hope the weather holds for your visit but it is looking changeable unfortunately. Never mind. Will give you a ring on Tuesday morning around the usual time if that's ok. Looking forward to our chat soon, luv

Maureen. xxx

6th September 2010
Subject: Re: phonecall

Dear Margaret,
Am having problems with my tablets again and have to go back to the hospital tomorrow morning for 9.25 a m so will have to miss the early phonecall—sorry. Will update you when I get back shouldn't be long. If I miss you I will ring again later. Don't stay in on my account and nothing for you to worry about regarding your visit. Cannot believe 3 days to go and counting! Pouring of rain here at the moment oh dear, but hope things will improve. Hope all is well with you. Bye for now, luv Maureen xxx

7th September 2010
Subject: Tablets etc.

Dear Maureen
Sorry to hear there is a problem with your tablets—do hope it is nothing too drastic for you. Please, please do not be afraid to say if you are not up for my visit. Honestly, there is no pressure at all. I would just leave it until things have settled down for you.
I have my Research Ethics Committee Meeting today and the last researcher is due in at 5.15 p m. This means we should finish the meeting approx 6 p m (all going to plan that is) and I would be home about 6.30 p m. I will be leaving to go about 1.15 pm. Dave will be here though as I am getting a lift from someone who lives in the next village. It saves Dave making four trips.
Weather has changed drastically here! Pouring rain and blowing a gale. I think summer has definitely gone now. It was just so dark this morning—shape of things to come.

You may not pick up this email but I look forward to hearing from you later.

Take care my love,

Margaret x x x

That is the full extent of the emails preceding my visit. On 9th September 2010, I travelled down to West Sussex with my friend, Pat, and I was glad of the company. We got chatting to someone on the train, a nurse, who had put a project before the Research Ethics Committee I sat on. What a small world it is. The journey went without a hitch and when going from East Croydon to Littlehampton, curiosity got the better of us when a young man, accompanying a huge, odd shaped case was standing beside us. "What's in the case?" I asked him, "A mountain bike", he replied. He then said that the hills in West Sussex were too small for his needs. I suggested he went to Scotland he replied "the mountains there are also too small." Further questioning revealed he actually cycled in the Alps, racing sometimes as well. Travel broadens the mind! You certainly meet some interesting people.

I arrived at Littlehampton and nervously alighted from the train. I needn't have worried. There was Maureen and Liam on the platform, ready and waiting for me. We hugged like old, old friends, not folk meeting for the first time. Magic.

Liam drove us to their bungalow and Maureen had cooked a lovely meal to welcome me. We talked non-stop and couldn't stop looking at each other, not believing that we were actually in each other's company after two years of emailing and phoning.

We had a short walk along the riverbank right outside Maureen's garden and from there you could see Arundel Castle and Cathedral. She lived in a beautiful area. We all felt set for a lovely weekend together.

The time came for Liam to drive me to their daughter Mandy's house where I was to stay. When we arrived and sat down, it wasn't long before Mandy said to her mother:

"How do you think Margaret would like a grand tour of The Royal Marsden tomorrow, and you could have a blood test thrown in for free?" Maureen was taken aback.

:

"What?" she exclaimed, "I'm not going up there tomorrow".

Mandy explained that her other daughter Leisha had noticed Maureen was looking a little jaundiced. She phoned the hospital and they said they wanted to see her the next day. There was no question of not going! And so it was arranged that we would leave West Sussex at 9.30 a m, and travel all the way back to London by car to meet with Maureen's Consultant. I could see Maureen was not very happy about this but I didn't mind at all as we would still be in each other's company. However, the day was to prove unbelievably long with a devastating outcome for Maureen.

10th September 2010

We had a good drive up to London. I had not slept particularly well. A church clock nearby was chiming every quarter and I counted 3 a m, 4 a m and 5 a m . . . I was quite comfortable sitting in Mandy's car for the journey.

We arrived at The Royal Marsden and Maureen was first sent for blood tests and she was also to have a CT scan. The Royal Marsden is a lovely hospital and all the staff very attentive. However, things naturally take time and we had a sandwich at lunchtime in the canteen and waited to see the Consultant. By this time, Maureen had had her scan and we were soon to get the results.

I was invited into the Consultant's room with Maureen and Mandy and we were told that Maureen had a blockage in her bile duct. They could not tell from the scan completely, but were of the opinion that because her last scan showed such an improvement in the liver tumour, it was more likely to be a gall bladder problem. I mentioned earlier that Maureen had been having trouble with gallstones but treatment for these had been shelved until the cancer was, hopefully, sorted out. The Consultant said that because her gall bladder problems had been dealt with by the hospital in Chichester, he would fax through everything to them and Maureen was to present herself at A & E there.

Maureen said "I'll go on Monday then", this being Friday, whereupon the Consultant replied "Er, no, I want you to go now!" Maureen was quite frustrated by this but between Mandy and myself, we made sure she felt more relaxed about the situation. And so, we had another long journey back to Chichester. We were expected, however, and led to a side room to wait for the doctor to come and see her. I actually took some photos here as I was determined to get plenty whilst I had the chance. It was a long while before the doctor came and he naturally had to go through all her history again. I was picking up vibes by now that she was going to be admitted, thinking there may be some emergency surgery on the horizon, if there was a gallstone blocking the bile duct.

True to my suspicions, Maureen was admitted, much to her disappointment. However, she was familiar with this hospital as this was where she started all her treatment. She was to be admitted to Richard Ward. But, there were no beds available until 9 p m. It was now about 7 p m and we had still only had a sandwich for lunch! A bed became available at about 9 45 p m so we got her settled in and made the journey home, arriving at about 10.30 p m totally worn out! Poor Maureen. She could not hide her disappointment that she was to be in hospital probably for the duration of my visit.

Mandy made some hasty phone calls to the rest of the family to put them in the picture and set about becoming the most wonderful hosts to me.

11th September 2010

The next day, Saturday, in the morning, I walked with Graham, Mandy's husband, with the dog into woodland right outside their house and up to a viewpoint where you could see for miles. It was a lovely walk. Later, after they had made arrangements with a neighbour to look after Fern (the dog), we drove into Chichester for some lunch and then visited Maureen in the afternoon. Chichester is a beautiful city, full of character and Mandy & Graham made sure I had my Soya latte, with lunch in a very trendy coffee shop. We visited Maureen and spent all the time talking non-stop. Chichester Hospital had decided they wanted to do another CT scan but we didn't know when this was to take place.

After visiting time, Mandy & Graham then took me to their church where there should have been Intentions read for Maureen but her priest, Father Peter, of whom she spoke so highly, and I would have really liked to have met, was away. However, it was a lovely service that took me back to my old church in Kent, St Barnabas. St Barnabas was high church but Church of England, not Roman Catholic. However, a lot of the responses were very similar and I enjoyed it immensely. We went round to the Lady Chapel before we left and this is where I lit two candles for Maureen, the second one in case the first one went out! This was in reply to her sending me two slaps in an earlier email, the second in case the first wasn't hard enough. I quoted this to Maureen when we visited her next and she laughed as she realised the significance of what I had said . . .

12th September 2010

On Sunday, before we went for lunch at Leisha's. I enjoyed a visit to see Mandy's beautiful horse, Holly, her pride and joy. I helped clear up the field with the biggest poop-scoop I had ever seen! Mandy then washed Holly's feet, brushed her magnificent tail and got her out for the day. Later we collected Liam and set off for Worthing. Here, I met Ruby, Maureen's delightful little granddaughter, Sheena and her husband and their two young sons, Shaun and Kieran. Kieran was in a bad mood, I was told. I said "We don't do bad moods, Kieran. Give us a high five" whereupon I brought out my gifts for them all and he cheered up.

We enjoyed a wonderful lunch and I felt so sorry that Maureen was missing this occasion. Leisha's husband was interested to know whether I had any breast cancer in my family. Like Maureen, no. The family seemed now to be of the opinion that Maureen shouldn't have received her "all clear" when she did as the cancer seemed to recur so soon after this. Indeed, it was less than 3 months. They also seemed to feel that my treatment in Scotland had been superior to that which Maureen had received. I could not argue with this, as it secretly was my own opinion. However, each case is different, with different outcomes and maybe I had just been a bit luckier than Maureen. Maybe my cancer was caught earlier. We shall never know.

We visited Maureen again on Sunday evening and as I was to return home on the Monday morning, we had to say our goodbyes. It was a sad parting for us. I sat and held Maureen's hand and we had a little weep together. She was becoming so anxious as to what lay ahead now. We promised each other we would keep in touch by text until she got home. She didn't have ready access to a landline phone here.

13th September 2010

Mandy's husband works on the railway and was called out on Sunday night to a derailment at Brighton. His job was to interview everyone concerned to try and find out what had happened and submit a report accordingly. I awoke on Monday morning. Mandy had gone to work and the house was very quiet. I wasn't sure where Graham was. Maybe he was walking the dog? I hadn't wanted to make myself breakfast so waited and at about 8.30 a m, he came downstairs and explained that he had been out almost all night with the derailment. However, he took me off to the station to get my train and saw me on board. Now it was my turn to be anxious as I had to change trains a couple of times before I got on the Kings Cross to Inverkeithing, my stop. I need not have been anxious as it all went very smoothly but I didn't feel comfortable travelling alone until I was on the Inverkeithing train and properly on my way home. It must be an age thing!

14th September 2010

On Tuesday morning my first text arrived from Maureen. I am reproducing her texts exactly as I received them even though they may seem a little disjointed at times, as text messages do. I still feel it is important to hear Maureen's side of the story.

14.9.10

11.11—CT scan this pm. Sitting with my crystals now xx

I must explain. I wanted to take a gift to Maureen and I visited the Mystic shop in the next village to ours, where all manner of interesting, if controversial, items are sold, including crystals of all sorts for ailments of all sorts, states of mind, etc. I decided to take some crystals down with me so that Maureen could hold them and maybe gain comfort from them. I can't remember the names of the crystals but I asked for advice from the owner of the shop who is a white witch, explaining what Maureen was going through. She gave me some that would help someone keep calm and deal with liver problems and some for coping with cancer. Maureen appreciated the thought behind this, as I thought she would, and did take some comfort from holding them whilst in hospital. She was a great believer in homeopathy and crystals are not that far removed from that.

Back to Chichester. The hospital had decided to do a further procedure—an ERCP (Endoscopic Retrograde Cholangiopancreatography)!! This would give them a look into the bile duct and would hopefully identify the obstruction . . . If it was found to be a gallstone, there was something on the end of the instrument that could dislodge it. If it was tumour, a stent would be inserted to bypass the tumour. This procedure was to take place the next day (Wednesday, 15.9.2010). However:

15.9.10
17.52—Threatened 2 walk out some of u has rubbed off on me all good! Now in 4 1.30 p.m. fri so fingers crossed. Luv keyring. God bless.

Yet another delay and more delays. The Pope was visiting Scotland about this time and there were some nice mementos on sale. I sent one to Maureen, a discreet picture of the Pope on a key ring. I was again hoping she would get comfort from this.

The ERCP arranged for Friday also did not go ahead and was re-scheduled for Monday 20.9.2010. It seemed quite unreasonable to me that Maureen had now been in hospital a whole week and nothing had been done for her. The next text I received sounded quite relaxed.

19.9.10

9.30—Morning. Electric bed v hard. Sore back. Quite noisy so didn't sleep 2 much. Lovely bfast soya milk and green tea. Also tele so am fine. Have a nice day with the family.

Monday 20ᵗʰ September brought a text to me from Mandy but not until 21.45. I had been on pins all day!

Hi Margaret, they only managed to have a look around inside today. Procedure now 2morrow in the afternoon. Fingers crossed Mx

How the time is marching on relentlessly.

21.9.10

6.42—Doing procedure 2day as a bit complicated. V sedated yest. Good nite. Update u later.

A second text arrived:

21.9.10

13.26—Still waiting 2 c if im on 2days list. Fasting and on drip. Watching tele

The procedure even then did not take place after all that fasting.

22.9.10

6.51—Morning. Just had bfast so am fasting 4 scan now. Cant tell u how sore rt arm is. How I hate needles

22.9.10

12.16—Lovely day here. Well done. Nothing happened here yet waiting around is tiresome. Leisha has gone to france this am.

22.9.10

18.23—Seen prof Johnson this pm. Ercp faild as tube 2 narrow. Going in on fri from outside. Mandy will update u better. So glad they were here when he came. Lovely supper

22.9.10

18.33—Got mri. Putting stent in. Couldn't do it mon as duct wouldn't open

This meant an operation rather than a camera down into the bile duct. Some of these texts are replies to questions from me but I have long since deleted them from my phone. I asked Maureen if Professor Johnson would be doing her operation.

22.9.10

18.43

No he wont. Dr Mcauley. Still in lot of pain but getting plenty of rest.

23.9.10

7.26—Cant wait to get some perm relief. Rollon 2moro. Watching bfast tv. Drip up. Will have a nice shower after bfast. Sorry its raining barney wont like that

23.9.10

14.35—Yes snoozetime. Vomited just before lunch. Will b glad 2 c back of 2day. Just a sandwich 4 t. Cant face anything else. Lots of luv.

I text Maureen to wish her goodnight and asked if she had managed anything to eat.

23.9.10

Thanks. Only managed soup. Nearly there. Cant talk 2day maybe 2morn.

I was becoming increasingly concerned at Maureen's condition and still found it incredulous that we were two weeks into her hospital stay and yet still nothing productive had been done.

24.9.10

7.21—Good morn. Had 2 get inject last nite 4 nausea. Felt ok this am On drip now as fasting. How r u.

Typical Maureen, always concerned less about herself and more about others. I sent a text to Mandy later on that afternoon to see if Maureen was out of theatre and she replied

24.9.10

16.21—Yes out of theatre. I am with her at the moment. Procedure went ahead. Just feeling a bit tired and groggy. Mx

I was relieved that at last Maureen was getting somewhere.

25.9.10

6.55—Morning. Just up in chair. Feel quite achy bit of pain not 2 bad. At least am going home soon.

25.9.10

7.06—Have a drain in so home mon all being well.

25.9.10

7.21—Just want to recharge battery today and feel better

I must have texted Maureen to say I had made a shepherd's pie for dinner as the reply came as follows. It was difficult to know what to text her apart from menus and clips of news.

25.9.10

16.31—Shep pie my fav. Appetite not great having beef cass and tom soup. Not in that order. Thought id feel better than

I do 2day. Back on oxygen. Bit under weather. Glad jude has a mini v.nice.

26.9.10

8.18—Sounds lovely. Got scrambled egg bacon beans and toms so im hoping 2 get my tastebuds going. Feel better. Pot (*potassium*) levels back 2 norm and antibiotics given in tab form now no drip. Looks dry outside.

26.9.10

8.24—Hope so. Fed up with being on the floor. Enjoy your fish

26.9.10

20.34—Not feeling great. Don't know what is rong hopefully a new day 2moro. Text 2moro.

I was feeling Maureen still had some optimism one minute and none the next. I so wanted to tell her everything would be all right in the end but things were not looking that way.

27.9.10

8.03—Had quite good nite. Watching tv since 7. Waiting 4 brekkie and then get moving. Let u no when ive eaten. R monitoring my fluid input and output. Fingers crossed I will feel better.

27.9.10

14.30—Feeling a bit better. Blood not rite yet. Wont be home 4 a few days Yellow (*jaundice*) going slowly. Bin 4 a little walk watch the world go by.

27.9.10

14.45—Priest coming later

I wondered if this was her own Priest, Father Peter, or the hospital Priest. There was a connection between him, Liam and Ireland.

27.9.10

14.54—Hosp priest. Apparently his gfather came from Clones. Liam met him last week when I got scan

28.9.10

7.35—Not 2 bad nite. Always glad 2 c morn. Put tv on at 5.45 passes time. Tummy bit achy. Have a nice day with Lucas. Wish I was home

28.9.10

7.40—Should no more 2day. Let u no any developments

28.9.10

14.24—Had bad diarrhoea so have bin moved 2 priv. Room. Pain gone. Enjoyed lunch 4 1st time. Maybe turn corner. Do feel so much better

29.9.10

7.33—Still in room. Awake at 7 as cudnt sleep for pain in tummy. Will text when doc bin. Have a nice day.

29.9.10

Will update tomoro as stent 2 be done on fri.

Maureen had heard that she was to have a stent put in. I gathered then it had been ascertained that tumour was blocking the bile duct. Bad news indeed.

30.9.10

7.45—Sorry not v chatty. Just don't feel great. Ething such effort. Have fluid on tummy now v painful. Maybe drained 2day. Thanks 4 being there.

This really brought home to me how far our friendship had come and we both shed tears and shared text hugs at this moment.

30.9.10

7.56—Thanks. Hugs 4 day with a tear.

30.9.10

21.30—Just had tube down my nose into stomach. V. uncomfie. Has 2 stay there all night. Luv.

I was suffering for Maureen and felt things couldn't get much worse but . . .

1.10.10

7.56—App loads of gas in tummy. Survived nite. C what 2day brings. Fingers crossed. Luv.

I still have a message to Maureen on my phone that I sent this day. I tried to encourage her and was willing her to get through her op and look forward to getting home.

1.10.10

8.00—Be glad when today is over for u. Hope no more tubes then and get home soon. Don't reply—just to know I'm thinking of u.

I later text daughter Mandy to see if Maureen was out of theatre.

1.10.10

15.21—Hi Margaret. I am with her now. Just back from procedure in an awful lot of pain. Just waiting for dr. 4 stents put in! Mx

Maureen even managed to text me later that evening

1.10.10
20.25—V tired but ok. Bp bit high

1.10.10
20.36—Nite nite

I was, of course, hoping Maureen would be feeling a little better the next day but it wasn't to be

2.10.10
8.26—No, in quite a bit of pain. On bed resting still v groggy. Luv

2.10.10
8.39—Have Leisha and Sheena. Wish I had your energy. Will c doc about pain relief

2.10.10
17.41—Got given morphine at ten am feeling much better. Sheena gave me a shower when she was here. Waiting 4 dinner

I had alarm bells ringing at the word morphine but Maureen did sound better for it and I emailed Mandy

3rd October 2010

Subject: Mum
Hi Mandy/Graham
Well, another week gone and Maureen doesn't seem to be improving. I am concerned she has to have morphine. It must be awful for her. She said Tracey & co had visited today. It would have been nice for her to see Sophie too.

Maybe there will be some further information forthcoming this week. Maureen will be desperate to get home but unless there is a rapid improvement, it doesn't seem likely at present, does it?

I hope everything is OK with you both, Holly and Fern. Are you still farming? My daughter said she had had several requests to start or join in with farming but she has resisted the temptation so far (I really mean she doesn't fancy it). *Farming was a Facebook pastime involving a virtual farm and one could sell livestock, or grain to other "farmers".*

We are away on Friday for a weekend break to Nethy Bridge which is near Aviemore. We went there years ago and decided to have another look to see if it has changed much. I believe Aviemore has had its first dusting of snow so not sure if we will get up the Cairngorm or not. Still, there are plenty of places round about to visit. I'll still be texting Maureen daily anyway but please let me have any news if there is any change or anything.

Bye for now. Love from Margaret xxx

3.10.10

8.29—Had morphine at half past ten pain v bad. Slept till 4 am. Sat in chair vomited at 5.30 am Got given anti sick. Went back 2 bed and dozed till now. What a life. Hope I have a better day.

I am only recording these messages in such detail as I am in awe of how Maureen was still concerned to let me know what was happening almost minute by minute, even though she was really going through the mill.

I know I text her to say how glad I was that we had met.

3.10.10

8.45—Yes did enjoy your visit though wasn't ideal we did spend sum time tog. Waiting 4 breakfast will get bflakes with soya and bread and marmie.

3.10.10

20.12—Had tracey and grant and sophie here. V dopey 2day and nauseus. Hope I have a better nite.

3.10.10

Nite, nite

We had got into a routine of texting first thing in the morning and last thing at night always to say good morning or goodnight

4.10.10

7.40—1ˢᵗ nite no pain turned a corner? Will be glad when get tubes out

4.10.10

16.57—Still tired. Prof j coming this pm. No pain glad u have had a nice day

5.10.10

8.56—Doc just bin round v pleased so far. Just need 2 get better blood results. Up at 4 a m in chair watching tv so late start. Having bfast

I must have text Maureen to say goodnight and asked her what she was watching on TV

5.10.10

20.38—Can only get BBC 1 and 2. Saw Leisha 2day. Nite nite luv.

I think I may have optimistically wished Maureen might be going home soon as her text came back:

6.10.10
8.25—I wish. Had 2 hav morphine at 12.30 a m pain was so bad but feel ok this a m.

I know I wished her a comfortable day as she simply replied "Will try"

6.10.10
17.20—Got drain removed this p m bit sore otherwise ok. Will be here 4 a few more days

6.10.10
17.26—Veg soup and jacket potato

7.10.10
11.04—Morn. Just up had 2 go 2 loo. Dressing leaked so have a soggy top. Watching tv. How wish could get rid of fluid in tum and legs

Maureen was suffering from a lot of fluid gathering in her stomach and legs. I, even with my meagre medical experience, knew this was not a good sign and she, likewise was so wishing she could get rid of it. I asked her if she knew how it would be drained.

7.10.10.
7.38—That's wot im worried about. Drain fitted? Cant bear thought of more pain. Such a wimp now.

Oh dear, dear Maureen. You are anything BUT a wimp, I know. We were due to go on our weekend break to the Highlands and I left making sure Maureen was going to keep in touch. I text Maureen as usual to wish her goodnight but got no reply. Neither did she answer my "good morning" text next day. I messaged Mandy:

8.10.10

Mum not answered texts last night or this a.m. Not like her. Forgive me if I am over anxious but is all ok. Don't say to Maureen. She'll think I'm fussing xx

I was relieved to get a text shortly after.

8.10.10

9.15—Had fone turned off early. Will update u of prog. Then perhaps I can get home.

8.10.10

18.58—Just got home. Tuf journey home.

I was surprised at this text but glad for Maureen as I know just how desperate she was to get home.

9.10.10

10.50—Got home at 7 p m. Tuf journey home but made it. Cat on lap. What u doing today

9.10.10

13.42—Thanks. Mandy doing lunch and dinner so well spoiled. Sheena doing shower later. V.warm here. Sitting in garden.

9.10.10

16.23—Yes R.M. (*Royal Marsden)* on Tues so will look 4ward 2 a call on wed if that is alright.

Maureen was due back at The Royal Marsden again on 12th October (Tuesday) so we were both looking forward to a phone conversation the next day.

There were no more text messages from Maureen. We did, indeed, have a telephone conversation on the Wednesday when I recall Maureen telling me she had been advised she was terminal. Although there could be no cure, she was still given hope that drugs could control the cancer. She said the girls were a bit upset but "I told them I've got ages and am not going to pop my clogs just yet!" Typical Maureen. We did both shed a few tears though. I also emailed Mandy.

13th October 2010

Subject: Mum

Hi Mandy and Graham

Was speaking to your mum this morning and she told me the devastating news. I don't think it was totally unexpected, but nevertheless it is still the worst news possible.

I know she will gain comfort from her wonderful family. She is quite looking forward to getting her wheelchair to get out a bit and is pleased she has a Macmillan nurse calling shortly. They are truly marvellous and know everything there is to know about medication, etc, so I am sure will be a great help, not only to Maureen, but to Liam and yourselves.

I am obviously keeping in touch with Maureen and I am not sure if she will be emailing as we used to. I shall email her and will telephone her. I would like to keep in touch with you too, just so I don't tire your mum at all so if you could let me know, now and then, how things are going, it would be much appreciated.

Well, Mandy, nobody knows quite what is ahead. It's a one day at a time thing me thinks and as long as Maureen is comfortable, we can cheer her up if necessary—although knowing her, she will be cheering us all up!

She is simply the best and I am so glad we met.

Love and regards,

Margaret x x x

14th October 2010

Subject: Update

Hi Maureen

How are you today? Hope the nausea not coming through. I found the Dexamethasone very good for the nausea but did give me really bad indigestion.

It's quite cold here today. We took Barney for his haircut and he is looking good. Jude will be calling him "stick legs" as she always does when he has been cut short. Not much going on otherwise today. Have got TV on—60 minute Makeover—they can come to my house any time.

Has your Macmillan nurse been to see you yet. And has your wheelchair arrived—I can just see you whizzing down the hills of Littlehampton (why not!!!) I dare you. Joking aside, it will be good for you to get out a bit and get some fresh air.

Jude still not got her new car. Apparently the previous owner had a private number plate and although the old plates are there, nobody can trace the documentation so it has all had to go to DVLA and wont be dealt with until 20th October. She is really deflated over it as was really excited at getting it. Arnold Clark have given her a courtesy car meantime so at least she is not without wheels. It is a KIA and not quite her style. Funny the things we think are important when we are young and healthy.

I do hope you are managing to relax and take each day as it comes. You will have lots of visitors I'm sure and I know Tracey came to see you today. At least nobody is too far away and can visit often.

Well, Maureen, obviously got you on my mind all the time. I hope you can email me the same as always. I will phone again, perhaps Tuesday if that's OK. I have to know how you are. I miss texting you funnily enough. It was part of my early morning routine and I was always glad to get one back.

Bye for now, get in touch when you can.

Best love as usual and loads hugs.

Margaret x x x x

I received another phone call from Maureen on Saturday 16th October, and we had a lovely chat and left on a cheerful note.

On Monday 18th I had a most uncomfortable feeling. All day, I kept wanting to phone Maureen but told myself not to be silly—I wasn't due to phone. However, at about 4.30 p.m. I decided I <u>had</u> to phone. It was Mandy who answered the phone. She was really upset, as her mother had been in so much pain that day. The doctor had to be called and he gave them the grave news that Maureen probably only had a few days of life left . . .

I was as shocked as the family at Maureen's sudden deterioration, although I had realised she wasn't improving. I asked Mandy to tell Maureen I loved her and begged her to keep me informed as to what was going on.

That evening, at about 9 p m my telephone rang and it was Mandy. She simply said:

"Margaret, she's gone".

I was devastated. I just felt so, so sad for the family, for Maureen, and for myself.

Personally, I had lost a true friend and soul mate. Maureen had become more like a sister to me than a friend and in two years, I got to know a most wonderful, caring, thoughtful and unlucky person. I had feelings of guilt that I was still here and she wasn't, but I was so, so relieved that we had met, albeit just once.

I must not dwell on the differences between our cancer treatment as I know everyone is an individual, but I can't help feeling that as Maureen had to wait so long between appointments, well, actually, for everything, it may have given her cancer more opportunity to spread. I really don't want to believe this. You cannot wait with cancer.

I still keep in touch with Maureen's family and hope to do so in future.

I am glad I kept most of our correspondence, as I would now like everyone to share our very unique friendship, our ups and downs, and how we were brought together through adversity but also found great happiness in each other. Maureen certainly made my life richer and I know I shall never find another like her.